Punishment in the Community
Managing offenders, making choices

Second edition

Anne Worrall
Clare Hoy

WILLAN
PUBLISHING

Published by

Willan Publishing
Culmcott House
Mill Street, Uffculme
Cullompton, Devon
EX15 3AT, UK
Tel: +44(0)1884 840337
Fax: +44(0)1884 840251
e-mail: info@willanpublishing.co.uk
website: www.willanpublishing.co.uk

Published simultaneously in the USA and Canada by

Willan Publishing
c/o ISBS, 920 NE 58th Ave, Suite 300
Portland, Oregon 97213-3786, USA
Tel: +001(0)503 287 3093
Fax: +001(0)503 280 8832
e-mail: info@isbs.com
website: www.isbs.com

First edition Longman Group 1997
Second edition published 2005

ISBN 1-84392-076-X paperback

British Library Cataloguing-in-Publication Data

A catalogue record for this book is available from the British Library

Project management by Deer Park Productions, Tavistock, Devon
Typeset by GCS, Leighton Buzzard, Beds
Printed and bound by T.J. International, Padstow, Cornwall

Contents

List of abbreviations

ACE	Assessment, Case management and Evaluation
ACOP	Association of Chief Officers of Probation
ASBO	Anti-Social Behaviour Order
CAFCASS	Children and Family Court Advisory and Support Service
CCETSW	Central Council for Education and Training in Social Work
CCTV	Closed Circuit Television
CP	Community Punishment
CPO	Community Punishment Order
CPRO	Community Punishment and Rehabilitation Order
CQSW	Certificate of Qualification in Social Work
CRO	Community Rehabilitation Order
CS	Community Service
DSPD	Dangerous Severely Personality Disordered
DTO	Detention and Training Order
DTTO	Drug Treatment and Testing Order
ECP	Enhanced Community Punishment
EM	Electronic Monitoring
HDC	Home Detention Curfew
ISSP	Intensive Supervision and Surveillance Programme
MAPPA	Multi-Agency Public Protection Arrangements
MAPPP	Multi-Agency Public Protection Panel
MPSO	Money Payment Supervision Order
NACRO	National Association for the Care and Rehabilitation of Offenders

NAO	National Audit Office
NAPO	National Association of Probation Officers
NOMS	National Offender Management Service
NPD	National Probation Directorate
NPS	National Probation Service
OASys	Offender Assessment System
OGRS	Offender Group Reconviction Score
PSO	Probation Service Officer
PSR	Pre-Sentence Report
ROC scale	Risk of Custody scale
ROM	Regional Offender Manager
SFR	Short Format Report
SIR	Social Inquiry Report
SOTP	Sex Offender Treatment Programme
SSR	Specific Sentence Report
STC	Secure Training Centre
STOP	Straight Thinking on Probation
YOT	Youth Offending Team

Acknowledgements

Anne Worrall acknowledges that many past and present colleagues in the probation service, Manchester University and Keele University have contributed to the thinking behind this book. She also wants to thank Neil Morgan and colleagues at the Crime Research Centre, University of Western Australia, Perth, for their support and for providing stimulating perspectives on penal policy and practice from the 'other side' of the world. Richard Harding, Inspector of Custodial Services for Western Australia, has offered encouragement and wise counsel on innumerable occasions. Beverley Hughes, as an academic colleague, friend and politician, has been a beacon of competence and integrity; as a Home Office minister, she represented the very best of New Labour. Finally, thanks are due to Andrew and Jennifer for their unquestioning love and tolerance.

Clare Hoy would not have taken on the challenge of co-writing this book without the knowledge that her colleagues in Cheshire Probation Area and South Cheshire Magistrates' Court would offer support. They have also clarified many practice and legal details and thanks are due to them – Cedric Fullwood, Steve Collett and the Senior Management Team at Cheshire PA, and Richard Holland and colleagues at Crewe Court. Tony Hoy's support has allowed much time to be spent in this endeavour.

Preface to the second edition

Writing a second edition of *Punishment in the Community* has been less straightforward than we anticipated. The timing of the publication of the first edition was unfortunate in the sense that it coincided almost exactly with the change of government in 1997. For that reason alone, a second edition, some seven to eight years on seemed appropriate in order to address the question, 'Has a Labour government made any difference?' But it quickly became clear to us that updating the references and adding a new chapter or two would not enable us to answer that question in the way that we wanted. It was also apparent that, while there was very little literature on community penalties when the first edition was published, that is no longer the case. Although it remains an after-thought in most of the penal literature, there are now a number of excellent texts addressing the main developments and debates in the field. We refer to these at many points in this book and a list of them appears at the end of the book as 'Recommended further reading'. So we had to ask ourselves whether a second edition of *Punishment in the Community* was necessary and whether it would be saying anything different from other texts. *Punishment in the Community* never pretended to be a comprehensive account of either non-custodial provision or the history of the probation service. In that narrow sense, it is not a 'text book'. Instead, the first edition aimed to be a critical and reflective appraisal of developments, offering a modest 'alternative' reading of the politics, policy and practice of sentences that do not involve imprisonment. It asked two central questions:

- Is it possible to explain (theorise) community penalties in ways that do not constantly have to make reference to prison?

- Why is it that, despite persistent attempts to 'strengthen' or 'toughen' community penalties, they remain 'soft options' in the eyes of the public – poor substitutes for the only 'real' punishment, which is prison?

In our minds, these questions remain highly relevant and the answers no less elusive than they were in 1997. In the first edition, it was argued that public opinion was not prepared to accept the blurring of the boundaries between prison and its opposite – freedom – and that all attempts to extend the constraints of imprisonment into the community would be met with scepticism. Government penal policy has moved inexorably in precisely that direction (while at the same time subjecting more and more offenders to imprisonment, thus creating a 'revolving door' between prison and the community) but we are not persuaded that public attitudes have become any more liberal or tolerant as a result – quite the contrary. The greater the levels of surveillance and monitoring imposed on offenders in the community, the more certain some sections of the press and public become that they should 'really' be in prison.

So we hope that this second edition will provide a new generation of criminology students, trainee probation officers – and possibly others with an interest in looking at what is happening from a slightly different perspective – an opportunity to reflect and argue. We have certainly tried to update the developments and arguments where appropriate and to remove some of the material from the first edition that has not stood the test of time. But we have retained the historical narratives where they are essential to contemporary understanding and we hope we have not changed the analytical and mildly irreverent tone of the first edition.

Anne Worrall
Clare Hoy

Introduction

'Small earthquake in Peru – not many dead.'

It is not considered very exciting to talk about the extent to which criminals are *not* sent to prison. Rather like the apocryphal headline above, the subject is lacking in news value, unless one already has an association with it. Consequently, when compared with the vast literature on prisons, there has been relatively little written about non-custodial penal measures. There is no market for the autobiographies of offenders' experiences of community service and there are no television series about 'bad girls' on probation.

Contemporary political (and academic) debate tends to assume that penality is synonymous with prison and that the most important theoretical and policy questions revolve around the nature, number and treatment of the (predominantly male) criminals sent to prison by our courts. Much attention has also been paid to the symbolism of the prison and its disciplinary effect on the populace at large. Penal measures that do not involve incarceration tend to be regarded by most criminologists as monolithic, unproblematic and invariably preferable to prison. Students consider them to be of only marginal and specialist interest.

Within the probation service there has always been much intro-spective analysis of the balance that can and should be maintained between caring for the offenders and controlling them. A perennial essay question set for trainee probation officers in the 1980s and 1990s asked 'Is the probation service still a social work agency?', the impli-cation being that its 'value base' was no longer compatible with the ethics of social work and that it was moving inexorably towards the American model of a corrections agency.

But that debate has been largely conducted within an apolitical framework that takes criminal justice policy as 'given' and which sees the role of the service as that of adapting to, or at least surviving, the vagaries of that ever-changing policy. Such debate is epitomised by the picture on the cover of one practice guide (Raynor, Smith and Vanstone 1994), which shows a probation officer and an offender standing outside a prison gate. The image is powerful yet contradictory. The offender is outside the prison, the prison is behind the offender, but the image of the prison is integral to the message that is to be conveyed. Probation is always practised in the shadow of prison.

About one and a half million people are sentenced for criminal offences every year in magistrates' courts and crown courts in England and Wales (Home Office 2003a). A further 250,000 who admit their guilt and are considered suitable for police cautioning never reach court. Of all these people, around 112,000 were sent to prison in 2002. Of the others, about 180,000 received supervised community sentences and the vast majority of the rest were either fined (1 million) or discharged (120,000), which means that they were reprimanded and warned of harsher consequences for any future criminal activity.

It is certainly not the purpose of this book to argue that concern about the increasing number of offenders being sent to prison is misplaced. On the contrary, its central argument is that we are so obsessed with the belief that imprisonment is the only 'real' punishment for 'crime' (and we rarely bother to define these terms with any care) that we are incapable of conceptualising other penalties except in terms of their relationship to prison. We talk of 'non-custodial' sentences and 'alternatives to prison' and imply that anything less than total loss of liberty must be merely 'a soft option'. Yet, as even the crudest of official statistics demonstrate, the vast majority of people who break the law – and get caught – still never go anywhere near the gates of a prison. And we would be outraged if it were suggested that they should!

It follows that any analysis of the role of non-incarcerative sanctions must go beyond technical discussions of their effectiveness (for instance, in reducing reoffending) by comparison with imprisonment and must address their social meaning. What, to use Garland's phrase (1990) are the 'moral values and sensibilities' which such sanctions encapsulate (or fail to encapsulate)? What are their sources of authority and from whence do they gain their (lack of) social support? In short, it must explore the conundrum posed by the widespread usage of penal measures which are discursively impotent. It needs to ponder Windlesham's observation that:

> if the belief, which had obtained such a hold on the British mind, that imprisonment was the only real punishment for criminal offences and anything else was a soft option was to be loosened, arguments with the power of dynamite [are] called for.
>
> (Windlesham 1993: 253)

Society's ambivalence towards punishment that does not involve prison can only be understood in the context of its deep-seated and increasing cynicism of the language of rationalisation. Non-incarcerative sanctions involve all the symbols of the modern state which arouse most suspicion – bureaucracy, professional power, unchallengeable claims to expertise, lack of public accountability – in an area of human experience which arouses extreme (if irrational) emotions of fear and anger. Far from being viewed as 'an index of the refinement and civility attained by criminal justice', such measures are deemed to have redefined the social meaning of punishment in such a way that it has 'been removed from direct public participation and involvement and ... cast in a form which de-emphasises [its] moral content' (Garland 1990: 184–5).

We have no generic term for such punishment that does not involve reference to prison. Each measure has its own name but, as we shall see in Chapter 1, the absence of a collective noun which is not ineluctably hitched up to incarceration means that our analysis is conceptually impoverished. We simply cannot think about punishment without thinking about prison because we do not have the words with which to do it.

The phrase 'punishment in the community' entered penal vocabulary with the government's Green Paper, *Punishment, Custody and the Community* (Home Office 1988). It was a deliberate attempt to dislodge prison from its central position in penal thinking. The reasons for this conceptual shift under a Conservative government (and the subsequent backlash) are complex and will be discussed later in Chapters 2 and 3, but the phrase came to signify a specific period of criminal justice policy-making in the late 1980s, culminating in the Criminal Justice Act 1991. According to Windlesham's account (1993), the architect of these developments was the then Home Secretary, Douglas Hurd, assisted by the then Minister of State, John Patten.

By the time the Criminal Justice Act 1991 was drafted, the phrase 'community sentences' had emerged but this referred only to sentences involving supervision by the probation service: probation and supervision orders, community service orders and the new combination orders. In the new sentencing framework, fines and discharges were each categorized separately.

Other attempts to find a generic term have included 'community corrections' (Haxby 1978), 'community penalties' (Raynor and Vanstone 2002) and 'community punishment' (Brownlee 1998). In 2001, with the creation of the National Probation Service, new names were introduced for the three main court supervision orders: community rehabilitation replaced probation; community punishment replaced community service; community punishment and rehabilitation replaced combination orders. In all these cases, the use of the word 'community' has been considered to be unproblematic. But 'community' has become a thoroughly promiscuous word, attaching itself to almost any activity formerly regarded as a responsibility of the state – and for a very cheap price. The significance of its usage in criminal justice discourse will be explored in Chapter 4.

Creeping into penal vocabulary from American literature in the 1990s were the terms 'intermediate sanctions' (see, for example, Tonry and Hamilton 1995) and, more chillingly, 'smart sentencing' (Byrne, Lurigio and Petersilia 1992). The latter phrase has been described as being 'the penal version of the neutron bomb which leaves the offender intact but destroys the offending behaviour' (Oldfield 1993: 32). Such terms refer to sentencing options which are intended to hold the middle ground between incarceration and what might be termed 'regular' probation, the latter being regarded as a welfare-orientated rather than punitive measure. Characterized by intensive supervision, surveillance and carefully targeted rehabilitative programmes, such as those to be discussed in Chapter 8, such sanctions had as their stated aims (see Byrne, Lurigio and Petersilia 1992: ix–x) to:

- save taxpayers money by providing cost-effective alternatives to prison;
- deter offenders and others from crime;
- protect the community by exercising more control than does traditional supervision; and
- rehabilitate offenders by using mandatory requirements and by the swift revocation of violated orders.

The unstated but equally important aims, according to Byrne *et al.* are to:

- create an 'appearance' of correctional reform;
- find a way of reclaiming limited resources for non-custodial sentences; and
- enable probation administrators and politicians to respond to the punitive mood of the public.

A decade on, the term 'intermediate sanctions' has fallen into relative disuse and one explanation might be that *all* community penalties now fit the profile described above. There is, arguably, no longer an 'intermediate' layer of sentencing. The aim of this book, therefore, is to unravel the complex of institutional goals (the role of community penalties in the criminal justice system), professional goals (what can be achieved by community penalties) and political goals (the packaging and 'sale' of community penalties to the 'law-abiding' public). Central to this analysis is the changing role of the probation service and its relationship to the courts, which will be examined in Chapters 5, 6 and 7. By way of illustrating these changes, Chapters 9 and 10 will discuss changing attitudes to two particular groups of offenders: sex offenders and young offenders. The concluding chapter will consider the future of punishment in the community in the twenty-first century.

The phrase 'punishment in the community' will be used to refer to the political and academic discourses which underpin discussions of non-incarcerative punishment, and the phrases 'community sentences' or 'community penalties' to refer to the concrete penal measures. The phrases are not mutually exclusive, as it is impossible to examine any discourse without also examining its effects in practice, but the distinction may be a useful one in making accessible the various elements of this complicated and under-theorized area of penality. The constraints of existing vocabulary will be identified and interrogated as the book progresses.

The first such constraint is that of gender. In the first edition of this book, the masculine pronoun predominated and this was quite deliberate. Men who are cautioned or sentenced for criminal offences outnumber women by at least four to one and the difference increases with the severity of the offence. For example, one in ten violent offenders and one in 40 burglars are women (as also are one in nine motoring offenders!). Sentencing patterns indicate that women represent less than one in five of all known offenders, less than one in six of those given community penalties and around one in 20 of all prisoners (Home Office 2004a). Crime remains overwhelmingly a male activity and community penalties, like prison, are a response to male offending. However, the increase in the women's prison population and the contemporary convention of insisting on the use of gender-neutral language have led us to concede that continued use of the masculine pronoun is unacceptable. But this does not detract from the book's aim of examining the gendered nature of community punishment and of arguing that a fully social analysis of punishment in the community must take account of community attitudes not only towards men and women who offend, but also towards the kinds of punishment which we, as men and women, wish to endorse as contributing to the well-being of the community.

Part I
The Principles and Politics of Punishment in the Community

Chapter 1

Introducing community penalties

Introduction

In attempting to provide a framework for understanding punishments
that do not involve prison, in their own right, there is a danger of
imposing a false coherence and rationale on a set of experiences and
events which have neither. But not to do so simply perpetuates the lack
of interest and analysis which currently characterize the field. It is not
without significance that Cohen's *Visions of Social Control* (1985), which
warns of a dispersal of discipline from inside the prison out into the
community, remains a more seductive text than Bottoms' more staid
analysis of 'Neglected features of contemporary penal systems' (1983).
The latter suggests that at least some of our most widely used punishments have very little to do with the creation of docile, compliant
bodies and much more to do with penalising rule infringement, much
as one might in a game of ice hockey (Bottoms 1983: 176). It will not do,
he argues, to make sweeping generalizations about non-incarcerative
sanctions, whether they be of the 'soft option' or the 'punitive city'
variety. But neither will it do, in reacting against such generalization, to
succumb to a nihilistic parody of postmodern analysis which claims
that there are no identifiable themes, no patterns or consistencies – only
gaps, illogicalities and fragmentations.

To make a start, then, it is possible to categorize community punishments in such a way as to enable an analysis of some underlying
assumptions about the relationship between the state and the
individual.

From segregation to normalization: the birth of community punishment

Before the end of the nineteenth century, the only non-custodial sentences (apart from the death penalty) used regularly by the courts were fines and release on recognizances (such as binding over, whose origins lie in the Justice of the Peace Act 1361). Since there were no facilities for paying fines by instalments, however, many people were imprisoned for non-payment of fines (Garland 1985). Release on recognizance usually involved giving sureties to guarantee future behaviour (rather like the present-day conditional discharge) or being 'vouched for' by a respectable citizen. Such undertakings were often given by the Police Court Missionaries, founded in 1876 by the Church of England Temperance Society and seen as the forerunners of the modern probation officer. The primary issues in imposing punishment, however, were concerns for formal equality before the law, uniformity of treatment and proportionality in the severity of punishment (Garland 1985).

During the period 1895–1914, however, there was a transformation in the relationship between criminals and the state. An increasing confidence in both their material wealth and their scientific knowledge led the late Victorians and the Edwardians to believe that crime was a social disease for which a cure was possible through 'specific practices of normalization, classification, categorization and discrimination between criminal types' (Garland 1985: 32). The reasons for such a transformation lie deep in the changing nature of Victorian industrial society and, in particular, attitudes towards the poor, but the result was the development of a complete sphere of punishment which focused on social control through attention to the material, social and psychological welfare of criminals.

By the second decade of the twentieth century, there was a separate court to deal with juveniles (Children Act 1908), a separate training institution (Borstal) for juveniles (Prevention of Crime Act 1908), a professional service to supervise offenders in the community (Probation of Offenders Act 1907) and a means for paying fines by instalments (Criminal Justice Administration Act 1914). Special institutional provision was also made for inebriates (Inebriates Act 1898) and for mentally defective criminals (Mental Deficiency Act 1913).

Since that time, the most significant developments in community sentencing before the Criminal Justice Act 1991 were the introduction of conditional discharges, attendance centres (Criminal Justice Act 1948, which also abolished birching), police cautioning (Children and Young Person Act 1969) and community service (Criminal Justice Act 1972). Compensation orders became sentences in their own right in 1988.

It is possible, therefore, to identify themes around which to organize community punishment conceptually. Those themes are:

- self-regulatory penalties
- financial penalties
- supervisory penalties

Self-regulatory penalties

The thread that joins police cautions and court discharges is the assumption that identification as a wrong-doer is sufficient to prevent further misbehaviour. Denunciation (which is private in the case of cautions but public in the case of discharges) of an otherwise upright citizen who has breached their contract with the local community (and thus with society) is seen to be enough to shame and reintegrate them with that community (Braithwaite 1989). They admit their guilt – or are found guilty – and frequently apologize and promise never to do it again. Their word is accepted (though often on condition that they prove their sincerity by not reoffending within a fixed period of time).

Financial penalties

The relationship between money and punishment, though ill-defined, is long established (see, for example, the Book of Exodus in the Old Testament) and taken for granted. The fine remains the most popular sentence imposed by courts, although its proportionate use has declined (Johnson *et al.* 2001; Home Office 2004a; Mair 2004). It is regarded by many as the most flexible of sentences since courts can match its amount both to the seriousness of the offence and to the offender's ability to pay (though in practice these two principles are often in conflict). At the same time, it is an impersonal sanction, implying no personal stigma. It is the only punishment whose obligations can be met by someone other than the offender themselves. It does not matter who pays the fine, as long as it is paid. So, while financial punishment may be effective in preventing further offending because 'it hits them where it hurts – in the pocket', it is not always seen as holding the offender sufficiently accountable for their breach of contract with the community. For this reason, it lacks the moral censure and personalized infliction of pain perceived to be essential in the punishment of serious crime (Young 1989).

This concern may be met to some extent through the payment of compensation, which may be linked to other sentences or (since 1988) imposed as a sentence in its own right. Compensation requires the offender to confront the harm done to their victim in a more direct way than a fine does, but the problem of devising a formula for the relationship between money and harm done (except in the most straightforward cases of theft or damage) is even more acute.

Supervisory penalties

The assumption underlying all punishments which involve an element of supervision is that the offender lacks the motivation or personal resources to repair their breach of contract with the community unaided. The exact nature of that aid is highly contested and its examination forms the central concern of this book. At this stage, therefore, it is perhaps sufficient to identify the main supervisory punishments as:

- the community rehabilitation order (which may include additional conditions relating to medical treatment, accommodation, programmes or activities and is available for anyone over 16 years of age)

- the supervision order (a similar order available for anyone under 18 years of age)

- the curfew order (restricting physical liberty with or without the addition of electronic monitoring or 'tagging')

- the attendance centre order (requiring fortnightly attendance for sessions of two or three hours, involving physical and educational activity run by the police and used for young people)

- the community punishment order (undertaking unpaid work for up to 240 hours and available for anyone over 16 years of age)

- the community punishment and rehabilitation order (which combines elements of community rehabilitation and community punishment)

- the drug treatment and testing order (which requires offenders to undergo regular testing and attend court reviews of their dependency)

- referral orders, reparation orders and action plans for young offenders aged 10 to 17 years

Other sentences

There are other punishments which do not fall neatly into any of these categories. Binding over, for example, is self-regulatory in that it accepts a verbal undertaking from the offender, but it requires a financial forfeit if that undertaking is broken. A deferred sentence (introduced under the Powers of the Criminal Courts Act 1973) offers a period of self-regulation to the offender – time to 'put their house in order' – but requires a return to court after that time with no guarantee of the nature of the eventual punishment. The suspended prison sentence might be regarded by some as self-regulatory insofar as no immediate pain, other than shaming, is inflicted on the offender. Nevertheless, the threat of imprisonment in the future is made more explicitly than in any other punishment, and the offender is left in no doubt that they have narrowly escaped incarceration, thus rendering the notion of self-regulation rather secondary to that of involuntary self-restriction. The use of the suspended prison sentence has declined and now represents only 1 per cent of all sentences (Newburn 2003), although they continue to be used to enforce payment of fines.

A hospital order relates specifically to offenders diagnosed as being mentally disordered and may be regarded, in theory, as being 'somewhere between' supervision and prison. In practice, however, many of these 'patients' experience imprisonment at some stage of the criminal justice process, either pre-trial or following sentence. The numbers of those who do not and are sentenced to 'unrestricted' hospital orders have reduced from about 750 a year in 1984 to 614 in 2001. Numbers receiving 'restricted' hospital orders (which frequently, though not necessarily, involve prison, secure units or special hospitals) have increased in recent years with annual admissions quadrupling from 284 in 1984 to 1074 in 1997, and reducing again to 980 by 2001 (Home Office 2002a).

Principles of sentencing and community punishment

Having identified the range of community disposals available to the courts, the next stage is to see the extent to which they can be said to satisfy the requirements of conventional 'philosophies of punishment' and 'principles of sentencing'.

It is usually argued that there are two broad philosophies of punishment known as *retributivism* and *utilitarianism*. Put very simply, retributivism (which can be traced back to ancient legal systems) maintains that punishing wrong-doing is a moral right and duty, an end in itself and an essential component of a civilized society. The obligations on the punisher are to ensure, first, that the person to be punished is correctly identified (that is, that guilt is established) and, second, that the punishment is proportionate to the seriousness of the crime (that is, that it is not excessive). Utilitarianism (whose most eloquent exponent was the philosopher Jeremy Bentham, 1748–1832) maintains that punishment is itself an evil which can only be justified if it brings about a greater good, namely the reduction of crime. Punishment is a means to an end, not an end in itself. The most obvious distinction between the two philosophies is that utilitarians have to demonstrate that punishment (or sentences) work, while retributivists only have to demonstrate that punishment is deserved.

There has been a tendency to associate retributivism with measures that are predominantly punitive, such as imprisonment and corporal punishment, and to associate utilitarianism with rehabilitative measures, but this oversimplifies the relationships. From these two broad philosophical approaches, a number of principles have developed which often result in contradictory and inconsistent sentencing. The implications for community punishment of the received wisdom of sentencing 'principles' require some examination.

Just deserts implies that the main purpose of sentencing is to denounce the crime and 'visit retribution' on the criminal, to the extent that they deserve it. Retribution must be distinguished from revenge, which is disproportionate punishment and supposedly has no place in any modern philosophy of justice, though observers of the tabloid press, and particularly of the mistakes made during the search for the killer of Sarah Payne in summer 2000, may wonder otherwise. In this case, the *News of the World* 'named and shamed' a convicted paedophile. Residents of a housing estate in Portsmouth sought him out and mob violence ensued. Other suspects were targeted, including a *paediatrician* in Gwent. The paper was prevented from printing further names. The crucial considerations for a *just deserts* approach are the seriousness of the crime and the culpability of the criminal (that is, the extent to which they can be held responsible for their actions). There is scope to consider aggravating and mitigating factors insofar as they relate to the offence and the offender's part in it, but wider considerations of the offender's circumstances are deemed to be less relevant. The government White Paper *Crime, Justice and Protecting the Public* (Home Office 1990a) sets out the philosophy underpinning the Criminal Justice Act 1991 and states that its aim:

is to ensure that convicted criminals ... are punished justly and suitably according to the seriousness of their offences; in other words that they should get their just deserts.

(para. 2.1)

It goes on to explain that this means that, while serious offenders should still go to prison, many others can be dealt with safely (and more cheaply) in the community. 'Seriousness' is still the basis of sentencing decisions despite the repeal of several sections of the 1991 Act. The Criminal Justice Act 2003 states that in order to determine the seriousness of an offence, sentencers should take into account the culpability of the offender and the harm caused, the offender's previous convictions and whether the current offence was committed whilst on bail.

Deterrence was the original concern underlying utilitarianism. It implies that the main purpose of sentencing is to deter people from committing crime. There are two elements in this principle: individual and general deterrence. Individual deterrence refers to measures which are intended to impress on the offender that the personal consequences of their actions in the form of the punishment received make it 'not worth' committing crime again. The most commonly used individually deterrent sentence is the fine, but any sentence that restricts offenders' liberty, inconveniences or shames them may have a deterrent effect. General deterrence refers to measures that are intended to set an example for other people in the hope of deterring them from committing crime. For example, a bout of criminal damage in a particular locality may result in an 'exemplary' prison sentence to demonstrate that local people have 'had enough'. One objection to deterrent sentences is that they may be disproportionate to the seriousness of the offence, in order to 'make a point'. A more fundamental criticism is the underlying assumption that crime is committed as a rational choice, with the offender weighing up the possible consequences of their actions before deciding to offend. Although this may be true in some instances, it is by no means the only explanation for offending. Much crime is impulsive or stems from what many people would view as irrational thoughts or feelings.

Protection and incapacitation are aims intended to protect the public from further harm from the offender. Rather than relying on the rational judgement of the offender that 'crime does not pay', a safer way of ensuring that no further crime is committed is to reduce the opportunity for crime by restricting the offender's liberty. The ultimate example of such a sentence is the death penalty. Imprisonment is less effective, since prisoners may escape and they will, in any case, be released at some point. Giving someone a community punishment order, placing them on a probation programme or even subjecting them to electronic monitoring may seem mild measures in comparison but the principles of restriction and surveillance are basically the same. The extent of the restriction has to be decided according to the seriousness of the offence and this means that the retributive principle of proportionality also has to play a part.

Compensation and reparation Just as deterrence may be either individual or general, so the principle of 'making good' harm done can include both the individual victim and wider society. Compensation (predominantly financial) is usually made to the individual victim of a crime. Reparation is a broader concept which involves the offender in doing something socially useful and morally exculpatory (such as community punishment), thereby demonstrating their remorse and willingness to put back something into society. Reparation orders became available for youths in June 2000 and can require a range of actions to be taken to ameliorate the harm done. In response to the perceived failures of the formal criminal justice system to either satisfy victims or deter/rehabilitate offenders, the concept of *restorative justice* proposes a new approach to repairing the harm caused by criminal activity within communities. Although the term is now used to describe a very wide variety of informal and semi-formal measures, the generally accepted 'umbrella' definition is that it is a 'process whereby parties with a stake in a specific offence resolve collectively how to deal with the aftermath of the offence and its implications for the future' (Marshall 1999). The underlying principles are concerned with healing, rather than with punishment (and some might therefore object to its inclusion in a book on punishment) and with restoring the real or metaphorical relationship between the offender, the victim and the community through 'moral learning, community participation and community caring, respectful dialogue, forgiveness, responsibility, apology and making amends' (Braithwaite 1999: 6).

Reform, rehabilitation and correction Bringing about fundamental changes to the personality, attitudes and behaviour of offenders, so that they no longer commit offences, not because they fear the possible consequences but because they appreciate that crime is wrong, has long been a utilitarian aim of sentencing. The distinction between reform and rehabilitation is not an easy one. Reform tends to assume that the individual has free will and is therefore capable of changing their attitudes and beliefs, given the right stimulus. As Hudson puts it: 'The criminal can repent, can become a good citizen, if only he will' (1987: 3). Rehabilitation assumes that the individual is determined more by circumstances (personal, social or medical) and that a change in these is required in order to produce a change in behaviour. 'Correction' is a term that has been imported from America. For some people, it has unacceptable overtones of coercion but Walker (1991) argues that it is a 'non-committal word' which we are adopting wisely because it implies an appropriate humility about the state of our knowledge about the reasons for which people stop committing crimes. (It is interesting to note that in 2003, the new post of Commissioner for Correctional Services in England and Wales was established.) In the past, people have viewed crime variously as a symptom of sin (which only religious conversion will remedy) or disease (which only medical science will cure) or an emotionally deprived childhood (which only psycho-therapeutic casework will resolve) or poverty (which only social and political action will alleviate). While all these explanations might provide some insight into understanding some crime, none provides a full explanation and few people now believe that such an explanation is either possible or desirable. People commit crimes for many reasons. They also stop committing crimes for many reasons and the sentence they receive may be only one (and possibly the least significant) of several influential factors. The study of why people stop – or desist from – committing crimes is now an important branch of criminological research (Farrall 2002; Maruna 2001).

Obstacles to community punishment

Attempts to uncouple the discourses of community punishment and imprisonment run into a number of recurring obstacles. First, and most familiar, is the obstacle of public and media perceptions that the demands of punishment can only be properly met, at the very least, by imprisonment (and for some only by the return of the death penalty). The principles on which state punishment is traditionally founded are interpreted within popular discourse as referring to corporal and incarcerative punishment. Other measures are viewed as poor substitutes, suitable only for the very young, the very old and the feeble-minded (and not even always for those categories, as will be seen in Chapters 9 and 10). Entangled with this popular reluctance to legitimize community punishment is the legacy of the Victorian principle of 'less eligibility'. Underlying all nineteenth century insti-tutional provision for the 'undeserving' was the belief that the standard of life enjoyed by inmates should not be greater than that of the poorest 'respectable' citizen. 'Less eligibility' remains a tenacious precept in penal thinking and surfaces in community punishment when offenders are perceived to be given better opportunities (for work, education or recreation) than the poorest non-offender.

Second is the obstacle of unfair or inconsistent sentencing. Despite increasingly sophisticated guidelines about the use of community sentences, there remain concerns that certain groups of offenders are over-represented in prison for reasons that have little to do with the nature of their offences. Community sentences, it is argued, are reserved in practice for those who are relatively advantaged socially – for those who have sufficient money to pay a fine, for those who are employed, for those who are perceived by probation officers to be able to 'benefit' from supervision, and so on. In other words, community sentences run the risk of being discriminatory, of being seen as justice for white criminals with homes, jobs and relatively few social problems.

Third is the obstacle of 'net-widening', a term which entered criminal justice vocabulary in the 1960s in the wake of labelling theory. With the proliferation of alternatives to custody, so the argument goes, comes the danger that instead of keeping more people out of prison, community sentences will simply draw more and more people into the 'net' of the criminal justice system and thereby increase the likelihood that they will eventually end up in prison. The treatment of juvenile offenders in the 1970s illustrates the point. Following the introduction of police cautioning with the Children and Young Persons Act 1969, the numbers of juveniles being cautioned rose steadily but so too did the numbers being placed under supervision and the numbers being sent to detention centres and borstals. Without the political will to reduce the number of offenders sent into custody, the introduction of new community sanctions tends to raise rather than lower the punitive stakes. Professor Rod Morgan, as Chief Inspector of Probation, widened this debate in 2003 by claiming that probation services were 'silting up' with low risk offenders, because sentencers were choosing supervisory community penalties rather than imposing fines (Home Office 2003a: 5).

Fourth, and finally, is the obstacle of enforcement. Fines are all very well if they are paid. Probation is all very well if appointments are kept. Community punishment is all very well if the work is done. But what if it is not? Surely, it is argued, community sentences must ultimately be 'backed up' with prison? There has to be a sentence of last resort for those who abuse the alternative opportunities they are given.

Traditionally, probation officers have been notoriously reluctant to institute 'breach proceedings' against offenders who fail to comply with the requirements of probation orders. Three per cent of community rehabilitation orders were terminated for this reason in 1993, but this figure has risen to nine per cent in 2002 (Home Office 2004a). Many probation officers see 'failure to comply' (which usually means failing to keep appointments) as a reflection on either their own inability to establish a helping relationship with the offender or on the offender's chaotic lifestyle (Hedderman 2003; Hedderman and Hough 2004). Returning an offender to court, with the possibility of a consequent prison sentence, is not an action which most probation officers relish, though some see it as an effective exercise of their authority, especially if they can persuade the court to allow the probation order to continue (Lawson 1978; Drakeford 1993). Breach enthusiasm has been more evident in relation to community punishment orders, where approximately 12 per cent of orders in 2002 were terminated for 'failure to comply' (Home Office 2004c) which, in this context, usually means non-attendance at work. However, a shift in approach with the commencement of the National Probation Service in 2001 has had an impact on the figures. A performance target for breaching non-compliance with orders is set at 90 per cent (National Probation Service and Home Office 2001). A recent research study has found that there is considerable variation in enforcement practices between probation areas but that there appears to be little difference in reconviction rates between offenders who have been subjected to a 'tough' enforcement regime and those subjected to a 'lenient' regime (Hearnden and Millie 2004).

The enforcement of fines is a less personalized process, though that seems to be no guarantee of its equity. Imprisonment for fine default is an extraordinarily expensive form of enforcement and courts would argue that they avoid it wherever possible, preferring to make money payment supervision orders (using probation officers to give advice and encourage payment) or attachment of earnings orders (stopping money out of pay packets and benefit payments). The number of receptions for fine default has decreased significantly since 1993, when it stood at over 22,000, or 30 per cent of all prison receptions. In 2001, fewer than 1,500 receptions were for fine default. Nevertheless, 1.6 per cent of prison receptions are fine defaulters and although most only spend a few days in prison (and therefore account for 0.2 per cent of the prison population overall) (Home Office 2003b), most studies show that the vast majority of these are unable, rather than unwilling, to pay their fines (Cavadino and Dignan 1997).

Discrimination, criminal justice and community penalties

As we have seen, the main criticism of utilitarianism is that it takes insufficient account of the relationship between punishment and the seriousness of the crime. The main criticism of retributivism is that it takes insufficient account of the differential effects of punishment. Both approaches run the risk, for different reasons, of making sentencing distinctions which are based on what are termed 'improper grounds'. By either taking account of, or failing to take account of, the range of personal and social factors that surround the commission of crime, sentencers and those who advise them are frequently accused of being unfair, inconsistent and discriminatory.

Since the mid-1980s, particular concerns have emerged about the over-representation of black and Asian people in prison and the inappropriate treatment of female offenders. In both cases, it is argued that sentencers and professional workers display discriminatory attitudes, based on stereotypical views of black and Asian people and women who commit crimes.

Concern about discrimination in the criminal justice system led the government to include a section (s.95) in the Criminal Justice Act 1991 which requires the Home Secretary to publish information annually which will enable those administering the system to avoid discrimination 'on the ground of sex or race or any other improper ground'. Critics point out that the drafting of the section makes this optional, since the Home Secretary has the incongruous alternative option of publishing information to assist administrators 'to become aware of the financial implications of their decisions'. Discrimination in public services, and particularly criminal justice, has been reviewed, challenged and monitored following the implementation of the recommendations of the MacPherson Report (MacPherson 1999). Following the murder of Stephen Lawrence in 1993, this report made clear that it should be a ministerial priority to increase the trust and confidence in policing amongst minority ethnic communities. It concluded that 'institutional racism' pervaded the Metropolitan Police. Performance indicators were to be set, and recording and reporting details defined. Its recommendations numbered 70, and one of the most significant was the definition for a racist incident, which was deemed to be 'any which is perceived to be racist by the victim or any other person'. The definition was to be used for police, local government and other relevant agencies. In fact, the report's recommendations became adopted throughout the public sector.

Discrimination on grounds of race and ethnicity

Black and Asian people (by which term is meant non-white minority ethnic groups of African-Caribbean and Asian origin) appear to be involved disproportionately in the criminal justice system as both offenders and victims of crime, though not as workers. Relative to their numbers in the population of England and Wales, black and Asian people (and especially those of African-Caribbean origin) are over-represented in prison. In 2002, 22 per cent of the male and 29 per cent of the female prison population were from minority ethnic groups (Home Office 2004b). These consist of both British and foreign nationals, the latter constituting approximately 10 per cent of the overall prison population. The over-representation of black and Asian people in prison raises two questions: do black and Asian people commit more crime than white people and/or are they discriminated against by the criminal justice system? (Cavadino and Dignan 1997; Harris 1992).

Those who argue that black and Asian people commit disproportionate amounts of crime range from those who claim that black and Asian people are biologically more inclined than white people to commit crime through those who argue that black and Asian people born in England and Wales tend to grow up without respect for 'British' ways, authority or law, to those who argue that the experiences of direct and indirect discrimination (that is, less employment, poorer housing and more poverty) make it more likely that black and Asian people will engage in criminal activity. It is not difficult to identify such beliefs as being racist, because they are based on prejudiced assumptions about a whole group of people which could never be shown to be true by objective enquiry. Pearson (1983) demonstrates that generations of white people have always maintained that Britain is 'by nature' a peaceful and law-abiding place and that they have always chosen to blame crime and public disorder on 'foreigners' (particularly young men) with 'alien cultures'.

There is more evidence, however, that black and Asian people tend to attract more attention and suspicion than white people, particularly from the police and particularly in public places. A number of research studies (predominantly in London) have indicated that black and Asian people (particularly those of African-Caribbean origin) are more likely than white people to be stopped and searched by the police and more likely to be arrested (Reiner 1989). The Census of 2001 showed that the population comprised 2.8 per cent black, 4.7 per cent Asian and 1.2 per cent 'other' minority ethnic – a total on 8.7 per cent of the resident population (Home Office 2004c). However, of those subjected to stop and search in 2003, 22 per cent were from black and minority ethnic populations. Black and Asian people were six times more likely to be subjected to stop and search in 2002/03 – an increase from five times in 2001/02. There is also some evidence that black and Asian young people are less likely than their white counterparts to receive a caution and no further action. (One reason for this might be that the young person denies committing the offence and therefore considers their arrest unjustified; the police, however, may then feel obliged to proceed with the charge.) Research suggests that interaction between police officers and black and Asian people is influenced by a 'canteen culture' based on racist banter and prejudiced stereotyping (Lea and Young 1984; MacPherson 1999).

Black and Asian defendants are more likely than whites to be committed to crown court for trial but this is often by their own choice because they deny the offence and believe they will get fairer treatment from a jury trial. Unfortunately, however, if they are found guilty, like all defendants, they are likely to receive a harsher sentence than they would in a magistrates' court. It has been difficult to find clear evidence that race plays an influential part in sentencing in the crown court but recent statistics show that the use of custody in the crown court was more common for black offenders (16 per cent) than for whites (14 per cent) and Asians (13 per cent) (Home Office 2004c). A study by Hood (1992) appears to demonstrate that at least some of the difference between the numbers of black men in the population at large and the numbers in prison can be accounted for by differential sentencing of black and white defendants. Hood claimed to find no similar evidence in relation to black women, a large proportion of whom he found to be drug couriers and therefore likely to be dealt with harshly for that reason alone (see also Carlen and Worrall 2004).

Hood also confirmed previous findings that black and Asian men were less likely than white men to be given community punishments such as community rehabilitation orders or community punishment orders. This appears to be partly due to an inability on the part of probation officers to make convincing recommendations for such options (Denney 1992). The situation had not significantly improved by the year 2000 when Her Majesty's Inspectorate of Probation found that race equality was lacking in the writing of Pre-Sentence Reports (Home Office 2000).

Discrimination is usually seen to be cumulative rather than specific at any one stage of the process but probation officers may be making a significant contribution. Unlike in studies on women offenders, however, the level of analysis has been rather simplistic – either black and Asian people are actually committing more crime than white people, as a result of their experiences of racism, or racism is responsible for constructing black and Asian people as being more criminal than white people (or, occasionally, as in Lea and Young 1984, the two arguments are combined to suggest a vicious circle). The focus has been on social reaction rather than an exploration of etiology. Two notable exceptions have been the work of John Pitts (1986, 1993) who has consistently rooted discussion of racism in understandings about youth justice and social inequality, and David Denney (1992) who has utilized discourse analysis to deconstruct professional assessments of black and Asian offenders and to provide insight into the difficulties which (white) probation officers have in transforming the black offender into the

> 'good subject' who can be conceptualized as having the 'potential' to become structured into and identify with probation discourses.
> (Denney 1992: 128)

A recent Home Office study (Calverley *et al.* 2004) confirms that there is no evidence to support the view that minority ethnic offenders have greater criminogenic needs (are more likely to commit crime) than white offenders. Many black and Asian offenders continue to experience the criminal justice system as discriminatory and there is a suggestion that they may receive community sentences at lower levels of 'criminogenic need' than white offenders. Nevertheless, black and Asian offenders' attitudes towards supervision were broadly favourable and not markedly different from those of white offenders.

Discrimination on grounds of gender

We do not know why there is apparently such a great difference between men and women in relation to criminal behaviour. Some people believe that men are genetically more aggressive and inclined towards deviant behaviour. Others argue that the difference is caused by differences of socialization. Girls tend to be brought up to be more conforming and to behave in ways that will not get them into trouble with the law. It is often assumed that adolescent girls are more likely to be 'in moral danger' because of sexual promiscuity than to become involved in criminal activity. When they are adults, women may have less opportunity to commit crimes because they are looking after their homes and their children. If they cannot cope with these responsibilities, they are more likely to seek medical or psychiatric help than to turn to crime. Heidensohn (1985) describes the ways in which modern society controls women's behaviour by communicating expectations that women will be feminine and domesticated. Some writers (see Adler 1975) thought that women's liberation would mean more women committing more serious violent crime but, despite media encouragement of a moral panic, this has not happened (see Chapter 10). Although more women are committing crime, in absolute numbers, it is generally less serious than that committed by men. In 2002, women were found guilty of 237,600 offences – an increase of some 15 per cent on 1997. However this increase was in summary, non-motoring offences. TV licence offences were the cause – these increased by 30 per cent over the five year period (Home Office 2003c).

Because so few women commit crime, it has been argued that women criminals are also abnormal women. Some people think there must be something biologically or mentally wrong with women who commit crime. In particular, they think that women criminals are 'more masculine' than 'normal' women. Others believe that women commit crime because they suffer from premenstrual tension, the menopause or postnatal depression. Yet others argue that women commit crime because they are sexually promiscuous or emotionally unbalanced. Although all these explanations may apply in a few individual cases, there is no evidence to support these ideas as general theories of female offending. (All these theories are discussed in detail in many texts on women and crime – for example, Gelsthorpe 2004; Heidensohn 1985; Morris 1987; Worrall 2002a.)

Carlen (1988) is one of several contemporary writers who argue that many of the women who commit crimes do so because they are poor. They steal food and clothes, often for their children, and defraud the Benefits Agency because they cannot live on the money they get. A lot of women in prison have been in care as children and find that they cannot look after themselves, as adults, on their own. Often they are homeless and many have drug or alcohol problems. Some women commit crimes out of greed or for excitement, just like some men, but these are a very small number. Women who commit violent crimes often do so after years of physical or emotional abuse. In recent years, a number of foreign women have been imprisoned for acting as drugs couriers, often under duress or as a result of poverty.

At first sight it may appear that female offenders are treated more leniently by the police and the courts than male offenders. In 2002, 44 per cent were cautioned by the police for indictable offences (and not brought to court) compared with 30 per cent of male offenders. Of those brought to court, 23 per cent of women were given discharges (compared with 13 per cent of men) and 19 per cent were put on supervision or community rehabilitation (compared with 11 per cent of men). On the other hand, 24 per cent of men were fined (compared with 18 per cent of women) and 9 per cent of men were given community punishment orders (compared with 7 per cent of women). Finally, 27 per cent of men and 15 per cent of women were sent to prison. One compilation of official statistics by Hedderman and Hough (1994) at the Home Office Research Unit argues that there is no evidence to support the claim that women are systematically dealt with more severely than men and that, overall, women seem more likely to receive lenient sentences even when previous convictions are taken into consideration. They do, however, concede that this does not rule out the possibility of disparities within gender and that individual women may receive unusually harsh treatment. The figures given here are from the Home Office Statistics on Women and the Criminal Justice System 2003 (2004b) and indicate that Hedderman and Hough's premise holds good, despite a narrowing of the gender differences in recent years. Hedderman (2004) has concluded that the greater use of custody for women over the past decade has not been driven by an increase in the seriousness of women's offending but by a more severe sentencing response.

Indeed, there may be a number of reasons for this apparent leniency. If a woman gets a 'light' sentence it is usually because her offence is not very serious. Occasionally a woman gets off 'lightly' because a magistrate thinks she is a good wife and mother – a respectable woman who has made one mistake. Magistrates often think that they are being kind to women by putting them on probation because they think it will help them to have someone to talk to. And often it does. Unfortunately, however, being on probation may have a stigmatising and 'net-widening' effect on a woman, making it more likely that she will go to prison if she commits another offence. Men often get the chance to do community punishment which has been considered less suitable for women. Women also get sent to hospital for psychiatric reports more often than men. Allen (1987) argues that psychiatrists seem very ready to label female offenders as 'mentally ill'.

There is evidence, however, that some women get heavier sentences than they should because magistrates think that women should not commit crime – that they are setting a bad example to their children and not behaving like proper women. Unmarried or divorced women, women with children in care and black and Asian women appear to get heavier sentences. They seem to get punished for who they are, rather than for what they have done. As we have seen, 29 per cent of women in prison are from minority ethnic groups, which is far in excess of their proportion in the population outside prison. Some of these women are drugs couriers who will be deported when they finish their sentence and may have to serve another sentence in their own country. But many black women in prison were born in Great Britain and commit the same offences as white women.

When the Criminal Justice Act 1991 was first implemented, there was some optimism that 'just deserts' for women would actually result in less punishment (because women commit less serious offences and have fewer previous convictions than men) and better provision (because access to community punishments had to be non-discriminatory according to section 95 of the Act). But the amendments of 1993 (see Chapter 3) and a wilful misinterpretation of 'equal opportunities' rhetoric has led to a rapid expansion of the female prison population and a reduction in the numbers of women receiving community sentences, especially the traditional community rehabilitation order. (For a fuller discussion of women's imprisonment, see Carlen and Worrall 2004.)

Social exclusion and discrimination on grounds of class

While attention has been focused rightly on discrimination against black and Asian people and women in recent years, it could be argued that class discrimination in the criminal justice system is so overwhelming as to be taken for granted. The vast majority of defendants appearing in court are from the working or unemployed classes, to the extent that some writers (such as Murray 1990) argue that there now exists an 'underclass' of poor, homeless and/or unemployed people with unstable family relationships who are responsible for most of the crime and disorder in our society. The first *National Prison Survey* (Walmsley, Howard and White 1992) indicated that people with these characteristics in their backgrounds are over-represented in prison. Critics of underclass theory point out that people in every social class commit crime and that the crime which damages society most is often committed by very rich people. The fact that lower-class crime is the most stigmatized is itself a form of discrimination. Gardiner argues that the Criminal Justice Act 1991 and its advocacy of punishment in the community was in reality 'a response in terms of the management of an aggregate group of people rather than individuals' (1995:363). It is, he argues, the 'underclass' which is being targeted by contemporary penal policy.

The term 'class' is used rarely these days – politically, it is regarded as too closely associated with 'Old Labour' – and the preferred term (although it is not synonymous) is 'social exclusion'. The definition of this phrase is widely contested but a useful 'working' definition is to be found in the Commission of the European Communities' *Background Report: Social Exclusion – Poverty and Other Social Problems in the European Community*, ISEC/B/11/93:

> Social exclusion refers to the multiple and changing factors resulting in people being excluded from the normal exchanges, practices and rights of modern society. Poverty is one of the most obvious factors, but social exclusion also refers to inadequate rights in housing, education, health and access to services. It affects individuals and groups, particularly in urban and rural areas, who are in some way subject to discrimination or segregation; and it emphasises the weaknesses in the social infrastructure and the risk of allowing a two-tier society to become established by default.

As far as crime and punishment is concerned, social exclusion also has a different meaning – a deliberate but spontaneous response to lawbreaking. Social exclusion of deviants is viewed by some as a necessary condition of social solidarity. In 2002, the Social Exclusion Unit in the Office of the Deputy Prime Minister produced a report identifying nine key factors of social exclusion that impact on reoffending by ex-prisoners:

- education
- employment
- drug and alcohol misuse
- mental and physical health
- attitudes and self-control
- institutionalization and life-skills
- housing
- financial support and debt
- family networks

The report claims that being in employment reduces the risk of reoffending by between a third and a half; having stable accommodation reduces the risk by a fifth. Many prisoners have poor basic skills and little experience of employment, few positive social networks, severe housing problems, and all of this is often severely complicated by drug, alcohol and mental health problems. And prison makes things even worse: a third lose their homes while in prison; two-thirds lose their jobs; over a fifth face increased financial problems; and over two-fifths lose contact with their families. Prison further socially excludes the already socially excluded and makes their reintegration into the community even harder.

Conclusion

This chapter has introduced the reader to the range of community punishments, their origins, development and use. It has included a discussion of the relationship between traditional sentencing principles and contemporary political debates about community punishment. But the analysis has also demonstrated some of the recurrent problems associated with non-incarcerative disposals, such as net-widening, enforcement, the image of the 'soft option' and the potential for discrimination on grounds of race, gender and class. In subsequent chapters, we examine these issues in more detail as they relate to specific historical and political developments, changes in legislation and the administration of justice.

Chapter 2

From alternatives to custody to punishment in the community

We should eschew the phrase 'alternatives to custody' for that acts subliminally to suggest that custody is the real answer and produces an expectation that we will supply a kind of custody in the community.

(Lacey 1984: 105)

Introduction

The early 1980s saw a number of apparently disparate political and academic developments that nevertheless worked together to suggest a strengthening of community punishment and an optimism about reducing the prison population and improving prison conditions. Attacks on the rehabilitative potential of institutions from across the political spectrum, centralising tendencies on the part of the Home Office and concern within the probation service to resist marginalization, together resulted in the discourse of 'alternatives to custody' in the mid-1980s and eventually to the idea of punishment in the community and the Criminal Justice Act 1991.

The demise of the rehabilitative ideal

Until the late 1960s, rehabilitation had been the dominant principle of criminal justice. It was an optimistic approach which held that offenders committed crimes for reasons rooted in their biological and psychological make-up or their social upbringing and that, with sufficient knowledge and patience, they could be cured of their criminal tendencies.

But that ideal came increasingly under attack from a number of directions. Loss of confidence in the treatment approach to deviance control, coupled with the rising influence of interactionist and Marxist theories, increased scepticism about the justification for executive discretion and led to a call for a return to 'fairer' tariff-based sentencing. Rehabilitation, it was argued, was disguised state control, part of the soft state apparatus to ensure conformity. Civil liberties were being infringed – because people could be 'treated' (often incarcerated) for an indeterminate period of time and often out of all proportion to the crime committed.

Pragmatists argued that rehabilitation did not work. Martinson (1974: 49) concluded that empirical evidence 'gives us very little reason to hope that we have in fact found a sure way of reducing recidivism through rehabilitation' (although one is no longer allowed to use this quotation without pointing out Martinson's later retraction in 1979 – see Raynor, Smith and Vanstone 1994). There were at least two damning pieces of research (Folkard, Smith and Smith 1976; Phillpotts and Lancucki 1979) which purported to demonstrate that offenders given intensive supervision did no better than those given ordinary or no supervision and in some cases did worse (see also Worrall et al. 2003). Others argued from a symbolic interactionist perspective that intensive intervention could do more harm than good by labelling offenders and amplifying their deviance, making it more likely that they would react by reoffending.

At the same time, the ideology of the New Right sought to buttress individualism, familialism and nationalism by encouraging the stigmatization of 'outgroups' and emphasizing the need for social discipline (Walker and Beaumont 1985). Right-wing critics argued that rehabilitation was soft and that what offenders needed was greater control and surveillance. They appealed to 'common sense' arguments that if offenders were to be kept out of prison then the alternatives had to be tough and demanding. The Criminal Justice Act 1972 introduced community service orders which involved probation officers in supervising offenders undertaking unpaid (often manual) work, with little obvious social work content in the relationship. It proved a popular sentence with courts and resulted in a dramatic decline in the use of probation orders.

With the tide of national politics turning towards an explicit 'law and order' agenda the probation service was obliged to revise its approach to offenders or risk the kind of swingeing financial cuts which Social Services experienced in the late 1970s. The changing role of the service will be discussed in more detail in Chapter 5 but these attacks left it unsure of its foundation and the issue of 'care versus control' came to dominate professional thinking in the early 1980s.

With the new Conservative government in 1979 began a fundamental review of the identity and ethos of the service. At one end of the spectrum, Haxby (1978) advocated the creation of a 'community correctional service', with the emphasis on punishment and strict 'alternatives to custody'. Other writers sought ways of reconciling the increasingly conflicting demands to care and control, the most influential being an article by Bottoms and McWilliams (1979) entitled 'A non-treatment paradigm for probation practice', which recommended abandoning the medical model of probation (based on notions of diagnosis, followed by treatment, leading to cure) and replacing it with the 'language of help, shared assessment and task-centred work'. At the other end of the political spectrum, Walker and Beaumont (1981) advocated a radical socialist approach to probation work, emphasising the role of capitalism, poverty and oppression in the perpetuation of crime. The views of the latter were widely embraced within the National Association of Probation Officers, the professional association and trade union for probation officers.

Alongside the developments in professional thinking based on broad political and criminological ideas came the rise of managerialism and accountability in the Thatcherite 1980s. Under the umbrella of the Financial Management Initiative which emphasised economy, efficiency and effectiveness, the Home Office, which had previously adopted a *laissez-faire* attitude to the 55 probation areas, decided to reassert its control. In 1984 the Home Office formulated its *Statement of National Objectives and Priorities*, which, according to Beaumont, established priorities 'by rationing resources between existing activities, rather than prioritising desirable improvements' (1995: 53). During 1985 and 1986 probation areas responded with their own *Statements of Local Objectives and Priorities* and, in an attempt to forestall further central government interference, engaged the services of financial management consultants. The implications of these developments for the role of the probation officer will also be examined in more detail in Chapter 5. At this point, it is sufficient to note that such developments had the effect of further undermining the notion of the probation officer as a 'caseworker', whose main professional skills lay in establishing helping relationships with individual offenders. Soon after the Labour government was elected in 1997, a review of the probation and prison services, entitled *Joining Forces*, served notice on the probation service that it would not be allowed to continue with its existing structure and culture (Home Office 1998). The commencement of the National Probation Service in 2001, with 42 probation areas being overseen, for the first time, by a National Directorate and Director, was indicative of further change. The objectives were set out and performance management was key. The culture changed, and with it the role and skills of probation officers and colleagues who had contact with offenders. Assessment for risk and suitability for programmes under the 'What Works' agenda became essential skills.

Meanwhile, a parallel and complementary debate was taking place over the role of Social Services departments in relation to juvenile delinquents. The history and development of this debate will be examined fully in Chapter 10 but it is important to note here that, following the ill-fated 'short, sharp shock' experiment at New Hall and Send Detention Centres in 1980 and the unprecedentedly high level of the youth custody centre population (7,700 in 1981), there was genuine concern about overcrowding in the youth custody system.

The 1982 Criminal Justice Act introduced criteria which courts had to be satisfied were met before sending a young offender to custody, and in 1983 the Home Secretary announced a new initiative to provide alternatives to custody for more serious and persistent young offenders. The Intermediate Treatment initiative launched by Local Authority Circular LAC 3/83 saw some £15 million invested in over 100 projects around the country. This, together with the increased use of police cautioning for minor offences, led to a dramatic reduction in the numbers of juveniles both entering the formal criminal justice system and being sent to custody. By 1990 fewer than 2,000 juveniles were being imprisoned annually.

But, as we shall see later, underlying this trend was a conscious move by juvenile justice social workers away from intervention which focused on the welfare of the child and towards a policy of minimal intervention designed to manage both the decisions made by the criminal justice system (systems management) and the criminal career of the juvenile (the alternative tariff approach) (Pitts 1992a). Since that time, changes have been wholesale. Attitudes towards young offenders changed in the early 1990s and the Labour government adopted a 'no excuses' agenda that led to the establishment of the Youth Justice Board in 1998 and multi-agency Youth Offending Teams. Particular emphasis was placed on identifying persistent offenders and implementing a particular version of restorative justice that focused on challenging young offenders to accept responsibility for the harm they caused and requiring active reparation from them (Crawford and Newburn 2003).

The decarceration debate

During the 1980s and 1990s, the various critiques of rehabilitation tended to confuse institutional rehabilitative approaches with non-incarcerative rehabilitative approaches. The argument for decarceration was based on the realization that prisons (and, indeed, other institutions) were wholly inappropriate environments in which to attempt to reform deviant behaviour. But such arguments begged two questions. First, is this the only (or even the main) reason for supporting decarceration? Second, what is the nature of 'rehabilitation' outside the institution? It was to these questions that four particular writers – Andrew Scull, Stanley Cohen, Thomas Mathiesen and Anthony Bottoms – addressed themselves in the early 1980s.

Identifying the gap between the rhetoric and the reality of deinstitutionalization, Scull (1977/1984) launched a scathing attack on those who advocated community treatment for mentally ill and criminal deviants. Isn't it miraculous, he asks, with feigned incredulity, that such programmes are not only more humane and effective, but also cheaper than institutional treatment? In a thesis that remains painfully relevant in relation to mentally ill people (but not, as we shall see, in relation to criminals), he argued that decarceration amounted to benign neglect as a consequence of under-resourcing and sheer lack of interest:

> Much of the time, it appears as if the policy makers simply do not know what will happen when their schemes are put into effect. Nor do they seem very concerned to find out. Often, they do not even know where those they have dumped back on the rest of us are to be found.
>
> (Scull 1984: 1)

In summary, then, Scull's concern was that decarceration would fail to provide mentally ill people and criminals with the care and supervision they require and thus render both them and the community vulnerable to danger and unacceptable behaviour. One of the consequences of this would be an increase in moral panics among the non-deviant community and a backlash of rejection and practices of exclusion which would be every bit as stigmatizing and non-rehabilitative as institutionalization had been.

The problem with Scull's thesis, however, was that he chose to build on Goffman's previous work on 'total institutions' (Goffman 1961), which had argued that there were certain characteristics which were common to many institutions (the asylum and the prison being among the most notable) and which resulted in the institutionalization of inmates. Scull mistakenly believed, therefore, that the deinstitutionalization of mental patients and criminals could also be subjected to an identical analysis.

But while mental hospitals were emptying and closing down, prisons were not. On the contrary, prison building was expanding and the prison population constantly rising. At the same time as the Home Secretary (then Leon Brittan) was attempting to regain centralized control over the probation service and arguably raise its profile as a credible provider of alternatives to custody, he was also announcing the largest prison-building programme ever. Far from seeing the convicted felon's chance of receiving a prison sentence grow ever more remote (Scull 1977/1984), it was clear that alternatives to custody were rapidly becoming no more than supplements to custody. And far from being supervised by probation officers 'with caseloads of one and two hundred persons' (Scull 1977/1984: 2), criminals were being subjected to a matrix of ever more complex social-control mechanisms in the name of community corrections. The argument that community corrections are undoubtedly cheaper than prisons was, and remains, fairly irrelevant. The fact is that people are prepared to pay for the punishment of criminals; they are not prepared to pay for their treatment. Community corrections will attract resources if they are dressed up as punishment but they will fail to attract even modest resources if they are perceived only as treatment.

Cohen's critique of decarceration (1979, 1983, 1985) owed more to Foucault's concept of the 'dispersal of discipline' than to Goffman's concept of the 'total institution'. His analysis of the history of 'social control talk' juxtaposed three different rhetorics, which made Scull's analysis appear simplistic. Accepting that, in an imperfect world, progress will never be unimpeded, Cohen describes, first, an optimistic conservative rhetoric which argues that penal reform has been steady and that decarceration represents the enlightened values of an ever more civilized society. By contrast, Cohen's second account of penal change reflects the liberal disillusion with rehabilitation, which characterized much of the symbolic interactionist literature on the sociology of deviance and the 'nothing works' approach to punishment. Rather than seeking reform, we should be looking for ways to manage – both the system and individual criminal careers – so as to cause the least damage, cost and inconvenience to the rest of society. But Cohen's third model presents a conspiracy of the powerful to mystify and obfuscate:

> Humanism, good intentions, professional knowledge and reform rhetoric are neither in the idealist sense the producers of change, nor in the materialist sense the mere products of changes in the political economy ... [T]he exercise of power itself creates and causes to emerge new objects of knowledge and accumulates new bodies of information.
>
> (Cohen 1983: 107)

The decarcerated criminal is one such new object of knowledge about whom new bodies of information must be accumulated. Community programmes, far from reducing the restrictions on criminals who might otherwise have been sent to prison, create a new clientele of criminals who are controlled or disciplined by other mechanisms. The boundaries between freedom and confinement become blurred. The 'net' of social control is thus thrown ever wider into the community, its thinner mesh designed to trap ever smaller 'fish'. Once caught in the net, the 'penetration of disciplinary intervention' is ever deeper, reaching every aspect of the criminal's life.

The particular insight which Thomas Mathiesen adds to Cohen's analysis is a prediction that the future of social control will involve a move away from the identification and punishment of individuals towards the criminalization of 'whole groups and categories – through planned manipulation ... of the everyday life conditions of these groups and categories' (1983: 139). From the growth of private security and CCTV to the 1994 legislation against travellers, to the creation of parenting and child safety orders, to the defining of persistent young offenders in the Crime and Disorder Act 1998 and to the civil and criminal types of Anti-Social Behaviour Orders, it is not difficult to find examples of the fulfilment of Mathiesen's prophecy.

The appeal of such radical critiques is undeniable. The spectre of George Orwell's *Nineteen Eighty Four* (1949) produces a frisson of resistance in most of us but the mundane reality of criminal justice is less spectacular or threatening. Most punishment, Anthony Bottoms (1983) argues, is not about the creation of docile bodies but the more routine business of disqualification from – and subsequent requalification to – full citizenship. Most offences are dealt with by means of monetary penalties – fines or compensation – and other disposals that do not involve supervision. The purpose is intentionally and openly to penalize unacceptable actions, to prevent repetition and to deter others by making examples of those who infringe the rules. There is nothing particularly sinister about the process and there is no congruence 'with a general thesis of a thrust towards indefinite discipline' (Bottoms 1983: 178). We must be as careful not to be carried away by moral panics about punishment as we are to resist moral panics about crime itself.

Enter discourse analysis

At this point, it is necessary to introduce some of the conceptual tools of discourse analysis in order to make sense of the paradoxical and inconsistent developments in both academic and policy thinking in the early years of the 1980s. Discourse analysis is concerned with the relationship between power and the production of knowledge (Worrall 1990). It is concerned with all aspects of a communication – not only its content, but its author (who says it?), its authority (on what grounds?), its audience (to whom?), its object (about whom?) and its objective (in order to achieve what?). What are the mechanisms whereby, in the face of a fragmented and contradictory reality, claims to know can be successfully translated into effective unified knowledge with over-determined consequences?

First, that reality has to be reconstructed as a field of recognizable (that is, unified and ideologically congruent) objects in which it is possible to intervene on the basis of prior existing knowledge. The observable phenomenon of people breaking the law has to be pro-grammed as people who break the law and about whom knowledge already exists, has always existed, and is waiting to be laid claim to. And that knowledge already contains within it (perversely hidden but ultimately reachable) its own inevitable consequences and 'correct' solutions (Worrall 1990).

The fragmented and contradictory reality of 'alternatives to custody' consists, *inter alia*, of the following elements:

- a consensus that prison can never be a genuine site of rehabilitation and that some attempt must be made to keep those criminals deemed capable of being rehabilitated out of prison

- a lack of consensus about the effectiveness of non-incarcerative rehabilitation and a concern about the effects (whether intended or unintended) of measures which blur the boundaries between prison and freedom

- a political decision to expand, rather than reduce, the number of places available in prison, thereby removing some of the pressure from sentencers to utilize alternatives to custody and

- consequent political pressure on the probation service to compete for its clientele either by proving its rehabilitative effectiveness or by demonstrating that supervision can serve other punitive purposes (such as surveillance and monitoring) which supplement prison but do so at less cost

Second, the programme of finding the 'correct' solution to the problem of 'people who break the law' requires a channel of conveyance. The *technology* of such conveyance is varied and disparate. It may consist of architectural institutions, like courtrooms, prisons or probation offices; it may consist of practices such as the provision of welfare, the ascription of motives or practices of exclusion (including surveillance and monitoring). Finally, it may consist of norms – technologies that have been internalized to the extent that they are no longer recognized as technologies at all. Self-regulation demonstrates the supreme success of a programme (Worrall 1990). An example of a practice of exclusion crucial to the conveyance of the programme of punishment in the community is the ejection from the discourse of rehabilitation of any legitimate concern for the welfare of the criminal. Instead, that concern is constructed as Other – the non-legitimated account of lived experience which threatens, and must be controlled by, the programme. The personal or social welfare of the criminal is explicitly detached from, and made discursively irrelevant to, the process of preventing recidivism. Offending is a matter of choice, not something determined by circumstances, and modern rehabilitation 'addresses offending behaviour' – it is not concerned with the offender's address (see Chapter 6).

Third, programmes and technologies are dependent for their success on *strategies* of intervention (Worrall 1990). Strategy is not the coherent, logical, overall planning of action (although it may be represented as such). Rather, it is an opportunistic and expedient means of exploiting the field of intervention. It is the means whereby the authority of programmes can be maintained (or denied) in spite of (and yet because of) their effects. Strategy is the process whereby individuals and agencies attempt to anticipate the effects of programmes and technologies and then utilize those effects to justify the continuation or cessation of such intervention. It is the means by which a programme 'caters in advance for the eventuality of its own failure' (Gordon 1979:

38). The tenacity of electronic monitoring, discussed below, is an excellent example of strategy.

The discussion which follows deconstructs the representation of punishment in the community as a coherent framework of response to crime and attempts to expose the absence of that which is represented as being present: namely, the political will to send fewer criminals to prison.

Greenpapering over the cracks

The process began with a strategy of consultation through the publication in 1988 of the Green Paper, *Punishment, Custody and the Community* (Home Office 1988). Responding to the rapidly increasing prison population which threatened to outgrow even the ambitious new prison-building programme, the government stated quite clearly that:

> Imprisonment is not the most effective punishment for most crime. Custody should be reserved as punishment for very serious offences ...
>
> (Home Office 1988: 2)

Within these two short phrases can be found the two crucial words which not only formed the foundation of the Criminal Justice Act 1991, but which simultaneously constituted the 'cracks' in that foundation – 'punishment' and 'serious'. It will be argued in Chapter 3 that it was the reliance on the ill-defined concept of 'offence seriousness' that brought about the demise of the 1991 Act. For the moment the focus will remain on the use of the term 'punishment' in official criminal justice discourse from the time of the publication of the Green Paper.

In a speech to the Annual Conference of the Association of Chief Officers of Probation (ACOP) in September 1988, John Patten (then Home Office Minister of State) attempted to define 'punishment' in such a way as to make it palatable to a professional group which, while accepting that its work included elements of control, had traditionally found it difficult to incorporate the word 'punishment' into its vocabulary. Patten's argument will be quoted in full because its logic is central to the theme of this book:

> I acknowledge straight away that there is an inherent tension between the concept of control – let alone punishment – and the

roles of the probation service which are variously described as 'welfare', 'caring' or 'helping' ... But I still use the word 'punishment'. My reason for this lies in some basic truths about the way the criminal justice system operates and how the public perceive it. Taking the public first, their concept of punishment, I suggest, is that of an offender being subject to restrictions on liberty, inconvenience and even to financial penalties; these restrictions to be proportionate to the degree of inconvenience the offender has caused for society or for his [sic] victims. They will be reflected in restrictions on his ability to do what he wants and when, and in the obligations which are put on him to face the reasons for his offending, the consequences for his victim and the need for reparation to society. The Green Paper recognises that in some cases the perception of punishment can be met only by a custodial sentence. It argues, however, that it would be adequately met in case of significant other categories of offenders, by... punishment in the community. *The fact is that all probation-based disposals are already in varying degrees forms of punishment. For example, the offender who has to report to a probation officer, or work specified hours on CS or spend 60 days at a day centre is clearly being punished. It is bizarre to scratch around to find polite euphemisms for what is going on.*

(Patten 1988: 12, original emphasis)

At one level, the logic of this argument is flawless. Whether one is reading the work of a radical writer like Foucault (1977) or a conventional criminologist like Walker (1991), no one pretends that the only definition of 'punishment' is the narrow one of incarceration of or inflicting pain on the physical body. According to Walker, punishment 'involves the infliction of something which is assumed to be unwelcome to the recipient' (1991:1). The infliction has to be intentional (deliberate) and for a reason (the breaking of a law) – accidental harm does not count. Nevertheless, no one would dispute that a conditional discharge or a fine are, *in a sense,* punishments, as are probation orders and community service orders, insofar as they are unwelcome inconveniences.

But what this technical definition fails to address is the purpose of punishment and it is here that Patten's definition so clearly (but implicitly) parts company from the traditional value base of the probation service. It is one thing to say that punishment is an inevitable (even desirable) by-product of placing an offender on probation. It is quite another to say that punishment is the purpose of such an order.

On the surface, Patten is arguing for the 'just deserts' philosophy that became explicit in the later White Paper – the imposition of proportionate restriction of liberty or inconvenience. But underneath is an attempt to appropriate a range of other, different, principles (deterrence, reform, rehabilitation) and to argue that they can be subsumed within a 'just deserts' discourse, because they are not incompatible with it.

What is being presented here is a falsely constructed politics of consensus. Instead of acknowledging genuine conflicts of interest and philosophy and arguing for a pragmatic compromise, the argument is presented in such a way as to pretend that *there is no conflict,* except in the minds of dangerously inflexible subversives, who apparently delight in the 'bizarre' practice of 'scratch(ing) around to find polite euphemisms'.

So one of the ways in which the government sought to greenpaper over the cracks of a penal crisis which was threatening to run out of control because of the lack of accountability of sentencers (Parker 1988) was to argue that 'we're all in the business of punishment'. There are no differences of principle, only differences of approach and language – and credibility. It is not, so the argument goes, that the government is opposed to non-custodial disposals. On the contrary, it wishes to enhance their status and extend their use by introducing the possibility of 'mixing and matching', to enable sentencers to make their own unique 'designer packages'. Apart from anything else, 'punishment in the community should be more economical in public resources' (Home Office 1988: 2). But in order to do this, it has to be recognized that 'not every sentencer or member of the public had full confidence in the present orders which leave offenders in the community' (Home Office 1988: 2). In other words, responsibility for making the new packages work lies not with sentencers but with those who provide what must now be referred to as 'tough and demanding punishment' for people who must no longer be called 'clients' but must now be referred to as 'offenders'. As John Patten rightly says, 'this is more than a semantic point' (Patten, 1988: 11).

Turning the clock forward a decade or so, this desire to show the punitive side of probation work was demonstrated by much of the language used at the inception of the National Probation Service (NPS) in 2001. Community service orders became community punishment orders and the NPS's five aims included 'the proper punishment of offenders'. It was no coincidence that the frontispiece of probation's *National Standards 2000* recorded Paul Boateng's speech as Minister for

Prisons and Probation: 'We are a law enforcement agency. It's what we are. It's what we do'.

A fate worse than prison?

The Green Paper made the fundamental mistake of assuming that offenders would (and could) do virtually anything in order to avoid a prison sentence. The later White Paper recognised that much crime was not committed after careful calculation of the possible gains and risks:

> Much crime is committed on impulse ... by offenders who live from moment to moment; their crimes are as impulsive as the rest of their feckless, sad or pathetic lives. It is unrealistic to construct sentencing arrangements on the assumption that most offenders will weigh up the possibilities in advance and base their conduct on rational calculation. Often they do not.
>
> (Home Office 1990a: 2.8)

But that eloquent insight was something for the future. In 1988, the government believed that it could make non-custodial sentencing almost as complicated and demanding as it wished. Admittedly, there was some acknowledgement that sentences had to be 'realistic':

> If the requirements are made too demanding, it is more likely that the offender will fail to complete it satisfactorily and this could result in his imprisonment. This would defeat the purpose of the order.
>
> (Home Office 1988: 14)

Despite this, the Green Paper goes on to suggest, as an example, that an offender in full-time employment or education could, nevertheless, be given an order which included a daily curfew, weekly community service, tracking (daily contact with a supervisor), paying compensation and having regular interviews with a probation officer to discuss his offending behaviour. For an unemployed offender, the package would include two days community service, two days at a day centre and two days 'prescribed activity' in addition to the daily curfew. It was this proposed punitive overload that prompted Pat Carlen to raise the question of sentence *feasibility* and the obligation that should be placed on sentencers 'in the cases of offenders bearing multiple social disadvantage [to]attempt to do least harm by making non-punitive and totally supportive orders' (Carlen 1990: 120). The development of intensive supervision and monitoring programmes for both young and adult offenders from the late 1990s onwards could be said to be bringing this punitive overload to some offenders (Worrall *et al.* 2003; Audit Commission 2004).

In the event, the proposed 'supervision and restriction order' did not materialize but the Green Paper did succeed in bringing about another highly restrictive measure, that of electronic monitoring. Tagging could not be used on sentenced offenders without specific legislation, but there was nothing to stop courts experimenting with it as a condition of bail. Again, the assumption was that offenders would put up with anything rather than be remanded in custody. Indeed, Tom Stacey (founder of the incredibly named Offenders' Tag Association) argued strongly that opposition to tagging was based on 'wilful ignorance' of the appalling nature of prison conditions and the 'vested interests' of the civil libertarian and penal reform lobbies. As well as wishing to avoid prison, offenders, he argues, would also prefer to be tagged than have to talk to a probation officer! (Stacey 1989). Leaving aside Mike Nellis' persuasive reply that tagging (by private security companies) is an 'effective means of control over the dispossessed communities – the underclass – who are surplus to capitalism's requirements' (Nellis 1989), it soon became clear in the three experimental schemes that, for some offenders at least, electronic monitoring was a fate worse than prison. Christopher Varney is reported to have asked a judge to return him to prison because he did not like the 'flea-ridden' hostel where he was ordered to live under curfew (*Guardian*, 29 November 1989). Richard Hart, aged 23, was the first person to be allowed to stay at home subject to curfew restrictions monitored by an electronic anklet. When he was first tagged, Hart had said 'Agreeing to being tagged was not an easy decision to make, because it could be like being a prisoner in my own home.' (*Guardian*, 18 August 1989) Difficulties with the technology of the equipment resulted in him returning to custody.

As we shall see in the next chapter, the attempt by the 1994 Criminal Justice and Public Order Act to revive the fortunes of electronic monitoring was little more successful in terms of numbers and considerably more expensive. It was not until 1999 that the Labour government felt sufficiently confident to make the electronic monitoring of curfew orders available nationally and, since that time, it has been used far more widely for the early release of prisoners on Home Detention Curfew (HDC) than as an alternative to a custodial sentence. In 2001, a total of 3,900 people were sentenced to curfew orders compared with around 14,000 prisoners released on HDC (Home Office 2002b; Nellis 2003a), although the numbers have increased to over 9,000 in 2004 (Home Office 2004a).

We should perhaps not be surprised that electronic monitoring took so long to be accepted in the UK. It was an idea we copied wholesale from America and, as Whitfield explained, 'the main message is that electronic monitoring in the USA is a shambles' (1995: 19). He suggested four factors which contributed to its inappropriate expansion: aggressive marketing by vendors; the promise that it would 'do something' about prison overcrowding; a belief that it might cost less than imprisonment; and a naive and totally unrealistic expectation of what the technology could achieve. Nellis (2002) has warned that rather than having a role in restorative and community justice, which he deems feasible, it could easily become part of the shift towards containment and surveillance where 'old probation ideals' are lost (Nellis 2002: 374). He also recognizes that the media do little to explain the punitive element of electronic monitoring (Nellis 2003a).

Crime, Justice and Protecting the Public

Following this period of 'consultation', the White Paper *Crime, Justice and Protecting the Public* (Cm. 965, Home Office 1990a) set out the government's proposals for 'better justice through a more consistent approach to sentencing, so that convicted criminals get their "just desserts" ' [sic] (1990a:2), though its public reception was not assisted by the persistent typographical error that invited jokes about porridge and prison puddings!

Joking aside, the shift in policy represented by the White Paper was hailed by the then Home Secretary, David Waddington, as heralding 'the most fundamental and far-reaching changes for at least half a century in the way offenders were punished' (*The Times*, 6 February 1990). Elsewhere it was suggested that the proposals 'will come to be compared to the introduction of the probation service in 1907 and the Labour government's abandonment of flogging in 1948' (*Independent*, 7 February 1990). The White Paper had a mixed reception and there was a recognition that the government was making a 'brave gamble ... a strange compromise, attempting to achieve real penal reform while appeasing judges and the law-and-order lobby' (*Independent*, 7 February 1990). A prophetic warning was given that the policy could 'backfire if sentencers failed to impose the new community-based penalties' (*The Times*, 7 February 1990). Nevertheless, commenting with the advantage of hindsight, the policies underpinning the Criminal Justice Act 1991 were very carefully considered and now look remarkably liberal for a Conservative government that had been in power for 12 years. As David Faulkner has since said:

> these policies had evolved gradually, through a process which took account of public feeling but which was largely driven by consultation with professionals, practitioners, academics and representatives of informed opinion ... there was a sense of continuity over quite long periods of time.
>
> (*Guardian*, 11 November 1993)

Professional groups greeted the proposals with a mixture of caution, scepticism and optimism. Some (such as NAPO) saw a dominant emphasis on retributivist punishment, indicating a fundamental change in the role and nature of the probation service, marking its end as a social-work agency. Others (such as the Prison Reform Trust) welcomed the underlying principle of reducing the prison population but regretted the continued wide discretion to be allowed to sentencers and the absence of concern about the needs of offenders. The probation service itself, however, seemed to accept that behind its tough language, the White Paper proposals were extremely pragmatic. They heralded an expanded role for the service, with more report writing, more supervision and more prison aftercare (and, it was hoped, more resources). If the service was prepared to concede the language of punishment, then it seemed that it would be allowed, by and large, to get on with the job it wanted to do.

Conclusion

The decade of the 1980s saw the gradual convergence of political, professional and academic discourses whose origins, authors and desires (or aims) differed widely. The broad sociological debates about decarceration and the demise of the rehabilitative ideal became elided with professional debates about managerialism and the political imperative for the Conservative government to be seen to be *successful* in controlling crime. For a brief moment in political history, there was a consensus that the best way to demonstrate success might be to reduce, rather than increase, the number of people being sent to prison. But, as with other such moments (notably the 1969 Children and Young Person

Act – see Chapter 10), by the time the consensus was set in the 'stone tablets' of legislation, the tide of public opinion was already turning. Reducing the prison population was soon to be seen as a sign of weakness, rather than strength, in the battle against crime.

Chapter 3

The Criminal Justice Act 1991 and its demise

So here we go again, on the punishment train with yet more trucks being coupled ... on to an already overburdened and lengthy express, hurtling nowhere quickly, with an inexhaustible power supply and seemingly infinite capacity to collect, reprocess and dump its perceived 'human waste' with little thought about the personal, social and environmental costs.

(Broad 1991: 22)

Introduction

The Criminal Justice Act 1991 came into force in October 1992 and was the first major review of criminal justice legislation since 1982. It aimed to provide a new coherent sentencing framework based on the principle of just deserts with only the most serious of offences being punished with imprisonment. Less serious offences were to be dealt with by means of three other categories of disposals: discharges (for the bulk of minor offences), financial penalties and community sentences.

The background to the Act was a growing concern with over-crowding in prisons and a related belief that alternative, non-custodial sentences were viewed by sentencers as being 'soft options'. It was accepted that some offenders were being sent to prison unnecessarily and some were being sent for too long. The Woolf Report into the prison disturbances of April 1990 (Woolf and Tumim 1991) and the Reed Report (Department of Health/Home Office 1992) into the treatment of mentally disordered offenders had both highlighted the dangers of inappropriate custodial sentences and of prison overcrowding. Attention was increasingly being paid to adopting appropriate criteria for custody, especially in the Juvenile Court. There was also recognition that sentencing lacked consistency and that this in itself was unjust. Evidence was growing that black and Asian people and women might be experiencing discrimination in the courts. Finally, there was dissatisfaction that courts appeared to make insufficient distinction between violent and sexual offences against the person and offences against property.

Key principles of the Act

The Act was based on six key principles (Sanders and Senior 1994):

1 *Sentences should reflect the seriousness of the offences committed (otherwise known* as *proportionality) and custody should be reserved for only the most serious offences* (1994: 124).

The Act required a court to focus primarily on the seriousness of the offence before it and to send the defendant to prison only if that offence and, if appropriate, one other associated offence were so serious that only such a sentence could be justified (section 1). This was intended to prevent courts from sending someone to prison for a number of minor offences, none of which in itself warranted imprisonment.

The Act also prevented courts from giving too much consideration to previous convictions, unless the circumstances of those offences should shed light on (or 'disclose') features of the current offence which make it more serious (section 29). This section was intended to restrict the powers of a court to send someone to prison for repeatedly committing minor offences.

2 *A sharper distinction should be drawn between property offences and offences against the person* (1994: 124).

This reflects the government's concern that people committing violent and sexual offences should be dealt with particularly severely. To this end, courts were permitted to consider the need to protect the public from serious harm when deciding the length of prison sentences for these offences.

3 *Community sentences stand in their own right and should not be seen as alternatives to custody* (1994: 125).

This principle refuted the popular misbelief of the 1980s that most offenders deserved to go to prison and that if they were given a non-custodial sentence, they were being 'let off' with a 'soft' alternative. The Act recognized that community sentences (that is, probation and supervision orders, curfew orders, community service orders, combination orders and attendance centre orders) constituted a sentencing band in their own right, providing a particular degree of restriction on liberty commensurate with a particular level of offence seriousness.

4 *Young people should be dealt with in a way that takes account of their maturity and stage of development* (1994: 125).

The Act replaced the Juvenile Court (which dealt with offenders aged 10–16) with the Youth Court (which deals with offenders aged 10–17). At the same time, however, it allowed courts to impose certain adult sentences (probation order, community service order, combination order) on 16- and 17-year-olds. This meant that courts could treat 16- and 17-year-olds as either juveniles or adults, depending on their maturity and stage of development. Very little guidance was given to courts to help them define and assess maturity objectively and there was some concern that the concept could result in prejudiced judgements of teenagers' circumstances and abilities.

5 *The intention of the court should be properly reflected in the way that a prison sentence is served* (1994: 125).

The Act introduced a clearly defined system of early release for prisoners serving sentences of less than four years, which replaced the much-criticised parole system. Put simply, the Act abolished automatic remission after two-thirds of the sentence and discretionary parole after one-third (or six months, whichever is the longer). Instead it provided that half of all sentences must be served in custody. Thereafter, there was a system of automatic release (with or without licence conditions) during which time a prisoner may be recalled to prison if they reoffend. Parole remained an option only for long-term prisoners – those serving sentences of four or more years.

6 *The whole criminal justice system should be administered efficiently and without discrimination* (1994: 126).

The Act contained a significant new provision (section 95) for monitoring the criminal justice system to ensure 'value for money' and the absence of discrimination on the ground of race or sex or any other improper ground. To these ends, the Secretary of State was required to publish relevant information annually. Cynics have pointed out the incongruous coupling of discrimination issues with concerns about financial implications.

The Act made two further major changes, one of which was later revoked. The introduction of *unit fines* was intended to force courts to give systematic consideration to offenders' means when imposing fines, recognizing that the same fine could be insignificant for a rich person while causing devastating hardship for a poor one.

The Act also replaced the *Social Inquiry Reports* (SIRs) prepared by the probation service with *Pre-sentence Reports* (PSRs). Such reports provide courts with information about the offender to assist in sentencing but, while SIRs focused primarily on social and personal information relating to the offender's welfare, PSRs were required to focus more clearly on the offence and to include only information that was relevant to it. Probation officers were also no longer allowed to make professional sentencing recommendations, but must instead discuss proposals for suitable options, making clear that the final decision rests with the court (as it always has).

Criticisms of the Act and amendments to it

The Criminal Justice Act 1991 represented the culmination of Thatcherite criminal justice policy and was surprisingly radical in its attempt to implement a 'just deserts' model of sentencing, which endorsed community penalties for the vast majority of offenders. Within six months, however, the key concepts of the Act had come under such vociferous attack that they were revoked. Yet the 1993 amendments were constructed within official discourse as being no more than a 'review'. According to a former deputy secretary at the Home Office in charge of criminal justice policy until 1992:

> there is now a serious void at the centre of the criminal justice system. There is no clearly understood set of purposes which it is meant to achieve or principles which it is meant to observe, and no effective and acceptable system of accountability for its operation.
>
> (Faulkner, *Guardian*, 11 November 1993)

The whole point of the 1991 Act was to reduce the prison population by decentring the prison from penal discourse. This was done in four ways: first, by focusing on the seriousness of the offence and limiting the extent to which previous convictions could be taken into account; second, by raising the status of community punishment; third, by making financial penalties fairer so that fewer people would go to prison for non-payment; and fourth, by explicitly outlawing discrimination and thus aiming to reduce the disproportionate number of black and Asian people in prison and the inappropriate use of prison for women.

The Act appeared to be very successful initially in achieving its objectives. Home Office Statistical Bulletin 25/93 indicated a fall in the proportionate use of immediate custody, especially among offenders with numerous previous convictions, a rise in the proportionate use of the fine (with average fines increasing for those in employment and decreasing for the unemployed) and a rise in the proportionate use of community sentences.

Within six months of its implementation, however, it was being described as a shambles. Three aspects in particular were claimed by sentencers to be unworkable:

1 The 'two offence rule', contained in section 1(2)(a), which required courts to consider only the offence and one other associated with it when deciding on a custodial sentence;

2 The admittedly obscurely drafted section 29 which had placed restrictions on the consideration of previous convictions;

3 The use of unit fines.

By August 1993, all three had been abolished, thus effectively reversing the whole ethos of the original Act. Section 66 of the 1993 Criminal Justice Act allowed courts, when deciding on a custodial sentence, to consider 'the totality of the offending behaviour' with which it is dealing (Magistrates' Association 1993). Courts were also allowed to take into account any previous convictions and any failure to respond to previous sentences. Finally, section 65 of the 1993 Act blandly required courts to inquire into the financial circumstances of the offender before imposing a fine.

The fall of the unit fine

There is no reason why the principle of unit fines (systematically relating fines to means as well as offence seriousness) should not have been acceptable in England and Wales. Similar approaches have been used in many other European countries and in parts of America (Tonry and Hamilton 1995). Experiments in English and Welsh courts indicated that the idea was feasible and an improvement on the previous system. It seemed that courts were happy to reduce fines for poorer people and that the fines were consequently paid more quickly, with less default and, therefore, fewer imprisonments for non-payment. With hindsight, there was perhaps insufficient attention paid to sentencers' reluctance to increase fines for richer offenders and this became one subsequent explanation for the downfall of unit fines. Old attitudes of charitable munificence towards the poor (which accounted for the initial welcome of unit fines) were misinterpreted by policy-makers as a willingness to embrace the principles of 'equality of impact' implied by unit fines.

There were undoubtedly some technical difficulties in deciding the minimum and maximum sums to be attached to units (Moxon 1995). In the experiments, the maximum had been about £20 per unit but the 1991 Act increased this to £100. This resulted in some anomalously large fines for only moderately well-off offenders committing minor offences. This was exacerbated by the discretion given to sentencers when offenders (particularly those who pleaded guilty by post) failed to provide proper information about their means. In theory, sentencers could then impose whatever fine they thought reasonable but some (perhaps to make the point) chose to impose the maximum. Inevitably, mistakes (possibly wilful) occurred. In one case, a motorist decided to go to court to defend himself against a fixed penalty for illegal parking and was fined £500. In another, an unemployed man was fined £1200 for throwing a crisp packet on the ground. In both cases the offender had failed to provide correct means information and in both cases the fine was properly reduced on appeal. Yet a few celebrated cases of 'unfairness' such as these were apparently all that was needed to abandon the venture.

Central to the downfall of unit fines was the perception of sentencers that their discretion in these matters was being eroded (Baker 1993). According to Baker, magistrates felt that the old system had worked well, that they had not been consulted about the new system and that it created insuperable problems. They found difficulty in 'thinking in units' and remained wedded to the notion of 'set worth':

> The magistrates saw certain crimes as being worth certain amounts of money ... they cannot be seen as more serious if one offender commits them than another. If double parking is worth £100, then it is worth £100, regardless of how much you earn.
>
> (Baker 1993: 68)

A few magistrates actually resigned because they felt they were being forced to adhere to rigid rules that resulted in unfair penalties. This much could surely have been anticipated and tolerated as 'teething problems'. That the whole system should be abandoned in less than a year suggests a studied lack of political will.

Swarming circumstances

So, was the whole punishment in the community era an aberration, merely a stop-gap measure or worse – a deliberate conspiracy to prove that liberalism must fail? The Hurd vision demonstrated a willingness by at least some members of the government to engage in Garland's rationalization of punishment (1990) but it could never eradicate the constant conflict, tension and compromise that has always character-ized penal history. As Garland reminds us, conflicts exist between ideological ambitions and financial constraints, between political expediency and established sensibilities, between the requirements of security and those of morality, between the interests of different professional groups. And 'these swarming circumstances are only ever resolved into particular outcomes by means of … struggles, negotiations, actions and decisions' (1990: 285) which involve com-promise and sacrifice.

The failure of the 1991 Criminal Justice Act was not due to its inability to achieve its objective of decentring the prison – it was initially very successful in doing that – but to its inability to establish the 'punitive city' outside the prison. Despite, or perhaps because of, the fear of an Orwellian society, there was a great deal of resistance to any discourse that appeared to 'blur the boundaries' and widen or strengthen the net of social control. Garland described a 'paranoid culture', indicating that 'the relations of the individual to the political community are pathologically out of sorts' (1995: 3) So rather than view the rise and fall of the discourse of punishment in the community as either a story of 'benevolence gone wrong' or 'mystification' (Cohen 1983), it can be seen as a period of strange and paradoxical but effective refusal or resistance by the courts and the public (but not by probation officers) to accept the programmes, technologies and strategies of power which sought to construct punishment or penality as a continuum of control. As we shall see, a decade later, the battle to establish 'seamless sentencing', in the form of the National Offender Management Service is meeting the same resistance. In 2003, in an attempt to examine some of the conflicting arguments, a Commission of Inquiry into Alternatives to Prison was set up by the Esmee Fairbairn Foundation to research the subject further. The Coulsfield Inquiry was charged with examining the 'adequacy and limitations of current provision for alternatives to prison for adults and children ... and the administration and levels of effectiveness of such alternatives' (Coulsfield Inquiry, Terms of Reference) and reported in the autumn of 2004. In the meantime, the Criminal Justice Act 2003 came onto the statute book, with a more complex range of community penalties available to sentencers (see Chapter 4).

Amid increasing concern about the perceived diminution of the powers of the courts by the 1991 Act, a new moral panic about young offenders gathered steam in 1992 and 1993. The riots of the summer of 1991, which were perceived to be largely the result of confrontation between young men and the police following attempts by the latter to clamp down on 'joyriding' (Campbell 1993), the media construction of 'rat boy' as the epitome of the persistent young offender responsible for a disproportionate amount of crime (Hagell and Newburn 1994) and the murder of James Bulger all contributed to a climate of public anxiety that could only be satisfied by a complete political U-turn. No longer would public opinion tolerate any blurring of the boundary between freedom and confinement. If you commit a crime, you deserve to be excluded from the law-abiding community. Michael Howard's infamous speech at the Conservative Party Conference in Blackpool in October 1993 caught the mood of public opinion brilliantly:

> Let us be clear. Prison works. It ensures that we are protected from murderers, muggers and rapists – and it will make many who are tempted to commit crimes think twice.

It is difficult to believe that only months before, the Royal Commission on Criminal Justice (the Runciman Committee) had reported, following the concern about miscarriages of justice that had been highlighted by the release of the Birmingham Six in 1991. Its two main recommendations – to set up an independent Criminal Cases Review Authority to consider allegations of miscarriages of justice, and to retain the suspect's right to silence – seemed out of step with public opinion by the summer of 1993 (although many of its other recommendations, such as ending the right to trial by jury and requiring defendants to disclose any defence prior to trial were criticized by radical lawyers for perpetuating injustices). But of much greater public concern by then was the perceived danger of acquitting the guilty or, at least, their overly lenient treatment.

The event that had finally confirmed the change in public opinion was the abduction and murder in February 1993 of two-year-old James Bulger by two ten-year-old boys, Jon Venables and Robert Thompson. The tragic and appalling event was wholly exceptional and might easily not have been constructed as being 'symptomatic of broader tendencies' in society (Hay 1995: 201). But it was. It became 'a mirror within which collective fears and anxieties [were] reflected and simultaneously a screen upon which they [were] focused' (Hay 1995: 200). As we shall see in Chapter 10, the event was taken to mark the end of the presumed and idealized innocence of childhood and the confirmation of the threat of children – *all* children were now potential killers.

The Criminal Justice and Public Order Act 1994

At the 1993 Conservative Party Conference, the Home Secretary announced his 27 pledges in an attempt to mop up all the outstanding problems of criminal justice as he saw them. Somewhere between 17 and 19 of these eventually reached the statute book in the 1994 Criminal Justice and Public Order Act (Morton 1994). The key provisions were extension of police powers, more detention options for younger offenders, changes to the court process and the inclusion of more behaviours under the banner of 'criminal'. Of interest also in relation to the arguments of this book is Schedule 9, which makes the following provisions:

- extension of the Attorney General's powers of appeal against 'unduly lenient' sentences

- removal of the mandatory requirement for courts to obtain pre-sentence reports before passing a custodial sentence or certain community sentences

- authorization for new pilot trials of curfew orders and electronic monitoring (by April 1996 a total of 65 offenders had been tagged in three pilot schemes, at a cost of £1.6 million, according to the reply to a Parliamentary Question reported by the Howard League magazine, *Criminal Justice*, in August 1996)

- provision for courts to bind over parents of a young offender to ensure that the child complies with the requirements of a community sentence

Disparate though its numerous sections may appear, the intended effects of the discourse within which the Act is constructed by the Home Secretary, are clear. 'The scales of justice have been tilted too far in favour of the offenders. Victims have had a raw deal. I want to redress that balance' (Home Office Press Release 166/94 cited in Morton 1994: 8).

By constructing the relationship between offenders and victims in this stark either/or way, the approval of public opinion is secured. The inclusion of one or two high-profile demands by campaigning groups (for example, abolition of the corroboration warning in rape cases, banning computer-generated pornography and creating a new offence of witness intimidation) distracts attention from the criminalization of whole new groups of citizens and a return to the highly damaging penal incarceration of transgressive children.

'Out go holidays': ejecting the Other of probation

Later in the same press release, the Home Secretary turned his fire on community sentences. 'These measures will mean an end to the approach which offers holidays for offenders,' he says. 'Out go holidays and in come tightly controlled community sentences.'

In March 1995 the government produced a consultation document entitled *Strengthening Punishment in the Community* (Home Office 1995c). Its main proposal was to replace existing non-custodial sentences with a single 'community sentence', the exact content of which would be decided by sentencers to suit the perceived needs and requirements of each individual case. The clearly-stated purpose of the proposal was to increase public confidence in non-custodial penalties; the less clearly stated aim (but one equally obvious to the initiated) was to bring the probation service once and for all under the control of the courts by making the purchaser–provider relationship quite explicit:

> The essential proposed change is that the probation service should provide community sentences which the courts consider to be required for individual offenders, rather than the courts having to select from the restricted range of sentences which the probation service is able to offer.

(1.4)

Much of the consultation document harks back to the 1988 Green Paper but its tone is one of weariness rather than innovation. If the Green Paper began a new debate then the later consultation document gave every indication of sounding its death knoll. It marked a final disingenuous gesture towards the preservation of the probation service as we know it. 'This is your last chance' is the phrase that seemed to leap from every page. Yet, simultaneously, opposition was anticipated and, with it, the perfect excuse to transform this troublesome service into the long-desired corrections agency.

The document's key proposal was the replacement of existing non-custodial sentences with a single 'integrated' community sentence. This was not a new idea. The 1988 Green Paper considered and rejected it on the grounds that:

> it might encourage the courts to impose too severe a penalty and make them more reluctant to use supervision a second time for an offender who had failed to complete an earlier order satisfactorily.
>
> (3.33)

Instead, an additional order was suggested – the supervision and restriction order – whose details were virtually identical to those being proposed in the 1996 document. One of the main arguments against such an order at that time was its lack of *feasibility* (Carlen 1989). The assumption that offenders are prepared to do almost anything – however restrictive or degrading – in order to avoid going to prison has been shown to be quite erroneous (see Chapter 2). Probation officers have always known that there are limits on the demands that can be made on offenders and have constantly cautioned against 'setting offenders up to fail'. The cynical reintroduction of such ideas smacked of 'setting up' the probation service to fail.

This idea has not gone away. One of the key community sentencing proposals of the Halliday review was to have an 'envelope' of community sentences to 'ensure tough, more intensive community sentences with multiple conditions ... to deny liberty, rehabilitate the offender and protect the public' (Home Office 2002c: 4). In 2004, further reforms were proposed by the government (Home Office 2004d), as a response to Patrick Carter's Correctional Services Review, *Managing Offenders, Reducing Crime* (Home Office 2003d). The government accepted the idea of bringing prison and probation services into one umbrella organization (the National Offender Management Service, NOMS), the separation of case-management from 'interventions' such as programmes, and the idea of 'contestability' for the provision of such. Carter wanted sentencers 'to have a full range of tough, credible and effective sentences that are properly enforced' (Home Office 2003d: 1).

But the impact of such a sentence on the *offender* was not the prime concern of the 1995 consultation document, nor of the government response to the Carter Review. Like the Green Paper before them, their main concern was to curry favour with the public in general and sentencers in particular. The 1995 document reiterated the Green Paper's concern that sentencing should focus on restriction of liberty, reparation and prevention of re-offending. The reintegration of the offender into the community (or 'rehabilitation'), reinstated as a sentencing principle in the 1990 White Paper, was dropped once again.

Like the Green Paper, the consultation document fuelled and reinforced a public perception of non-custodial sentences which it had itself helped to construct. Compare these two excerpts:

> Not every sentencer or member of the public has full confidence in the present orders which leave offenders in the community.
>
> (Home Office 1988: 2)

> Community sentences ... have failed to command the confidence of the public ... probation supervision is still widely regarded as a soft option.
>
> (Home Office 1995c: 11)

Almost a decade on, New Labour has realized that 'talking up' lack of public confidence in the criminal justice system is not necessarily a vote-winner. The tone has changed and the Carter Review (Home Office 2003d) asserts that 'public confidence in sentencing has improved but remains fragile ... the proportion of people believing sentencing to be "much too lenient" has fallen from one in two to one in three' (Home Office 2003d: 3).

But there has always been little evidence to support the view that sentencers want to be more involved in the detailed content of supervision programmes. Developments in pre-sentence report-writing which set out more explicitly than before what the probation service can offer have undoubtedly been welcomed. And the least contentious aspect of the 1995 consultation document was probably the proposal for the provision of feedback reports to courts on offenders' progress. Nevertheless, it seemed quite unrealistic to expect sentencers to draw up individualized packages of supervision for every defendant and the danger was that an informal 'tariff' would develop which may be every bit as inconsistent and court-specific as previous practice.

The document's one genuinely new proposal was the removal of the requirement for consent before the imposition of a community sentence. It could be argued that this was entirely consistent with the nature of the proposed 'community sentence'. Since the impact of the sentence on the offender is no longer a matter of concern to the court, there is no reason to perpetuate the myth of contract. It is also true, as the document argued, that what matters is not formal consent at the point of sentence 'but the offender's willingness to comply throughout the sentence' (11.4). Where the logic of this argument breaks down is in the assumption that the removal of formal consent will make no difference to the offender's co-operation. One cannot imagine anyone arguing that witnesses should not take an oath (or affirm) when they give evidence because what matters is not the oath but their 'willingness' to tell the truth! Many aspects of our criminal justice system are dependent on the significance of public declarations – it is part of our basic belief that 'justice should be seen to be done'. We know that the giving of consent to a probation order was no more than a residual ritual but it may have meaning for some offenders and it was, in any case, a useful negotiating tool for probation officers at the pre-sentence report stage. Its removal, by contrast, was highly significant, for it demonstrated not only that the offender's consent does not matter but, yet again, that the probation officer's consent (to the wishes of the court) does not matter either. The consent requirement was finally removed by the Crime (Sentences) Act of 1997, except for those orders that required drug or alcohol treatment, or the treatment of a mental condition (Crime (Sentences) Act 1997 s.38).

The introduction of the generic term 'community sentence' by the Criminal Justice Act 1991 provided a helpful clarification of the role of non-custodial penalties in the sentencing framework, but it is difficult to see how 'the transparency of community sentencing' (5.2) could be increased by blurring the distinctions between existing disposals. On the contrary, an obvious criticism of the 'integrated' community sentence was that no one except the sentencing court and the supervising probation officer (and, it was hoped, the offender) would know exactly what it entailed in any individual case. As far as the public was concerned, an integrated community sentence (and, indeed, the 'generic' community sentence introduced by the Criminal Justice Act 2003) could mean anything – or nothing. The price of reducing public confusion about the differences between probation orders, community service orders, curfew orders and so on could be the reduction of all non-custodial penalties to their lowest perceived common denominator – the soft option.

Yet another truck on the punishment train

By August 1996, yet another truck had been coupled to the punishment train in the form of a White Paper entitled *Protecting the Public: the Government's Strategy on Crime* in *England and Wales* (Cm. 3190, Home Office 1996a). The Paper was not dissimilar in style and format to the 1990 White Paper which preceded the 1991 Criminal Justice Act. It set out the state of the art of criminal justice policy in the 1990s before making its four main proposals:

1 Abolition of automatic early release and its replacement by earned remission;

2 Automatic life sentences for second-time serious violent or sexual offences – 'two strikes and you're out', in popular parlance;

3 Mandatory seven-year prison sentence for third-time drug trafficking offences;

4 Mandatory three-year prison sentence for third-time burglary offences.

The result of these proposals, it was admitted, would be to increase the prison population by nearly 11,000 by the year 2011, a statement that prompted (the then) Lord Chief Justice Taylor to describe the Paper as 'a bonanza for prison architects' (cited in Baird 1996), though it now seems a very modest prediction. Unlike the 1990 White Paper, which admitted that prison 'can be an expensive way of making bad people worse' and that 'nobody now regards imprisonment as an effective means of reform' (Home Office 1990a: 6), the 1996 Paper stated that 'the government firmly believes that prison works' (Home Office 1996a: 4). Prison, it was now being argued, prevents crime by taking offenders out of circulation, it protects the public from dangerous criminals, its threat acts as a deterrent and it *'can* be used to rehabilitate offenders' (our emphasis). Perhaps most tellingly in relation to this book, we were told that 'criminals sent to prison are no more likely to reoffend than those given community sentences'. It may be for this reason that the chapter on community sentencing is notably thin and vague. The White

Paper and the Crime (Sentences) Act 1997 that resulted from it gave the distinct impression that the government was about to give up on punishment in the community.

Developing debates – risk

During the early 1990s, arguments developed about the realistic management of crime. A rising crime rate, static detection and conviction rates, overcrowded prisons and a public antipathy to spending public funds on crime that was not associated with putting more police officers on the beat or offenders inside, resulted in a recognition that if crime could not be stopped, then at least effort should be put into preventing the offending of the most serious and persistent offenders. In order to do this, actuarial risk assessment became a key concept and Feeley and Simon described the ensuing approach to the management of crime and the criminal as the New Penology (Feeley and Simon 1992).

The New Penology depended on advanced statistical methods and an actuarial language that shifted the emphasis from the re-habilitation of offenders to the control of crime. The focus was not on individuals, but centred on the identification and management of unruly groups:

> Its goal is not to eliminate crime but to make it tolerable through systemic co-ordination.
>
> (Feeley and Simon (1992) in Muncie, McLaughlin and Langan 1996: 368)

Feeley and Simon argue that parole and probation were seen as cost-effective means of managing the dangerous in the long term, rather than being seen in their traditional role of reintegrating offenders into their communities. In order to do this, it was essential to have an accurate (or as accurate as possible) risk profile of the group to which the individual belonged:

> But once the focus is on categories of offenders rather than individuals, methods naturally shift toward mechanisms of appraising and arranging groups rather than intervening in the lives of individuals.
>
> (Feeley and Simon (1992) in Muncie, McLaughlin and Langan 1996: 371)

This implied changes to the nature of the work of the probation officer. There was a more formalized need for probation officers to assess the risk that offenders presented. Kemshall (2002) defines risk as the probability that an adverse event will occur, and with it must be balanced the impact that the event would have. If that can be predicted, what steps can be taken to avoid its occurrence? In the light of the global risks of postmodernity, as evidenced by the terrorist events of September 11th 2001, Giddens and Beck (quoted in Kemshall 2002) would say that contemporary risks are largely incalculable. However, in the criminal justice system, attempts have been made to make those calculations. Kemshall states that:

> Risk, in the era of the 'justice model', was used predominantly to rescue offenders from the over-use of custody, and to allocate offenders rationally to intervention programmes.
>
> (2002: 101)

Later, re-offence predictions were assisted by the use of tools such as the Offender Group Reconviction Score (OGRS) which shifted the emphasis from the offender him/herself being 'at risk' (of facing custody) to the offender being the site of risk that would lead to criminal behaviour. Risk assessment has become one of the most important topics covered in a probation officer's interviews for writing a pre-sentence report on an offender. It must address risk of harm to self and to others as well as the likelihood of reoffending. The tool that is now used, in common with the prison service, is called OASys (Offender Assessment System). Kemshall believes (2002) that whilst energy has been placed in such systems, insufficient attention has been given to communicating with local communities about effective community risk management. She says:

> At heart, the issues are about reintegration and inclusion of risky people, the risk perceptions of communities and public perceptions about the acceptability and tolerance of community risks.
>
> (2002 :109)

Conclusion

The 1991 Criminal Justice Act was one of the most significant pieces of criminal justice legislation of the last quarter of the century. At the time, there was much criticism of it, but, in retrospect, there was probably more thought and consultation involved over a period of several years than one might have expected from a Conservative government that had been in power for over a decade. That it failed so spectacularly and so quickly was not the result of any long-term political conspiracy. Rather it resulted from a particular constellation of events occurring before the 'teething problems' of the Act had been resolved. In the prevailing political and economic climate of 'short-termism' (Hutton 1995) it was perhaps inevitable that knee-jerk reactions would gain more credence than measured analysis. But 'events' take place against a backcloth of longer-term trends in penal attitudes and, with the benefit of hindsight, it is possible to see that the concepts of risk assessment and the management of dangerousness were steadily embedding themselves in the thought processes of sentencers, making the more liberal aspects of the Criminal Justice Act 1991 impossible to sustain.

Chapter 4

Constructing the punishing community under New Labour

Introduction

This chapter will analyse the political and legislative changes that occurred at the end of the twentieth century and in particular, the contrasts and similarities between Conservative and Labour social and penal policy agenda. It will become clear that 'community' has been central to many recent debates and changes – from the use of the term 'community charge' for what was popularly known as the 'poll tax' early in the Thatcher reform period, to the use of community wardens to assist the police in 'beat' duties in the new millennium. Because this book is concerned with punishments that take place in the offender's 'community', a consideration of its meaning is appropriate.

The term 'community' is one of the most promiscuous words in contemporary political usage. It is attached to concepts hitherto regarded as falling within the spheres of either the private or the public. It is prefixed to innumerable 'feel good' words, such as care, centre, home, school, health, provision, transport, crime prevention, service and, of course, punishment. Thus located, it beguiles and seduces 'because it readily evokes images of neighbourliness, mutual aid, and a positive sense of "belonging" ' (Smith 1995: 93). At the same time, critics would argue, it blurs the boundaries of responsibility (which is part of its appeal) and consequently (to continue the metaphor) it cheapens and degrades the original concept.

The word may appeal to a warm, nostalgic sense of 'belonging' among the self-proclaimed law-abiding but its promise of inclusivity can be interpreted in contradictory ways when applied to those who break the law and are criminalized. Far from demonstrating that it is resourceful, tolerant and healing, the community is then rejecting, excluding and intolerantly punitive. What, then, constitutes the 'community' in which offenders are to be punished?

Communitarianism, community and the individual

The term 'community' is rarely defined. It is a nebulous concept, which may be used to describe neighbourhood groups or whole nations, people with a community of interest (as in 'the gay community' or 'the deaf community') or people sharing a geographical identity and so on. Willmott's three-fold distinction between territorial communities based on geography, interest communities based on non-geographical common characteristics and attachment communities based on relationships with people or places is frequently cited (Willmott 1987). This definition, however, ignores the politics that have underpinned the use of the term since Thatcherism. Crawford reminds us that, under the influence of neo-liberal ideology, the term 'has become a metaphor for "rolling back" the state and "freeing up" collective voluntarism and entrepreneurship' (1998: 126).

However it is used, it implies at least two things. First, it *assumes* an element of homogeneity based on common social characteristics, histories, traditions or beliefs. Second, it *presumes* that this homogeneity will manifest itself in a sense of mutual responsibility – a willingness to 'look after' or 'deal with' the needs of the members of the community. As Stanley Cohen says:

> The iconography is that of a small rural village in pre-industrial society in contrast to the abstract, bureaucratic, impersonal city of the contemporary technological state.
>
> (Cohen 1985: 118)

There is nothing new about these assumptions and presumptions but their proliferation in political discourse has been a feature of the last two decades of the century and, in particular, a feature of the ideology of both the New Right and New Labour, emphasizing less the community's collective responsibility *for* its members and more the responsibility of its members *to* the community (Fatic 1995; Ireland 1995). In particular, it has stressed the 'rights' of the community to require certain standards of behaviour from its members and, ultimately, to exclude members in the interests of the whole community. According to Crawford:

> The 'community' constitutes an acceptable collective imagery for activating and responsibilising individuals.
>
> (1998: 126)

This brand of communitarian discourse does not in any way guarantee equality of access to the community's resources (Frazer and Lacey 1993; Raynor 2001). While it claims that moral and political values are generated and maintained by the community itself and are changed only through internal discussion, argument and conflict, the insularity of communities and the absence of 'debate across traditions and on the basis of values external to prevailing cultures' (Frazer and Lacey 1993: 144) may result in the maintenance of sexist, racist or other discriminatory values and practices. There is nothing in the appeal to community that offers any fundamental criticism of oppressive traditional sexual divisions of labour or social practices of racial intolerance and exclusion. Community 'club' membership is not equally available to all, despite the powerful rhetoric to the contrary.

When we talk, then, about crime control being a matter for the community, or a community responsibility, it is by no means clear which particular brand of communitarian values are being expressed (Fatic 1995). On the one hand, we may be arguing that crime and criminals are a product of the community, that the causes of crime can be found in the material and social inadequacies of the community, that criminals are produced when individuals are denied their rightful share of the community's wealth and welfare. On the other hand, we may view the community as the upholder of positive values and moral virtues, as an environment of trust that is betrayed by the actions of criminals. Either way, the relationship between the criminal and the 'law-abiding' community is problematic, since the decision has to be made whether the criminal can or should be excluded from the community or reintegrated within it.

The connection between crime, community and the economy has perhaps been argued most accessibly in recent years by the economist, Will Hutton. His damning indictment of what he perceives to be a society based on the worship of short-term profits and the dominance of shareholder interests blames our obsession with market processes for the creation of 'more and more poorly socialized children, teenagers and young adults' (1995: 225). Unlike Charles Murray (1990), Hutton identifies the structural preconditions, rather than the personal inadequacies, which exclude many young people from educational and employment opportunities and condemn them to impoverished life chances and incomes. The result is a perfectly predictable breakdown of the informal control mechanisms which prevent most of us from committing the more visible and most publicly condemned acts of lawbreaking:

> With the collapse of local communities there is less stigma attached to criminality, the informal sanctions and expressions of disapproval which offenders fear are no longer there; and they have little reason to empathize with their victims. There are fewer inbuilt deterrents and greater incentives to criminal behaviour.
>
> (Hutton 1995: 225)

Involving the community in crime prevention has been a central concern of all governments since the 1980s. The symbols of such involvement have been closed circuit television (CCTV) and Neighbourhood Watch schemes. Despite the civil liberties objections, CCTV has been very widely accepted by the public (Groombridge 1995), though the problems of displacement (that criminals will simply go elsewhere) are beginning to be recognized. While CCTV is predominantly confined to high streets and shopping malls there may be few objections, but its extension to residential and semi-residential areas has met more resistance and recent research highlights the need for the management of CCTV schemes to engage with stakeholders, such as local businesses, and the local community (Scarman Centre 2003). 'Freeborn Englishmen' do not readily subject themselves to invasions of their privacy and Garland's 'paranoid culture' (1995: 3) lurks not far beneath the surface. It is one of the central arguments of this book that public opinion requires clear boundaries to be observed between conditions of freedom and conditions of custody, between public and private spheres.

Community and the victim of crime

Public opinion also requires clear boundaries between victims and offenders, with the latter being held accountable to the former. Accusations that the criminal justice system pays too much attention to offenders, while neglecting the needs and rights of victims, resulted in the publication of the *Victim's Charter* in 1990, which ostensibly set out the standards of service that victims should expect from criminal justice agencies, but also made a clear statement about the future priority of victims in criminal justice discourse. In line with its development of the concept of social citizenship and the obligations of the individual to the community, the document constructs the crime victim as a consumer of localized criminal justice services – as a stakeholder with rights as well as needs. Probation officers, for example, were required to take account of victims' views on the release of life-sentence prisoners. The setting up of a victims' helpline in 1994 to allow victims to ring prisons and express their fears about prisoners being released on home leave put additional pressure on probation staff both in assessing prisoner risk and in supervising home leave. The revised National Standards, produced in 1995, required probation officers to take account of victim impact when preparing pre-sentence reports. Probation services have been encouraged to enter 'partnerships' with Victim Support schemes at a local level (Kosh and Williams 1995; Williams 1996). The work of the National Probation Service with victims is now measured by a specific target of making contact with certain victims, and doing so within a prescribed timescale was a cash-linked performance objective in 2003/04. *Bold Steps* (the National Probation Service Business plan for 2004/05) states that 'victim awareness and empathy are central to what we do' (NPS 2004a: 7). Spalek (2003) identifies three areas of victim-focused work: helping victims to cope with their situation, taking account of the victim's perspective in work with offenders and developing restorative justice strategies.

But the victim to whom all this refers is not every victim. This victim is constructed as structurally neutral (Mawby and Walklate 1994; Spalek 2003), without age, gender or class – the 'legitimate victim'. In order to be a legitimate victim, one is assumed to be a particular kind of person: an innocent child (who is abused), a helpless old person (who is mugged), a virgin (who is raped), a law-abiding pillar of the community (who is burgled). In other words, an image is created of a victim who is randomly selected and who in no way contributes to their own victimization. As soon as we move away from that pure and irrational image, we begin to rationalize why some people are victims and we begin to consider how they might have contributed to their fate. So the relationship or interaction between offender and victim starts to be constructed as significant and an object of examination and theorizing. Judgements begin to be made about deserving and undeserving victims. Those deemed by the community to be undeserving may fare little better than offenders when it comes to seeking support and access to local resources.

New Labour: new focus?

After 18 years of Conservative government, it would be tempting to presume that the Labour government of 1997 brought a completely different set of goals and priorities for law and order and, particularly, for criminal justice and sentencing. This was not the case. In 1996 and 1997 their 'five pledges' for a new government included the fast track punishment of persistent young offenders. In order to make itself electable, the Labour party had described itself as 'New' and had promised to match several of the Conservatives' aims, especially the economic ones of keeping inflation, interest and income tax rates low. Downes (1998) feels that abandoning 'the hostages to fortune' was a prime objective of New Labour policy prior to 1997 – to abandon those ideas which were 'symbolic issues central to Labour's history' (Downes 1998: 191) but which were seen to have clouded the party's image and made it appear 'soft' on crime.

A key tenet of the Labour government from 1997 was to espouse the 'Third Way' in politics. This approach recognized the limits of delivery of social goods through a welfare state and the pressures of globalization. As Crawford says:

> The reformed state ... will establish a new relationship between risk and security, on the one hand, and individual and collective responsibility, on the other.
>
> (Crawford 2001: 54)

Stenson (2000) explains how the Third Way represents a means of balancing liberal government with 'joined up' strategies. Joined up working was manifest in the role of regions and local authorities, and in the development of partnerships for the delivery of services and social goods. In Sparks' (2003) view, populism and punitivism have come together in late-modern politics. A review of the most significant crime legislation since 1997 will reflect these different interpretations of Labour's philosophy.

One of the first legislative actions of the New Labour government in 1997 was the enactment of the Crime (Sentences) Act, which had been progressed by the Tories. Its key provisions were mandatory sentences for second burglary and drug dealing offences, and for certain violent and sexual offenders ('Two Strikes'), as well as an attempt at 'truth in sentencing', with clarification of determinate custodial sentences. Downes (1998: 192) observed that this was 'being as tough as (or even tougher than) the Tories on crime', reflecting Tony Blair's mantra, first used in 1993, to be 'tough on crime and tough on the causes of crime'. Another key piece of early legislation was the Sex Offenders Act 1997, which required convicted or cautioned sex offenders to register their address with the local police. Failure to do so can result in custody. Public opinion and a desire to minimize risk drove this populist law onto the statute book. Since 2001, the most serious sex offenders are now monitored by local MAPPPs (Multi-Agency Public Protection Panels) as well – the 'community' is considered an appropriate place for these people to reside, but the 'community' has a role in monitoring their behaviour and risk (see Chapter 9 for further discussion).

The Crime and Disorder Act 1998 developed from the White Paper *No More Excuses* of November 1997, whose stated aim was to reform the youth justice system, by bringing a focus on prevention, accenting the acceptance of responsibility, taking action on racially motivated offending, providing early intervention with young offenders, promoting efficiency and establishing partnership working. The implications for dealing with young offenders will be dealt with in Chapter 10, and here we will concentrate on the measures pertaining to adults.

One of the key provisions of the Crime and Disorder Act was the Anti-Social Behaviour Order (ASBO) – a civil measure that responds to behaviour that may not be criminal but with the provision that a breach of the order may result in criminal proceedings (Harradine *et al.* 2004). Local authorities and others make the orders and some would say there is a human rights issue about bodies other than courts being in a position to restrict people's liberty concerning where they may go. The purpose of the order is to make neighbours respond more sensitively to each other, and as many of the behaviours relate to noise, it explains the thinking behind making the local authority the sanctioning agent. As local authorities are also the focus for Community Safety Partnerships (see below), there was a degree of logic to this move and it provides evidence to support Sparks' view, tapping into the populist appetite for punishment.

Drug Treatment and Testing Orders (DTTOs) were also created by the 1998 Act and are a new sentence to be served in the community. They contrast with the 'tough' measures taken against young offenders and present a means of dealing with the causes of crime. They demonstrate a recognition of the amount of small/medium scale acquisitive crime that is required to feed a dependent drug habit, and make an attempt to help offenders break their cycle of offending. A DTTO requires the offender to undergo regular drug testing, and to have contact with the probation service and other partner agencies on a daily basis, as well as having the order reviewed regularly in court. The strict regimen means that only those ready to give up their habit will have hope of success; but, if they keep trying, there are practical supports to assist them.

Lack of neighbourliness and the ready availability of drugs were regarded as two of the three main 'causes of crime' that the Labour government intended to be 'tough on'. The third was poor parenting. Parenting Orders also came into being under the Act. The measures include counselling and guidance sessions for the parents of children subjected to ASBOs, child safety orders, convicted young offenders and those who have failed to attend school regularly. The order restricts the parent's freedom, in that attending the sessions would impact on their liberty; but their stated purpose is reformative, though it could be said that parents are being punished for the misdemeanours of their children (Drakeford and McCarthy 2000). Downes (1998) sees great potential for these orders to result in taking young people and their parents 'up-tariff' in the sentencing frame. He says:

> These punitive and net-widening aspects of the UK Crime and Disorder Act make it even more important that the restorative justice components are given the maximum feasible chance to succeed.
>
> (Downes 1998: 195)

The parts of the Crime and Disorder Act of 1998 that pertain to adults are all community-based sentences, which might suggest that the New Labour government was keen to see rehabilitative sentences in the forefront of practice. The other key part of the Act is its setting up of the structures for community safety partnerships, which place the responsibility for local crime prevention, reduction and action on local authorities and police, with co-operation from probation and health services. It demands a co-operative method of working to bring long- and short-term strategies to fruition. The role of the community is therefore centre-stage, both as a location for the prevention of crime, by making changes to the environment that will restrict the opportunities for crime, and as a platform for representatives of the local community to have a voice in crime reduction policies and practices.

Chronologically, the next significant legislation was the adoption of the European Convention on Human Rights under domestic law in the form of the Human Rights Act 1998. Coming into effect in October 2000, it was telegraphed as having the potential to change the face of criminal justice, as defence lawyers would use the law to claim abuse of their client's rights. In practice, this has not been the case, although there have been a few judgements that were required to set case law – particularly well-publicized were those to do with driving, speeding and camera matters (www.parliament.uk/post). Fullwood (2002) reminds us that there is a need to review and consult on the impact of human rights law on community penalties. Scott (2002) provides a useful framework to identify risks of human rights abuse in probation practice (for example, failure to protect, inform or provide; degrading treatment; discrimination) – its notable omission being the failure to identify the human rights of probation staff as they attempt to manage offenders. He goes on to quote Hudson (2001: 112), who argues that 'the culture of rights is a culture of social inclusion, where no one is outside the constituency of justice'.

In 2000, the Criminal Justice and Court Services Act made provision for making the probation service a national body, wholly funded through the Home Office. The 'new' service commenced in April 2001, and will be discussed in detail in Chapter 5. Along with its set-up costs, there was an increase in funding and thereby, a recognition of the contribution that community penalties can make. (A 31 per cent cash increase in funding was promised over the first three years, according to the executive summary of 'Criminal Justice: The Way Ahead'.) As mentioned above, the Act required all probation areas to work jointly with the police in their lead roles in MAPPPs, to assess the risk and take action in relation to the most serious offenders released from custody. This was indicative of New Labour's approach to partnership working and 'joined up' government. In effect, this sort of collaboration between senior police and probation staff had always happened, but its new formalized activity was part of the new approach to public protection.

Public protection was also implicit in the support for certain victims, which became a statutory duty for probation services under this Act. As certain longer-term prisoners are released back into their community there is a requirement on probation staff to inform and liaise with the victims. Here the community is envisaged as clearly not such a 'safe' haven when its criminals are again at large. The Act also brought into force two further community orders – exclusion orders and drug abstinence orders. The former allows the court to prevent an offender entering a certain area, for a period up to 12 months. The drug abstinence order is aimed at the non-dependent drug user of Class A drugs. How popular and successful these orders are deemed to be is yet to be seen: the latter is still being piloted.

The government was returned for a second term in 2001, retaining a large parliamentary majority and continuing to make substantial changes to the criminal justice system. During 2001, there was much consultation on change to two of the major elements – sentencing and the organization of the courts. The Halliday review looked at the sentencing powers of magistrates' courts and made proposals for increased sentencing powers, a rehabilitative element for shorter-term prisoners, intermittent custody (weekends only?) and a new way of suspending custodial sentences ('custody minus') among its many proposals. Sir Robin Auld was charged with reviewing the criminal courts system, and looked at various ways in which efficiency might be improved. He proposed a unified criminal courts system, in three divisions, to replace magistrates' and Crown courts. The government's response was that the system should be: 'modern, in touch with the community, efficient and fair' (www.dca.gov.uk).

The Criminal Justice Act of 2003 was the embodiment of Halliday's proposals, though Auld's are only partly included. Like most Criminal Justice Acts, it comprises much legislation that 'tidies up' and clarifies previous Acts. But it is mostly concerned with making the court system and sentencing more effective.

There are several reforms that have implications in terms of the Human Rights Act. These include the adjustment of the 'right to bail', the use of live links and three which caused much debate in the House of Lords before final enactment of the Bill – not requiring a jury to hear complex or lengthy fraud cases or if there is a likelihood of jury tampering; the opportunity for serious offences to be re-tried if there is new and compelling evidence; and the rules of evidence being revised, so that hearsay evidence may sometimes be admissible and a defendant's previous record may now be revealed during a trial. These reforms are very much in line with the government's wish to see a reduction in the abuse of the courts and legal system – by all parties.

For the purposes of this book, the most significant reforms relate to sentencing. For the first time in statute, the purposes of sentencing are laid out: the punishment of offenders, the reduction of crime (including by means of deterrence), the reform and rehabilitation of offenders, the protection of the public and the making of reparation by offenders. (It is interesting to note that these five aims are the same as those for the National Probation Service stated in A New Choreography in 2001, but in a different order. Has the order been changed for a different audience, or is punishment now in the ascendancy as an aim?) An important new initiative is the formation of the Sentencing Guidelines Council to be informed by a Sentencing Guidelines Panel to look at sentences and allocations (Crown or magistrates' court). The Council must have regard to the need to promote consistency of sentences imposed, the cost of different sentences and their 'relative effectiveness in preventing reoffending' (www.legislation.hmso.gov.uk s.170) as well as the need to promote public confidence and take account of the Panel's views. For the National Probation Service, the cost and effectiveness issues will represent measures of their work, especially in the light of the 'contestability' requirement in the work to be carried out under the new correctional service, NOMS (see Chapter 11).

Also of great relevance to probation staff is the reform of custodial sentences. Extending magistrates' powers to a 12-month sentence (s.181) might be seen as an attempt to become more punitive. But in fact, all custodial sentences are reviewed in the Act. Custodial sentences of over a year in length will have half the term spent in custody and half under the supervision of the National Probation Service with a range of community orders to be followed. This is closer supervision on release than previously. Prison sentences of less than 12 months will be termed 'custody plus' – with a 28-week minimum. The custody period will be between 2 and 13 weeks, and offenders will be on licence (supervised by Probation and undertaking community orders or tagged curfew or exclusion orders) for at least 26 weeks. The Explanatory Notes to this Act state that there are new 'intermediate sanctions' in the form of intermittent custody and suspended custodial sentences. (In Halliday's report (Home Office 2002c: 4), the latter were referred to as 'custody minus', but this was clearly not seen as an appropriate name for a new sentence requiring strict compliance.) Intermittent custody will require the offender to be on conditional licence when not in custody. Sentence length will be 28 to 51 weeks, and the custodial days can range from 14 to 90 days. The suspended custodial sentence will also be for 28 to 51 weeks of imprisonment, but the offender will only be incarcerated if they fail to comply with one or more of the community orders during the supervision period, or if, during the 'operational period' they commit a further offence. Suspended sentences of imprisonment may be reviewed by courts and amended according to progress. This sentence is distinct from a community order. For the new, generic community order, sentencers will be able to specify the requirements of the order, selecting from those managed by the probation service and other providers..

The Criminal Justice Act 2003 is going to make more work for probation staff, for the number of offenders under supervision is going to increase. The Act attempts to give supervisory help to offenders who find themselves in the 'revolving door' of prison. Community sentences have become tougher, more varied and able to be tailored to an offender's needs. This is clearly part of the political rhetoric. The government was faced with a prison population of 74,000 in early 2004, but anticipates having nearly 79,000 places by 2006 (Home Office 2004d). According to Travis (2004) the projection is that it could rise to 93,000 by 2009. As he says, 'replacing ineffective short-term prison sentences with robust and intensive community programmes, could keep that figure to 80,000' (Travis 2004: 5).

David Blunkett, as Home Secretary, had been faced with the results of the 'tough' policies of the Labour government since 1997 – recognizing that prison and probation sentences have increased from 85,000 and 133,000 respectively in 1996 to 112,000 and 186,000 respectively in 2002 (Home Office 2004d). Will the provisions of the 2003 Act be sufficient to get the focus back on community punishments and away from prison as the sentence of choice? The government must hope so – the costs of incarceration are too high (especially as, overall, crime has been falling in recent years) – and the reforms in this Act and the Carter review (see Chapter 5) will not be cheap to implement. Harding (2003) says that 'custody plus' will be popular with sentencers as it combines stick and carrot and that the impact of blurring the edges between custody and community penalties will be threefold:

> First, these measures will not reduce prison expansion, but add to it; second, we will create a new round of net-widening; and finally, we perpetuate values that support imprisonment. Seductive seamlessness raises the spectre of custody as the first resort of the courts rather than the last.
>
> (Harding 2003: 371)

The new sentences roll out from 2004 onwards, so the effects of the Criminal Justice Act 2003 and, alongside it, the merging of correctional services as in the Carter proposals (Chapter 5), will not be seen for some time.

The evidence from this legislative outline suggests that the Labour government is as preoccupied with law and order as its predecessor – if not more so. There have been, and continue to be, major changes to the criminal justice structures, and the rhetoric against persistent offenders and the need to 'put victims first' continues. Meanwhile, incarceration rates have continued to rise, community sentences have increased in number, whilst recorded crime and people's experience of crime has fallen, with little change in detection rates (Johnson et al. 2001; Simmons and Dodd 2003). The role of the community has been enhanced with a range of new community-based orders and more partnership and collaborative working across communities, but this has not made the community an inclusive place for offenders. It is the place where they are singled out to report, be tested, attend courses and programmes, do unpaid work, be assessed for risk, register with the police and be excluded from having the freedom to go where they choose.

Conclusion: the punishing community

The discourse of punishment in the Community presupposes a mythical community which, to use Faulkner's analysis, is 'inclusive' (1996). Such a society seeks to 'put things right' rather than punish, recognizing the capacity of individuals to change and the obligation of the community to support and protect the vulnerable and disadvantaged. By contrast, the reality of community is 'exclusive'. The criminal is seen as the enemy. We are engaged in a 'war' against crime, where there are two clear sides: the respectable law-abiding citizen and the feckless criminal outsider. *This* sense of community reflects an insecure society, suspicious of, and hostile towards, anything and anyone who is different. Community means segregation, prejudice and the desire for revenge.

The 'exclusive' community is the result of faith in the efficacy of the worst excesses of capitalism – unregulated competition and the survival of the fittest. Hagan (1994) parodies the language of capitalism by talking about *capital disinvestment:* the lack of will to invest in programmes that build up *social* and *cultural* capital.

In addition to *physical capital* (the tools, machinery, equipment, buildings and so on that are necessary for wealth production) and *human capital* (the skills and knowledge which are normally developed through education and training), Hagan argues that we stockpile *social capital*. This refers to the capabilities that are developed through social relationships, primarily through the family but also through other social attachments and commitments. *Cultural capital* refers to the ways we adapt to our heritage and our environment – whatever it is that we 'value' in our culture or cultures, over and above the imperatives of survival and wealth creation.

In order to maintain these forms of capital there must be *investment* by society. It is only through this investment that we will become *embedded* in the legitimate social and economic networks of our society. The notion of *embeddedness* means that we take for granted both the existence of certain structures and our own obligation to abide by the norms and values generated by those structures. At a personal level, it simply does not occur to us to behave in any other way. Bottoms' theory of compliance (which aims to explain why people comply with the law) divides this into 'normative compliance', based on a 'felt moral obligation, commitment or attachment' and 'compliance based on habit or routine'. He contrasts these with two other modes of compliance: 'instrumental/prudential compliance' based on 'self-interested calculation' and 'constraint-based compliance' based on physical and structural restrictions on individual freedom (2001: 90).

Hagan argues that we are experiencing instead *capital disinvestment*, by which he means the deliberate enhancement of inequality through policies of residential segregation (coupled with growth in private security), non-investment in poorer communities and collusion with racial discrimination. Such policies are destructive of social and cultural capital and lead to a dangerous process of *recapitalization*. Recapitalization refers to a reorganization of available, diminished resources and the supplementing of these with illicit new resources in order to achieve goals. The most significant example Hagan gives of new illicit resources is that of drugs. The development of alternative structures and economic networks based on the economy of illicit drugs results in a new and oppositional kind of embeddedness, that of *criminal embeddedness.* The punishing community, far from encouraging reintegration and conformity, may instead be creating a 'parallel universe', reinforcing for some an embeddedness that takes for granted that the only way to behave is criminally.

Part 2
The Changing Role of the Probation Service

Chapter 5

From 'advise, assist and befriend' to 'enforcement, rehabilitation and public protection'

Introduction

The role of the probation service in the criminal justice process represents at least two theoretical dilemmas: the extent to which criminal courts are obliged to follow the advice of non-legal professionals and the extent to which a balance can be maintained between care for an offender and control of an offender. It has been said that the probation service represents a mechanism whereby courts can institutionalize their ambivalence (Millard 1982). When requesting reports and when placing offenders on probation, they are admitting that they are unsure whether an offender should be punished or should receive help.

This chapter will focus on the history and traditions of the probation service and the impact of policy and legislative changes since the mid 1970s. It will also engage with the debate about the training of probation officers which, it will be argued, has done more than any piece of criminal justice legislation to change the way in which the occupation is viewed. The removal of training from a specific area of higher education (social work education) and Home Office calls for more ex-servicemen and 'mature' people with 'authority' and 'common sense' to be recruited in place of liberal do-gooders has had significant implications for the whole identity of the probation service. What sort of people do we now have as the community punishers of the future and are these the people we want to be doing the job?

What the probation service does

The probation service is the major organization in England and Wales for dealing with offenders in conditions of freedom. (In Scotland, the probation service ceased to exist as a separate organization when it was incorporated into the new Social Services departments in 1968; Northern Ireland has its own Probation Board which was set up in 1982). Probation officers supervise adult offenders placed on probation by the courts and some young offenders under 18 years through their partnership arrangements with the Youth Offending Teams (YOT). Probation service staff also supervise offenders placed on community punishment orders and staff approved premises (hostels). They provide what is called a 'throughcare' service for offenders sent to prison, which includes staffing a probation office in each prison and young offender institution, and supervising prisoners on early release or parole, which is known as 'resettlement'. Probation officers prepare pre-sentence reports on offenders to help courts to arrive at the best sentencing decision, and for certain sentences, a specific sentence report is prepared by a court officer (for further discussion see Chapter 6).

A community rehabilitation order is a community sentence that requires an offender to be supervised by a probation officer for a minimum of six months and a maximum of three years. Under the Criminal Justice Act 1991 such an order may be made on any offender over the age of 16, although the juvenile equivalent, a supervision order, remains an available option for 16- and 17-year-olds.

The probation order (the previous name for a community re-habilitation order) has a long history dating back to the Probation of Offenders Act 1907. It was originally intended to be an *alternative to a sentence* and remained so, technically, until the Criminal Justice Act 1991. Its traditional purpose was to offer advice, assistance and friendship to offenders, in the belief that they could thus be reformed or rehabilitated. More emphasis is now placed on restricting offenders' liberty, although under the Criminal Justice Act 1991, the objectives of an order still include the rehabilitation of the offender, as well as protecting the public and preventing reoffending. The conduct of community rehabilitation orders is governed by National Standards, issued first in 1992 and revised regularly thereafter. Their significance is discussed later in this chapter.

Offenders sign a contract that, while on probation, they will keep in touch with their designated probation officer through regular office appointments and, possibly, visits at home. They must also notify their probation officer of any change of address or employment. If they fail to meet these requirements they may be subject to breach proceedings, which means that they are taken back to court and may be resentenced. Probation officers have been very reluctant in the past to institute breach proceedings because they have viewed it as undermining their rehabilitative role (Lawson 1978), but now probation officers generally adopt the view that breach proceedings are just, beneficial to the offender and, most importantly, raise the credibility of the probation service as being able to deliver 'tough' sentences (Drakeford 1993). The Director General of the National Probation Service said in her Performance Report in November 2003:

> The cultural issues about enforcement have been addressed.
> (National Probation Directorate, 2003: 5)

For many years the proportion of community rehabilitation orders terminated for failure to comply with requirements (where no new offence was committed) ran at 2 per cent annually. Since 1989, however, this proportion has crept up and was 9 per cent in 2002 (Home Office 2004a).

Since 1948 it has been possible for courts to add conditions to a basic order requiring an offender to live at an approved residence or to undergo psychiatric treatment. When courts now make a community rehabilitation order, it is open to them to make specific additional requirements and in 2002 they did so in 37 per cent of orders – an increase from 26 per cent in 1992 (Home Office 2004a). Of those sentenced to community punishment and rehabilitation orders 33 per cent had additional requirements. The most significant additional requirements concern medical (that is, psychiatric) treatment, residence, treatment for alcohol dependency, and attendance on an accredited programme. A wider range of rehabilitative accredited programmes is deemed to be responsible for the sharp increase in these figures (Home Office 2004a).

Advocates of the traditional probation order extol its flexibility as a sentencing option. They argue that it can be used for relatively minor and serious offences (although the 1991 Criminal Justice Act required that the offence be deemed 'serious enough' for a community penalty by the court) and can be tailored to the particular needs of an offender. However, it has been hard for the order to shake off its image in the eyes of the courts as a 'soft option', suitable only for less serious offences. After the introduction of community service in the 1970s (now known as community punishment), the use of the probation order declined dramatically. In response, the probation service emphasised its value as an *alternative to custody* for serious offences. After the Criminal Justice Act 1982, the use of the probation order for men increased from about 29,000 in 1984 to 40,000 in 1994 and to 46,000 in 2002. By contrast, orders for women declined in the same period from about 11,000 to 7,000 in 1993, but increased again to 12,000 by 2002 (Home Office 2004a). The decline in orders may be explained by the success of probation officers in persuading the courts that most offences committed by women are insufficiently serious to warrant supervision, but the steadily increasing numbers of women sent to prison suggests that a more contradictory logic of 'bifurcation' is in play. The more recent increase in probation/community rehabilitation orders and custodial sentences may illustrate that sentencers are being more egalitarian in selecting disposals for women and not distinguishing between the genders (Worrall 2002a; Carlen and Worrall 2004). By comparison, while an equal number of community punishment orders (CPOs) were made on men in 2002 (46,000), only half as many CPOs as community rehabilitation orders (CROs) (6,000 compared with 12,000) were made on women (see Chapter 7 for a fuller discussion).

Since the 1991 Criminal Justice Act, community rehabilitation orders can now be combined with community punishment orders. The rationale for community rehabilitation and punishment orders is to provide courts with an additional community sentence which offers help to the offender while also exacting reparation. Such orders have proved popular with the courts, their numbers having increased from 1,400 in 1992 to 15,500 in 2002 (Home Office 2004a).

Prior to the creation of the National Probation Service, there were 54 probation areas in England and Wales (mostly coterminous with counties), employing around 7,800 probation officers, 1,900 probation services officers (PSOs, formally known as ancillary workers), 4,800 clerical and administrative staff, and 900 non-probation officer staff in approved probation and bail hostels (Home Office 1996b). In 2002, the total number of probation officers was about 8,000, including 1,600 trainees. Other staff numbered 9,300, of whom 4,100 were PSOs (Home Office 2004a). So the balance in staffing has changed. (It should be remembered that losing the Family Court Welfare Service to the newly created Children and Family Court Advisory and Support Service in 2001 resulted in a drop of probation officer numbers.)

In the ten years from 1984 to 1994, the proportion of female probation officers rose from 39 per cent to 52 per cent, and had reached 61 per cent by 2002 (Home Office 2004a). It is notable that in 1992, eight of the 54 chief probation officers were female. By 2002, 18 of the 42 chief officer posts were held by women, and the percentage in senior positions was 50, compared with 33 per cent in 1992. In 1994, approximately 7.5 per cent of all probation staff were recorded as belonging to a minority ethnic group; by March 2003 that had increased to 11.2 per cent – higher than the Labour Force Survey of 2001 which shows 9 per cent (NPS 2004b). The proportion that were Asian or Asian British remains low at 2.5 per cent (in 2002).

Responsible to the chief officer of each probation area are deputy and assistant chief officers, who usually have responsibility for particular aspects of service (for example, training, performance, prisons) and/or geographical regions in the area. Senior probation officers are in charge of teams of probation officers, covering a geographical 'patch' or a specialism such as courts, community punishment or approved premises. Most teams include probation service officers, who often have an NVQ Criminal Justice qualification to level 3, as well as clerical and administrative staff. Attached to many teams are probation service voluntary associates and mentors, who are ordinary members of the public, assisting probation officers in such tasks as befriending and transporting clients.

In the past probation areas enjoyed relative autonomy to develop their own policies and practice but in 1984 the Home Office published the *Statement of National Objectives and Priorities*. Since that time, central government has sought to standardize practice across England and Wales and probation officers work within the framework provided by National Standards, which set out the expectations and requirements of all aspects of the supervision of offenders. The new national service has centralized the strategy and objectives.

Throughout the 1980s and until the mid-1990s, there was considerable disagreement about the extent to which the probation service could be regarded as a social work organization. Until that time, in order to be appointed as a probation officer it was necessary to have a professional social work qualification (the Certificate of Qualification in Social Work, the Certificate in Social Service or the Diploma in Social Work) but the Home Office Green Paper *Supervision and Punishment in the Community* (1990b) argued that more emphasis should be placed on the service's role as a criminal justice agency and, for the first time, hinted at the possibility of significant changes in training and recruitment. Before pursuing that particular debate, a brief account of the history of the probation service will illustrate how the service found itself facing such a threat to its professional status.

The history of the probation service

The probation service has its roots in the work of the nineteenth-century police court missionaries, first employed by the Church of England Temperance Society in 1876 to 'reclaim' offenders charged with drunkenness or drink-related offences. The Probation of Offenders Act 1907 gave magistrates' courts the right to appoint probation officers, whose job it was to *advise, assist* and *befriend* offenders placed under their supervision.

The Criminal Justice Act 1925 made it obligatory for every court to appoint a probation officer, and during the first half of the twentieth century the work of the service expanded to include work with juveniles and families, as well as adult offenders. Part of that work included dealing with matrimonial problems and it was through this aspect of the work that the role of the Divorce Court Welfare Officer developed. By the mid-1960s the service had also taken responsibility for the welfare of prisoners, both inside prison and on release. The distinctive professional skill which probation officers developed was that of Social Inquiry (or Enquiry) Report. This was a social work assessment of an offender in their social environment, with a specific purpose of assisting courts to make sentencing decisions.

The 1991 Criminal Justice Act changed the name and, some would say, the purpose of reports. The content of pre-sentence reports is laid down in National Standards and must include offence analysis, offender assessment and an assessment of risk of harm to the public by the offender and their likelihood of further offending. The report concludes by proposing possible appropriate sentences, bearing in mind their suitability and motivation. The main difference between a social inquiry report and a pre-sentence report is that the former traditionally placed greater emphasis on the personal and social circumstances of the offender, while the latter is primarily concerned with the seriousness of the offence and the offender's attitude towards it, though this is a rather crude distinction, as will be seen in Chapter 6.

Although there had always been a degree of tension in the role of the probation officer between *caring* for offenders and *controlling* their criminal behaviour, these two aspects of the work were viewed as part and parcel of both the psychoanalytic casework and the paternalistic 'common sense' advice which combined to characterize the typical probation officer of the early and mid-twentieth century. By the end of the 1960s the probation service had grown from the status of a localized mission to that of a nationwide, secular, social work service to the courts. Its expansion had been unselfconscious and the concepts of care and control had not been incompatible. The service's three-fold function apparently caused no crises of conscience:

1 Advisers to courts – both criminal and civil;
2 Supervisors of offenders in the community;
3 Supporters of prisoners and supervisors of ex-prisoners.

From the 1970s onwards a number of developments had paradoxical consequences for the service and resulted in a loss of identity, or, to use Harris's (1980) term, 'dissonance'. Harris argued that probation officers were experiencing three kinds of dissonance in their work:

1 Moral dissonance, resulting from conflicting ideologies about the purpose of probation;
2 Technical dissonance, resulting from discouraging empirical evidence about the effectiveness of probation in reducing criminal behaviour;
3 Operational dissonance, resulting from tension inherent in managing the 'care and control' aspects of the daily probation task.

Three ideological conflicts permeated the probation service in the 1970s. These can be summarized as, first, the conflict between *genericism* and *specialism;* second, the conflict between work with *low-risk* and *high-risk* offenders; and, third, the conflict between *ideological trade unionism* and *pragmatic trade unionism.*

The Seebohm Report of 1969 heralded the age of genericism in social work and by 1971 the new Social Services Department had been established. The ideology of Seebohm was that the new social workers should be able to offer a comprehensive generic service to families in need, rather than a series of specialized interventions. To complement this radical change in service delivery, a new national training body – the Central Council for Education and Training in Social Work (CCETSW) – was created and, along with it, a new generic qualification – the Certificate of Qualification in Social Work (CQSW) – located in universities, at a mixture of undergraduate, postgraduate and non-graduate level.

The equivalent development in Scotland was introduced a little earlier by the Kilbrandon Report in 1968, and the probation service in Scotland agreed to be incorporated into the new Social Work Departments. In England and Wales, however, the probation service fiercely defended its independent identity and remained separate. It did, nevertheless, join in with the new training proposals. Prior to the

79

establishment of CCETSW, probation officers had been trained on a short specialist course run by the Home Office. Increasingly, recruits to both Social Services Departments and the probation service were young, academically able and politically radical. The Home Office, which had supported the retention of a separate probation service, became increasingly alarmed at its inability to control the content and tone of the training of probation officers.

On the same day as the new Social Services Departments came into being, the 1969 Children and Young Person Act was implemented – or, at least, as much of it as was ever implemented. This landmark piece of legislation will be discussed in more detail in Chapter 10 but the important point to note here is that it aimed to remove juvenile offenders from the stigmatizing effects of courts and probation service supervision. Instead it invested the power to care for juvenile offenders in the new Social Services Departments. The logic of this lay in the belief that juvenile delinquency is a product of unsatisfactory up-bringing and socialization within the family and that the welfare of juveniles should be of greater concern than their punishment.

But the new breed of generic social workers was viewed with distrust by the police and magistrates when it came to their ability – and their willingness – to control the behaviour of troublesome young people. Magistrates frequently compared social workers unfavourably with probation officers. Brown (1990) identifies three reasons why magistrates were uncomfortable about social workers. First, they had a fear of unfamiliar colleagues and they did not understand the social work 'culture'. Second, they perceived social workers as lacking expertise in the 'rules of the game' in court (see Carlen 1976). Third, social workers were perceived to be too theoretical, jargon-bound and idealistic – they were viewed as driven by left-wing ideology, lacking 'common sense', making 'unrealistic' recommendations in their reports.

The upshot of this was that magistrates were reluctant to commit juvenile offenders into the care of social workers. The original intention of the 1969 Act was that very few offenders under 14 years of age would be brought to court at all and that offenders aged 14–17 would be supervised by social workers. Very quickly it became apparent that courts wanted probation officers to continue to supervise older juveniles and, because of the confusion about responsibilities between the two agencies, the safest option for magistrates seemed to be to send increasing numbers of juveniles to detention centres or to the Crown Court for borstal sentencing (which was outside their powers), so that they would eventually be released on 'after-care' to the probation service. This was totally contrary to the spirit of the 1969 Act and was certain to bring about its failure. True, the numbers cautioned rose dramatically, but the numbers placed on supervision or in care declined and the numbers sent to detention centre or borstal escalated from 2,500 in 1968 to 7,500 by 1978 (Pease and Bottomley 1986). It was a classic case of 'net-widening' and 'up-tariffing'. The welfare approach so widely condemned as a feature of the 1970s did not, in reality, ever happen.

The consequence of 'hiving off' juveniles to Social Services was that the probation service was enabled to work with more 'high-risk' offenders. The 1972 Criminal Justice Act introduced community service (see Chapter 7) and day-training centres (see Chapter 8), planting the seed of 'alternatives to custody' rhetoric and the greater surveillance of offenders. But the most controversial development was to be found in the recommendations of the Younger Report in 1974, based on the belief that to reduce the numbers of young people in custody one had to 'strengthen' community supervision (a familiar net-widening fallacy). A new 'supervision and control' order was proposed which did not require the offender's consent and also gave probation officers the power to request the police to detain a 'client' already on supervision for up to 72 hours in order to forestall the commission of an offence. The recommendations were greeted with alarm by most probation officers (for a discussion of the arguments, see the Special Younger Report Issue of *Probation Journal*, Vol. 21, No. 4, December 1974) and were never implemented but a re-reading of the Report 30 years on will demonstrate that many of the contemporary debates about 'care versus control' are by no means new.

The third continuing conflict concerned the development of the probation service's sense of its own occupational identity and its relationship with other workers – and not just those in the criminal justice system. During the 1970s, the National Association of Probation Officers developed from a 'cosy' professional association to a trade union representing an increasingly well-trained profession. Politically increasingly left wing, it was concerned to promote the ideology of radical social work within the criminal justice system and beyond. But this was set against the constraints of the general economic climate of the 1970s and the decline in the use of traditional probation orders. In order to avoid cuts, the probation service identified with the 'law and order' lobby of the new Thatcherite government and sold itself directly as a service that could help reduce numbers in prison by offering effective alternatives.

The rise of managerialism

Following the 1984 *Statement of National Objectives and Priorities*, and their own subsequent local responses, the probation service began to engage the services of financial management consultants. In this it was reflecting the increased use of management science in the public sector, but the most visible effect on probation officers was their perceived loss of professional autonomy and a greater emphasis on accountability through the devising of team and area objectives, action plans and so on.

In 1989 the Audit Commission reviewed the service and concluded that it was not giving value for money. A similar, but lower-profile exercise went on in relation to probation training, which was funded through sponsorship by the Home Office. As a result of the Coleman Review, the Home Office decided to be far more directive about the content of probation-training programmes in an attempt to socialize students better into the ideological and bureaucratic demands of the service and rid them of left-wing indoctrination by ivory tower academics. It paid scant regard to the fact that CCETSW itself had already embarked on a major overhaul of social work training that was to go some way towards answering the Home Office's concerns. The new Diploma in Social Work required every course to be accountable to a local consortium, or partnership, of social work agencies, to ensure that students were being trained appropriately to meet the demands of an ever-changing social work scene. Local probation services became the driving forces behind a number of these partnerships and, as a result, expressed increased confidence in social work training – a message that did not please the Home Office!

Alongside the White Paper *Crime, Justice and Protecting the Public* (Home Office 1990a), which set out the government's philosophy for criminal justice, based on the principles of 'just deserts', came two further Green Papers: one on the organization of the probation service and the other on partnership with voluntary agencies.

Supervision and Punishment in the Community (Home Office 1990b) was designed to rationalize the structure and organization of the service and to limit the autonomy of individual probation areas. It proposed greater central control and possible amalgamations of smaller services. It also reinforced the role of the service as a criminal justice agency (rather than a social work agency), which should relate primarily to other criminal justice agencies, the police, prisons and, above all, the courts. It stated that the probation service must be so organized as to ensure:

- responsiveness to criminal justice policy;
- a clear framework of accountability;
- effective management;
- value for money;
- confidence of sentencers;
- effective links with other organizations in the community.

It raised again the question of probation officers' training and suggested that social work training might not be the most appropriate route to qualification. It made a number of alternative proposals, including a free-standing probation qualification, and asked for views.

Similarly, the (pale) Green Paper, *Partnership in Dealing with Offenders in the Community* (1990c), was intended to make clear to the service that it did not have a monopoly on punishment in the community and that the privatization of community sentences might well follow prison privatization (Matthews 1990). When the probation service had refused to have anything to do with electronic monitoring during the 1989 pilot schemes, the government saw a golden opportunity to begin thinking about contracting out the supervision and surveillance of offenders. Fourteen years on, the emergence of NOMS has the idea of 'contestability' at its heart.

To complete the chronology of this particular round of multi-coloured papers, a blue 'Decision Document' entitled *Organising Supervision and Punishment in the Community* was published in April 1991, which dealt with structural organizational changes aimed at rationalizing the service, limiting its financial resources and making it more accountable to other criminal justice agencies, especially the courts. The full impact of this review process was not felt until the Labour government of 1997 had been in power for some time. Whilst accountability was still a key tenet, the enactment of the Court Services Act 2000 that created the National Probation Service in 2001 also signified a sizeable expansion of financial resources.

The loss of professional autonomy

However, we might argue that all these developments, while affecting the managers and policy-makers in the service, would still leave the grass-roots probation officer with her professional autonomy in respect of her individual cases. Even the 1991 Criminal Justice Act did not impinge directly on that.

But National Standards did. From 1989 to 2002, the Home Office compiled a series of National Standards directing practice in relation to all aspects of probation service supervision: report-writing, supervision and probation orders, community service orders, new combination orders, the management of hostels, and supervision during and after imprisonment. They cover not just broad policy guidelines, but detailed instructions about the administration of orders. They cover frequency of contact, record-keeping, rules about enforcement and the taking of breach action, and the content of supervision sessions.

There were some good professional justifications for the National Standards, and few disputed the need to standardize some very variable and inconsistent practices across the country and between individual officers. Professional autonomy had undoubtedly been used in the past as an excuse for poor practice. Also, if anti-discrimination was to be taken seriously, then there had to be an attempt to ensure minimum standards of service delivery.

However, National Standards must also be seen as the government's attempt to make individual probation officers more accountable to management and management more accountable to the government. It is not without significance that the revised National Standards progressively downplayed their value to offenders and other service users. While the 1992 version stated that offenders 'should have access to a fair and effective complaints system if they are dissatisfied with the service they receive' (Home Office 1992b: 3), the latest version stresses that National Standards 'inform offenders of what is expected of them and the action which will be taken if they fail to comply' (Home Office 2002d).

The overriding point about the introduction of National Standards was that they limited the discretion of the individual probation officer and focused on the management of supervision rather than on its content. And it followed that the need for probation officers to undertake two years' training as social workers, when all the procedures they would ever need to follow were now laid out in a glossy ring-bound booklet, must be open to question.

The stage was set for the final onslaught on probation training. In 1994 Vivienne Dews of the Home Office reported on a training scrutiny and recommended the removal of sponsorship from most Diploma in Social Work programmes, despite widespread satisfaction among local probation services (Ward and Spencer 1994; Williams 1994). She favoured the retention of a few centres of excellence but expected most recruits to the service to be trained on the job, perhaps through the competence-based framework of National Vocational Qualifications (NVQ). Both routes would lead to a new 'Diploma in Probation Work'.

In February 1995, the Home Secretary took the decision to repeal the legal requirement for all new probation officers to hold the Diploma in Social Work, thus ending the control of higher education over probation training. The decision was justified on two grounds: first, that since Social Service social workers are not required by law to have a social work qualification, why on earth should probation officers be required to do so? Second, it was argued that existing training selection discriminated against mature students, particularly men who had relevant experience and skills (for example, in the armed forces). The first argument was, logically, the stronger but politically weak, since most people agreed that more social workers, rather than fewer probation officers, should be professionally trained. The second argument was disingenuous in the extreme, since the probation service has always recruited a proportion of older second-career men. But it has insisted on retraining them. Even more invidious was the appeal to broader recruitment on implied equal opportunity grounds, which temporarily seduced some into thinking that there might be more opportunities for black and Asian people and women to join the service. This was emphatically not what Michael Howard had in mind – indeed, the Dews Report had identified the high proportion of younger women joining the service as a 'problem'.

There were many campaigning comings and goings but, by 1996, there were no Home Office sponsorships for Diploma in Social Work programmes and on-the-job training was developing fitfully. Probation services themselves largely gave up the battle because financial restraints were so severe that there were no jobs to recruit into anyway. On the contrary, services were 'downsizing' and looking for early retirements among existing staff. Some might say that in this, as in other aspects of the job, the probation service precipitated its own downfall with its constant criticism, over the previous decade, of social work training. Particularly damning was research undertaken in the late 1980s by Davies and Wright (Hardiker and Willis 1989) that purported to show that probation students on social work courses considered themselves ill-equipped and inappropriately trained for their future employment. The long-term impact of this was that there was still a chronic shortage of trained probation officers at the inception of the National Service, when there was funding available for employing more staff. Only in 2003 was this trend reversed.

However, in this respect, if in no other, the change of government *did* make a significant difference. Recognizing the potential damage of the training vacuum created by the Conservatives, the then Home Secretary, Jack Straw, announced new training arrangements in 1997. The new Diploma in Probation Studies was to combine an under-graduate university degree with an NVQ Level 4 award. The award was to be employment-led and run by consortia of probation services and higher education institutions. A new awarding body, the Community Justice National Training Organization was established which would, once and for all, distance probation training from social work training (Knight 2002).

There is little doubt that probation training as it now exists is extremely demanding (Schofield 1999). Whitehead and Thompson describe training as 'coaching a [trainee] in a particular mode of behaviour and/or performance' (2004: 22) and liken the process to that of training an athlete. But there is disquiet among some who deliver training that the specificity of the roles and tasks for which trainees are equipped may not produce the flexible, reflexive and creative employees that are needed to work imaginatively with offenders in the twenty-first century (Nellis 2000). As an experienced deliverer of training in a university, Knight (2002) worries that trainees may be encouraged to view themselves too much as employees and too little as students. She expresses the hope that:

> Sadly, in times of excessive work pressure and low morale arising from the pace of change and lack of consultation, workers frequently lose [the] thirst for knowledge and give up on the process of 'thinking' ... As students, [trainees] have permission to think the unthinkable, to challenge current orthodoxy, and to hear the views of a wide range of academic staff and experienced practitioners, who feel free to express their opinions on current developments.
>
> (2002: 296)

Problem-solving to impression management

For a number of decades, probation officers saw themselves, rightly or wrongly, as professional social workers, working in the specialist setting of the criminal justice system. They believed they possessed a body of knowledge, had developed particular skills and had an ethical base to their work. As such, they had a right of discretion and control over their own work. That professional autonomy has been steadily eroded to the point where many probation officers see themselves as nothing more than criminal justice operatives, concerned only with the technological aspects of a bureaucratic job.

An example of concern for many officers was the introduction of Specific Sentence Reports (SSRs) for courts in 2001. These 'on the day' reports are commonly written by court officers (Probation Service Officer grade) rather than probation officers – they will be discussed fully in Chapter 6. Many probation officers felt that sentence recommendation, following full offence and offender analysis, was their area of expertise, which was being undermined by the new system. The significant difference is that with SSRs, sentencers select the order for the offender and ask the court officer to report that he/she is a suitable candidate. So there was a perceived loss of requirement for professional expertise. Many probation officers were, however, persuaded that their skills lay in offender and risk assessment for the more serious culprits.

Shaw (1987) writes about the erosion of control which school teachers have over their work and he argues that the same analysis could be applied to social workers. Shaw's concern was that the loss of control and the acceleration of managerial and bureaucratic demands meant that workers were so preoccupied with the minutiae of their jobs that they either lost sight of, or were too exhausted to take interest in the wider social, economic and political influences that ultimately shaped the nature of their work. If they managed to remain aware of them, then they would be broadly integrated into the hegemonic establishment as a service class of junior partners. Shaw argues that the mass professions like teaching and social work are unavoidably untidy, indeterminate and unpredictable because they are dealing with human beings in changing social circumstances. Attempts by the government to tidy up probation and make it more efficient and effective are linked with the desire to reduce opposition to government criminal justice policy and to locate the blame for its failure to reduce crime at the lowest level possible – namely, at the level of face-to-face contact with offenders.

The probation service was therefore shifting from being what May calls a 'problem-solving' organization to a 'performance' organization:

The clients' problems are not then considered central, but impression management for the government and the Home Office is.

(May 1991: 169)

This was a prophetic insight on the part of May, for with the commencement of the National Probation Service in 2001, Eithne Wallis, as national director, set the strategic framework for the service. One of the nine objectives for the first three years was: 'Building an effective performance management framework' (National Probation Service and Home Office, 2001: 3).

Critique of the management ideal

There were a small number of voices seeking to resist the hegemony of managerialism and the foreclosure of the management debate in the probation service (including Humphrey 1991; Humphrey and Pease 1992; May 1994; Beaumont 1995). Perhaps the most persistent was that of McWilliams (1990, 1992). He argued that the management ideal masquerades as a set of 'value-neutral techniques with claims to the detachment of a science' (1990: 60). It is, on the contrary, a system of thought which incorporates ideas about the nature of relationships – in the case of relationships with offenders, that they should be tough and confrontational – and on the ethics of actions – that they should be procedurally standardized, efficient, economical and capable of being monitored.

National standards, he argued, were a mixed blessing for three reasons. First, they legislate only for minimum standards, discouraging innovation and diversity; second, they relocate discretion up a hierarchy away from the professional practitioner, stifling initiative; third, they shift attention away from the intrinsically individual nature of the rehabilitative and reformative processes.

The management ideal, he argued, makes the probation service vulnerable to change imposed from outside because it starts at the top with policy that is 'given'. The role of managers is merely to translate that policy into instrumental objectives and to ensure, through evaluation and monitoring, that organizational practice is com-mensurate with those objectives.

McWilliams proposed an alternative model of organizational arrangement that he called an 'Administrative/Professional Leadership Model'. This model is based on an appreciation of the nature and purpose of the probation service that is concerned more with its identity – what it is – than with what it does. This involves a leadership that embodies the values and professional practice of the service, leading by example, and an administrative framework that enables those who work within the organization to express those values in their tasks and practices. Improvement in performance standards comes through feedback, dialogue, encouragement and critical analysis. Supervision is characterized by consultation and advice, rather than by its contemporary characteristics of line management. Officers would be held *substantively accountable* for their professional decisions and actions, rather than *formally accountable* for the procedures they follow. In short, he yearned for a return to a participative model of organizational accountability.

Perhaps unsurprisingly, McWilliams was perceived as an idealist by many in the probation service. Shepherd (1991), in his response to McWilliams, argued that his critique of management was simplistic, vague and unduly negative and that his alternative model was so nebulous that it was extremely difficult to imagine how it would work. He argued that what McWilliams was talking about was bad management, not management *per se.* On the contrary, he believed that good management benefits the probation service in the following ways:

- recognizing that staff are an organization's most valuable asset and maximising their potential

- recognizing that staff work best if they are clear about what is expected of them

- holding staff accountable

- ensuring staff have the resources to do the job

- encouraging creativity within the boundaries of policy

- ensuring that decisions are made on the basis of the service's values and not individual whim

In summarizing New Labour's project to 'modernize' criminal justice, Raine (2002) identifies five main facets: new policy priorities; new information and communication technologies; new organizational architecture of corporate governance; new performance management frameworks and new relationships with the professions. New policy priorities include not only the 'what' of criminal justice policy but also the 'how' of management policy – for example, the shifts from outputs to outcomes (not just what is *done* but what is *achieved*), from cost efficiency to cost effectiveness (not just what it *cost* but whether it was *worth the effort*). The impact of ICT has transformed both the levels of information and the nature of interaction within criminal justice (see also Mair 2001), though by no means unproblematically. The new architecture of corporate governance has been characterized by two seemingly conflicting principles: co-terminosity of boundaries (using the 42 police areas as a template) and centralization (as in the nationalization of the probation service). The proliferation of performance measures and targets in the National Probation Service has, arguably, improved the quality of service to some consumers but Raine suggests that the relentless emphasis on performance measurement may have encouraged both partial (or even dishonest) reporting and a 'sapping of staff morale' (2002: 339). Finally, he suggests that the new relationship between government and the professions is characterized by the dominance of a management perspective and the continued curbing of professional discretion.

In short, it soon became clear that, far from making any radical break with the attitude of the previous government towards the probation service, New Labour intended to introduce legislation and pursue policies that, had they succeeded, would have brought an end to it altogether.

The beginning of the end for the probation service?

In August 1998 the Home Office launched what might, facetiously, be termed a new national game called 'Rename the Probation Service' (Worrall 1998). It invited suggestions for a name that 'is capable of inspiring public confidence in the work of that Service' and, while expressing 'no strong preference', provided a number of suggestions to stimulate ideas. These were:

The Public Protection Service
The Community Justice Enforcement Agency
The Offender Risk Management Service
The Community Sentence Enforcement Service
The Justice Enforcement and Public Protection Service
The Public Safety and Offender Management Service
The Community Protection and Justice Service
(Home Office 1998: para.2.14)

The call to rename the probation service, despite the acceptance by the Home Office that probation 'is a long established concept, well understood internationally' (1998: para 2.13), arose from the determination of the new Labour government to abolish any terminology that might be 'misunderstood' or 'associated with tolerance of crime' (1998: para 2.12). This was rhetorically compatible with their now famous manifesto pledge to be 'tough on crime and tough on the causes of crime'. Nonetheless, the proposal that a service with (then) 7,200 probation officers and a total of fewer than 15,000 employees (including clerical and administrative staff) could provide 'public protection' was difficult to take seriously (NAPO 1998).

The Prisons-Probation Review had been set up in July 1997, shortly after the new government took office, and was intended to explore the possibility of integrating the prison service and the probation service. The consultation document reporting on the review was entitled *Joining Forces to Protect the Public* (Home Office 1998). The review rejected a merger of the two services, partly for reasons of principle (that there was insufficient overlap of responsibilities) but predominantly, one suspects, for reasons of cost (delicately phrased as 'disruption to staff and the difficulties of renegotiating major IT initiatives' [para.2.38]). In fact, very few of the review's recommendations affected the prison service. The probation service, however, as well as being renamed, was to undergo a major restructuring. Of most significance was the proposal to create a unified national service with national leadership directly accountable to the Home Secretary. This proposal was long overdue and welcome and, of itself, could go a long way towards remedying the perceived shortcomings and lack of credibility of the service. That the new leadership would not be leading a recognizable probation service, however, rather undermined the gesture.

The desire of the government to erase the concept of 'probation' from the collective conscience was the surface manifestation of a more fundamental desire to blur the boundaries between freedom and confinement and extend the disciplinary effects of imprisonment wider and deeper into the community. As the review put it, 'we are interested in looking at ways of replacing the present cut-offs with a more flexible set of sanctions based on a continuum of loss of liberty, reparation in the community and correction of offending behaviour' (1998: para.1.8). Community-based sentences were no longer to be viewed as alternatives to custody (as they were in the 1980s as a response to prison overcrowding and the decarceration debate) or as sentences in their own right (as in the Criminal Justice Act 1991, which sought to reduce the prison population directly by limiting the powers of sentencers) but as part of a continuum which allows smooth and easy movement between prison and the community. The state of tension – indeed of healthy conflict – that had hitherto been assumed to exist between advocates of imprisonment and advocates of community-based penalties had been rendered redundant. As John Patten had predicted a decade earlier (see Chapter 2), we were all in the same business now – the business of punishment – with no differences of principle. Retribution, deterrence, restoration and rehabilitation could be fitted neatly together within a socially constructed consensus about the purposes of punishment. The only remaining differences were those of approach and even differences of approach were being eroded.

By December 1999, the government had decided on the name, 'The Community Punishment and Rehabilitation Service'. The change received no support from any probation organization (NAPO 1999) and probation officers feared that offenders would quickly find a mischievous (if admittedly inaccurate) abbreviation that would soon make it the subject of ridicule (CRAPOs working for CRAPS!) (NAPO 2000a). Following Early Day Motion No 346, the government reconsidered and, to everyone's delight, abandoned the name change (NAPO 2000b).

But the more serious business of changing the culture of the probation service continued apace.

Enter the National Probation Service

In April 2001, the National Probation Service for England and Wales was created and its national director, Eithne Wallis, could be said by some to be demonstrating the Administrative/Professional Leadership Model for which McWilliams had argued so many years before. Or perhaps it better reflects Shepherd's model of good management? This new organization of 42 Areas (which are coterminous with county boundaries) plus a National Directorate, is wholly funded by and responsible to the Home Office. For the first time in its history, the service has become a national body, centrally led and centrally funded. Each Probation Area is administered by a Board of 15 people, comprising independent members, a Lord Chancellor's representative (a Crown Court judge), magistrates and community representatives. The chief officer (who is the accountable officer and responsible to the Director General), treasurer and secretary, and the Board chair make up the 15 members. The Board employs all the Area staff (except the chief officer) and is responsible for ensuring that staff deliver services, for performance management and for the governance and the probity of the deployment of the Area's resources. The Areas are grouped in 10 regions, which are mapped on those of the government offices of the regions and the Welsh Assembly.

One of the obvious changes that came with the new national service was the altering of the names of orders that offenders undertake. Probation orders became Community Rehabilitation Orders, Community Service Orders became Community Punishment Orders and Combination Orders (comprising elements of both) became the cleverly titled Community Punishment and Rehabilitation Orders! At the inception of the national service, it was only the names that changed: the content did not differ from what had gone before. But there was a significant change in bringing the words 'Community', 'Rehabilitation' and 'Punishment' to the fore. The creation of the public perception of a tough law and order agency was behind these changes. This was assisted by taking the Family Court Welfare Service (where specialist probation officers had looked after the needs of children in civil proceedings) away from probation, to the newly created Children and Family Court Advisory and Support Service (CAFCASS). In addition, a more collaborative approach was required, with the high profile chief officers for each area having to liaise formally with their police colleagues to manage dangerous offenders in the community, using the forum of the Multi-Agency Public Protection Panels (MAPPPs). Local Criminal Justice Boards are another manifestation of collaborative working.

In order to bring together these previously disparate probation services, the National Director set out her strategy in a document called *A New Choreography* (NPS/Home Office 2001). The major part of this document had been circulated earlier and had laid down Wallis's vision for the new service. The final version, endorsed by Tony Blair and Home Secretary, David Blunkett, outlined the aims and objectives for the service and put these into financial context by including the spending budgets until 2003/04 (which show a significant increase of some 30%, from a total of £542m in 2001/02 to £713m in 2003/04). It is worthwhile considering this document in some detail as it had a great bearing on the operation of the new service.

A New Choreography states that the aims of the National Probation Service are:

- protecting the public
- reducing reoffending
- the proper punishment of offenders in the community
- ensuring offenders' awareness of the effects of crime on the victims of crime and the public
- rehabilitation of offenders.

(NPS/Home Office 2001: iv)

It links these into the Home Office aims of ensuring the effective delivery of justice and delivering effective custodial and community sentences to reduce reoffending and protect the public. The text attempts to create an impression of 'joined up' government and collaborative working. Wallis did not shirk from her new responsibilities:

> Sometimes, however, I shall be leading the Service against the grain of its past history and traditions, to achieve this delivery of new services to high levels of specified performance.
> (NPS/Home Office 2001: 5)

She thereby admitted that there was a new direction for the service and a new philosophy for its people to uphold. The strategy then outlines nine 'stretch objectives' for the NPS. These are:

- accurate and effective assessment and management of risk and dangerousness

- more involvement of victims of serious sexual and other violent crime

- offender programmes that have a track record in reducing reoffending

- intervening early to take young people away from crime

- enforcement

- providing courts with good information and pre-trial services

- valuing and achieving diversity in the National Probation Service and the services it provides

- building an excellent organization

- building an effective performance management framework.

It should be noted that these are not just called 'objectives'; the adjective suggests that these are aims which it will be difficult for services to deliver and will put them under pressure to achieve the desired performance. A challenge indeed! The language used elsewhere also indicates that this is a new era with managerialism at its heart: 'We want the image of the Service to be that of a "hawk-like professional", sharp and keen-eyed' (NPS/Home Office 2001: 8). So why was this all enshrined in a document called *A New Choreography*? The author says that it is 'to capture and communicate the essence of the macro change programme' (NPS/Home Office 2001: 6).

But how does it do that? Choreography is the art of arranging or composing dances. Sometimes dancers are directed by the choreographer to rehearse and perform these composed dances. But many notable choreographers in the world of ballet left their notated dance compositions for others to direct and rehearse the artists. Did Wallis see *A New Choreography* as her template for the operation of the NPS, or did she see herself in the role of choreographer directing her own composition? The latter would seem more likely, as this dance metaphor has pervaded much of the early work of the NPS: *Heart of the Dance*, *Next Steps* and *Bold Steps* are all NPD strategy documents. But having a *new* choreography suggests that there was an *old* one. And this is clearly not the case, as there was no national co-ordination of probation before 2001. But there had been past history and traditions, as Wallis had noted, so perhaps *A New Choreography* was really there (to continue the metaphor) to tread all over the past and stamp it out? Maybe the term 'choreography' was used to suggest a 'softer' form of managerialism, with its artistic connotations and association with music. After all, an alternative theme could have been chosen, such as 'A Blue-Print to Engage', and associated with a military operation, campaigning and drill. Wallis's title is more subtle.

A less subtle change came in February 2003 when Martin Narey, formerly director general of the Prison Service, gained permanent secretary status and became the first Commissioner for Correctional Services in England and Wales, 'with responsibility for Prison and probation services, oversight of the Youth Justice Board, and policy responsibility within the Home Office for correctional, rehabilitation and sentencing issues' (NAPO 2003: 8). 'Correctional Services' is an Americanism that doesn't sit very happily with the traditional ethos of probation (Travis 2004). The National Director of the NPS had her title changed to Director General and became accountable to Narey. So suddenly the probation service was linked, as never before, with the prison service – despite the attempts in 1998. This was clearly in preparation for anticipated changes following Patrick Carter's review of correctional services: *Managing Offenders, Reducing Crime* (Home Office 2003d). Many of Carter's recommendations had been anticipated by NAPO members at their 2003 AGM – they saw the writing on the wall with Narey's earlier appointment (www.napo.org.uk/agm2003).

The government's response to Carter (Home Office 2004d) makes it clear that decisions had already been made about changes *before* asking for public comment. The need for change is justified by the politicians by a continually high prison population – 74,000 in 2003 (Home Office 2004d) despite a reducing crime level – and the consequent costs of this.

The new strategy is for prisons and probation services to work ever more closely together as the National Offender Management Service with two clear objectives: punishing offenders and reducing reoffending. ('Punishment' seems to be higher up the agenda than first espoused as an NPS aim in *A New Choreography*.) Regional Offender Managers will become more important – a part of the present government's strategy in all matters. The Sentencing Guidelines Council has been created to try and bring about a greater consistency in sentencing, whilst not impinging on the independence of the judiciary. However, the Council, in making recommendations to sentencers, is expected to take account of capacity of both prisons and probation (Home Office 2004d).

Having arguably undergone more change in the last four years than in the previous 40, the National Probation Service is now on the brink of more fundamental change. In the day to day work of managing offenders, running programmes and writing court reports, the work of the front line officer may not vary too much. In fact, early pronouncements suggest that there will be a shift of emphasis to community punishment from custody (Home Office 2004d). But which organizations will provide the programmes, punishments and reports is the key question. The Home Office states that 'Regional Managers would contract with providers of prison places, community punishment and interventions (such as basic skills or health) – whether in the public, private or voluntary sector' (Home Office 2003d: 36).

Conclusion

The probation service has developed in little more than a century from being a localized, voluntary, evangelical outreach provision to being a profession whose work is integral to the criminal justice system. Having consciously adopted the 'high-risk' strategy of focusing on 'high-risk' offenders and having conceded the right of central government to dictate its priorities, it was bound to become vulnerable if the penal climate were to get any colder – as it has done. Once the need for probation officers became politically open to question, it was perhaps inevitable that the service would have to face the de-professionalization of its workforce.

The readiness with which most probation staff adapted to the new regime of the NPS in 2001 is indicative of a cultural change. The 'strapline' of the new, national service was 'enforcement, rehabilitation and protecting the public' – highlighting the new role of the service as a criminal justice agency designed to get public and sentencer confidence in community sanctions as a means of reducing incarceration rates. The recommendations of Carter (Home Office 2003d) suggest that this confidence has not yet been established. But the argument of this book is that it never will be because the public perception that community punishment is never 'real' punishment is tenacious. The policy of 'bifurcation' (separating out the 'minor' from the 'dangerous' criminals) has been a feature of the politicization of crime in the past two decades and has allowed successive governments to sustain a paradoxical rhetoric of supporting alternatives to custody while arguing that there are many 'dangerous' criminals for whom alternatives are simply not suitable. Since 'dangerousness' (as politically defined) is very much 'in the eye of the beholder', this line of official rhetoric has given rise to the concept of 'populist punitiveness'. Raynor and Vanstone (2002) argue that the impact of this on community penalties is that 'crime-related issues [are] defined by political elites as problems of insufficient punishment or as being "soft" on criminals' (2002: 69). By playing on understandable public concerns about crime, supporting biased media coverage and fuelling moral panics, politicians use crime-related issues to manipulate public opinion. Within this discourse, the only acceptable kind of community sentence is a 'tough' one, administered by 'tough' people – certainly not by traditionally-trained, liberal-minded, university graduates who have been taught to criticize and challenge anything that smacks of managerialism and accountability.

Chapter 6

Taking the 'social' out of inquiry reports

Introduction

This chapter will discuss the role of the probation officer and the probation services officer in court as 'expert witnesses' and their relationship with sentencers. The social inquiry or enquiry (there was never any logical reason for the different spellings) report was the traditional mechanism for the reconstruction of a criminal within professional discourse as a 'treatable' or 'manageable' offender. It symbolized individualized sentencing based on the positivistic (or humanistic) belief that an understanding of the offender's personal and social background and circumstances may contribute towards helping them to stop offending. The 1991 Criminal Justice Act replaced the social inquiry report with the pre-sentence report and this represented much more than a change of nomenclature. It represented an uncoupling of the relationship between crime and 'the social', locating it firmly in the realm of 'the moral', the main focus being individual intentionality, remorse, risk and capacity to respond to normalizing instruction.

Over a quarter of a million reports are prepared every year, mostly for magistrates courts; about 21 per cent are for Crown courts. The figure of 253,000 reports in 2002 (Home Office 2004a) includes both pre-sentence reports (PSRs) and specific sentence reports (SSRs). The latter are short court reports, produced by court officers on the day, for specific sentences. They were introduced nationally in 2000. It usually takes probation officers three weeks to prepare PSRs (and there is a service performance measure that 90 per cent of them will be prepared within 15 working days), although they can be written more quickly if this is considered essential. Probation officers normally interview a defendant twice and one interview may be at the defendant's home in order to assess their circumstances. Relevant personal information is gathered and then verified as far as possible. The defendant's attitude to the offence is assessed and possible sentences are discussed. The format of PSRs is prescribed in National Standards. Probation officers have to try to ensure that they conduct the interviews and write the reports in a way that accords with anti-discriminatory and anti-oppressive practice (Whitehead and Thompson 2004). They have to take account of the fact that black and Asian people and women may experience discrimination in the criminal justice system.

Until the 1994 Criminal Justice and Public Order Act, courts were required to obtain reports before passing certain sentences, such as custodial sentences and certain community sentences. Since that time, they have had wider discretion to pass a custodial sentence without reports but they still often ask for reports in these and other cases (Charles, Whittaker and Ball 1997).

Harris has said, 'Social inquiry reports are the main vehicle for routine interchange between the probation service and the courts' (1992: 148). Their content, structure, style and philosophical under-pinnings are symbolic of the whole relationship between social work (in the form of the probation service) and criminal justice. Their significance is much greater than the factual accuracy of the information they contain about an individual offender, although criticism of their role has often focused narrowly on that aspect. Their origins are clearly rooted in the rehabilitative individualized approach to sentencing which emphasises personal histories and circumstances, and it has not been easy to adapt them to a 'just deserts' approach which focuses more on the offence than the offender.

The history and development of court reports

Providing personal and social information on an offender to a court has always been a key feature of the job of the probation officer. Le Mesurier (1935) talked of 'investigation' and described its purpose as being 'to strengthen the hands of the court in dealing with the individual offender' (1935: 89). She talked about the importance of magistrates understanding the offender's personality, needs and potentialities. She set out guidelines on both the content of a report (under the two headings of 'environment' and 'personal history') and the process of information-gathering. The probation officer should 'avoid too much direct questioning' and 'over-insistence on points of detail'. In short:

> He must be a good listener, sympathetic but unbiased, neither critical nor condemnatory, but unemotional and quite 'unshockable'.
>
> (Le Mesurier 1935: 95)

So, although from the outset reports were intended as sentencing aids, they were also much more than this. They were intended to be diagnostic tools, similar in many ways to the social histories taken by a doctor or psychiatrist. Probation officers saw themselves as professionals making diagnostic assessments about the causes of offending and the treatment appropriate for each individual offender. Although Le Mesurier talks about the interests of the offender and the interests of the community, she does so in the same breath and makes no reference to any conflict between the two. What is the right treatment for the individual offender is also assumed to be in the best interests of the community.

This optimistic, positivistic, scientific approach reached its zenith with the Streatfeild Report of 1961. Its purpose was to examine the role of probation reports in the context of what was perceived to be a changing sentencing climate – a gradual shift from backward-looking concerns about culpability to concerns about how to influence future behaviour (Bottoms and Stelman 1988). The key to this influence was seen to be the provision of information that was comprehensive, reliable and relevant to sentencing. The probation report (renamed the social enquiry report by the Morison Report of 1962) had to provide three kinds of information:

(a) Information about the social and domestic background of the offender which is relevant to the court's assessment of his culpability;

(b) Information about the offender and his surroundings which is relevant to the court's consideration of how his criminal career might be checked; and

(c) An opinion as to the likely effect on the offender's criminal career of probation or some other specified form of sentence.

(Bottoms and Stelman 1988: 23)

The assumptions underlying Streatfeild were that such information existed and that it was obtainable, communicable and useable. The belief was that sentencing was rational and scientific and that probation reports could both reflect and contribute to scientific research about explanations for crime and the efficacy of particular treatments for particular sorts of offenders. Reports were therefore professional documents of the assessment of culpability and risk.

Unfortunately, attacks on rehabilitation in the 1960s and 1970s called into question the existence of any reliable knowledge about the effects of treatment on offenders. In addition, critics were increasingly pointing to a gap between rhetoric and practice. Research suggested that even basic information was gathered and presented in a haphazard and inconsistent manner (Perry 1979; Thorpe 1979). Academic courtroom observers commented on the strategies used by probation officers to maintain their credibility with magistrates while appearing, to the untrained eye, to be seeking lenient sentences for their clients (Carlen and Powell 1979). Radical socialist probation writers Walker and Beaumont (1981) wrote a searing indictment of social inquiry report practice, claiming that probation officers had neither the time nor the skills to make the kind of claims that were routinely made in reports. They identified a 'front region account' corresponding to the Streatfeild model, which was presented to magistrates and researchers and which contrasted with the 'back region account' of interviews conducted in competition with children, television, neighbours and animals:

> It is not easy to concentrate with a demented budgie sitting on your head or a large Alsatian sniffing up your skirt.
>
> (Walker and Beaumont 1981: 16)

Probation officers were increasingly criticized for making personal moral judgements in the guise of professional assessments and of contributing to erratic and discriminatory sentencing. Harris concludes:

> Empirical research into the quality, content, consistency and impartiality of SERs found them wanting and probably incomprehensible to their subjects, disappointingly few of whom possessed the social science degree which would have enabled them to have understood the more linguistically and conceptually complex of these documents.
>
> (Harris 1992: 146)

He quotes Barbara Wootton, who was on the Streatfeild Committee, as saying in 1978:

> I welcome social enquiry reports because they make me feel cosy, inasmuch as they transform a 'case' into a human being but, sadly, I am driven to the conclusion ... they do little to make me in any sense a better sentencer.
>
> (Harris 1992: 146)

Bottoms and Stelman (1988) suggest that, in addition to Streatfeild's model, there are two other ways of looking at the significance of social inquiry reports. The first is within the penal analyses of Foucault (1977) and Garland (1985), based on notions of hierarchical observation and normalizing judgements. The second (to be discussed later in this chapter) is the administrative, systems-management approach advocated by Tutt and Giller (1984) and containing the seeds of pre-sentence reports.

In *Discipline and Punish,* Foucault (1977) talks about the 'examination' which combines 'hierarchical observation and normalizing judgements'. He talks of the 'normalizing gaze' that makes it possible to qualify, classify and punish by making individuals visible and then differentiating and judging them. The purpose of social inquiry is therefore to control or discipline offenders by placing them in preconceived categories which trigger particular responses – a sophisticated way of distinguishing between the deserving and undeserving. Much of the advice offered to social workers about conducting social inquiry was designed to enable the worker to 'catch out' the individual being investigated. Bottoms and Stelman cite Donzelot (1980) who, in turn, quotes a 1920s article on social inquiry. The article contains the same advice as that given by Le Mesurier but Donzelot interprets it very differently. The investigator was advised to find out everything on record about a person before visiting them, to talk to anyone respectable who might know them, to make surprise visits – first in the afternoon to catch mother alone and then in the evening to see if father gives the same story – to examine the home for evidence to support or refute the offender's story. But all this was to be done pleasantly, in order to encourage the person to talk as much as possible – and presumably to give themselves away!

This pessimistic approach to social inquiry fits the model of the disciplinary society constructed by Cohen (1983, 1985). What matters here is not so much the detailed accuracy of the content of a report but the image of the offender that is represented by the report. This analysis has been particularly relevant to reports written on women and black and Asian people where stereotypical representation has been seen adversely to affect sentencing practice.

Social inquiry reports, women and black and Asian people

In the early 1980s, the main concern among those practitioners who were prepared to cast a critical eye over their practice was that too many women were being placed on probation at too early a stage of their criminal careers. Although women offenders represented between 15 and 17 per cent of all known offenders, they accounted for about one-third of all probation orders. With increasing awareness of the dangers of net-widening (thanks largely to the insights of writers in the field of juvenile justice) an optimistic view emerged that reducing the numbers of women on probation would result in a reduction in the numbers of women being sent to prison. (This optimism proved quite unjustified, as will be discussed later.) The social inquiry report was identified as a key document in the social construction of female offenders as suitable candidates for supervision. Worrall (1981) and Eaton (1985, 1986) drew attention to the dangers of seeking to locate such women within the ideology of the nuclear family and of portraying (or failing to portray) them as good wives, mothers or daughters. By comparing reports on men and women, and the differential use of home visits by probation officers preparing reports, Eaton (1986) also highlighted the significance of differing gender role expectations in reports. Such expectations go beyond a description of a conventional division of labour in the home to the belief that women have a responsibility for the emotional well-being of everyone in the domestic sphere. Even when they themselves are law-abiding, they are expected take some responsibility for – or at least shed light on – the offending behaviour of male partners. The reverse is rarely the case.

In a statistical comparison of court disposals of male and female defendants, Mair and Brockington (1988) concluded that women tend to be referred for social inquiry reports more readily than men (when offence and previous record are matched) and are more likely to be recommended for (and to receive) probation orders. Mair and Brockington observe that there is some evidence that referral for reports is in itself likely to move a defendant 'up-tariff' and that this should be a matter of concern for a service seeking to target reports on specific groups seen to be at risk of custody.

Deciding when a female offender is 'at risk' of custody, however, has been a vexed issue. Jackson and Smith (1987) found that many women are in prison for an accumulation of minor offences, having been considered unsuitable for community service as a result of domestic responsibilities. Similarly, Dunkley (1992) found a lack of consensus among probation officers about the appropriateness of referring women to probation centres. Consciousness of sentencing discrimination may lead one officer to recommend attendance on a probation programme to forestall a custodial sentence, while another officer may view such a recommendation as collusion with that same discrimination.

Representing women in social inquiry reports as 'programmable' – as motivated towards and able to benefit from the resources of the probation service – requires their construction within the discourses of domesticity, sexuality and pathology (Worrall 1990). It is an exercise fraught with dilemmas:

> The trap for probation officers who might want to construct female lawbreakers within alternative discourses is that, in an area where such stereotypes dominate, they run the risk of seriously disadvantaging their client. Hence many officers justify their continued writing of gender-stereotyped reports on the grounds that they are working tactically in their clients' best interest.
>
> (Worrall 1990: 116)

Stephen (1993) confirms the view that female offenders are 'muted' (Worrall 1990). Although their own accounts of their offending differ little from those given by men (and are predominantly based on external social factors), they are more likely to find their accounts disregarded by probation officers, who apparently still tend to prefer seeing women's crime as the result of 'underlying emotional problems'. Female offenders are still not being listened to (Horn and Evans 2000; Prison Reform Trust 2000; Malloch 2004).

Very little research exists which is specifically concerned with the portrayal of black and Asian women in social inquiry or pre-sentence reports. Denney (1992) suggests that probation officers tend to write assessments of white women offenders that are more detailed and sympathetic than those of black women. There is a tendency to assume that at the root of black women's offending lies a problem of identity resulting from not belonging to the dominant culture. While white women may be portrayed as neurotic and irrational, black women are portrayed as unpredictable and 'suffering from a peculiarly "feminine" form of "silliness"' (Denney 1992: 109). Chigwada (1989) argues that racism in social inquiry reports is more overt:

> Black women may be seen as over-protective, over-religious or over-punitive, and labelled as "bad" mothers. Expressions of emotion, whether anger or affection, may be misinterpreted. Similarly, value judgements concerning issues such as sexual or family relationships, work status, parental responsibility based on a Eurocentric view of society, are then used to justify prison sentences.
>
> (Chigwada 1989: 104)

In her later work, Chigwada-Bailey (2004) also comments that this 'distortion of perception' is particularly in evidence in relation to foreign national women who are judged not as poor women going to extreme lengths to support their families 'but as women who have left their families and who have neglected their responsibilities to their dependants' (2004: 194).

Although little has been written specifically on black and Asian women, a number of small-scale research projects in the 1980s were concerned to identify any differences in reports written on white and black men that might account for the disproportionate numbers of black people given custodial sentences. The details of these, sometimes conflicting, studies have been well-documented (see, for example, Reiner 1989; Denney 1992; Durrance and Williams 2004; Calverley *et al.* 2004) and it is possible to extrapolate from them three broad conclusions, reflecting a lack of understanding and confidence on the part of white probation officers when faced with black (often young and usually male) offenders.

First, there was a tendency for probation officers to fall back on racial and cultural stereotypes, attributing offending to unconventional family structure and socialization, or to cultural tensions and conflicts, especially among 'second generation immigrants'. Second, probation officers tended to include information which might appear routine and morally neutral, such as nationality and place of birth, but which might nevertheless serve to create an image of the offender as different – as Other – and as requiring special treatment by the court. Third, several studies found that probation officers were reluctant to make firm recommendations for non-custodial sentences for black and Asian people. This was not necessarily attributed to direct racism on the part of probation officers, but more to an inability to develop sufficient rapport with an offender to create the kind of relationship in which supervision might be seen as having any potential. Unfortunately, some of the anti-racism training given to probation officers during that time made the situation worse rather than better. White probation officers lost their professional confidence and came to believe that they did indeed have very little to offer young black and Asian offenders. Consequently, recommendations for probation became even fewer with the result that more black people were given prison sentences.

Following the 1991 Criminal Justice Act and, in particular, section 95 (see Chapter 2), probation officers were provided with a 'Checklist for Anti-Discriminatory Pre-Sentence Reports' (Sanders and Senior 1994: 156-7). The checklist addressed five broad areas of discrimination – race, gender, sexual orientation, poverty/unemployment and disability – and took the officer step by step through the process, content, proposals and outcomes of the report. It offered some sound practical advice such as allowing adequate time to discuss issues of discrimination, telling the offender what is going into the report in good time so that any errors could be corrected, creating a 'conducive' environment for interview and not being oppressive (shades of Le Mesurier?). It also, however, poses some unanswerable questions such as:

> How can structural inequalities re housing, education, benefits etc. be included when relevant, without stereotyping?

> Check out own value judgements/belief systems to see how they influence content.

> Check that any community sentence proposed will not further contribute to discrimination.
>
> (Sanders and Senior 1994: 156–7)

If we could answer these questions, we should undoubtedly go a long way towards the elimination of discrimination!

Since the 1990s, and in the light of the publication of the MacPherson report in March 1999, much work has been done in all public services to try to root out institutional racism. HM Inspectorate of Probation undertook a thematic inspection of probation services, producing the report *Towards Race Equality* in June 2000 (before the National Probation Service was in place). This inspection report was followed up with a re-inspection that reported in January 2004 (Home Office 2004e). Despite progress on 17 of the original 19 recommendations of 2000, sadly only three were considered to have been 'well met' (Home Office 2004e: 9). Pertinent to this discussion is that the original recommendation that 'probation committees and chief probation officers should take action to improve the overall quality of PSRs on minority ethnic offenders' (Home Office 2004e: 21) was deemed to be only 'partially met' in 2004. Of particular note is that:

> reports on minority ethnic offenders tended to be of a slightly poorer quality on virtually every variable. This negative finding needs to be set against the overall significant improvement since the original inspection.
>
> (Home Office 2004e: 24)

Tutt and Giller and the Home Office

In response to criticism about the value of social inquiry reports, the Home Office issued guidance during the 1980s which was aimed at making them more focused documents, concerned with very specific issues rather than claiming to be all-purpose generalized assessments of people and their lives. In doing this, they were influenced by work at Lancaster University that Norman Tutt and Henri Giller (1984) did in relation to juvenile justice and court reports. This work was based on three assumptions:

1 That behaviour is often situation-specific rather than being the product of enduring personality traits;

2 That reports can contribute to stigma and labelling and thus amplify deviance;

3 That rehabilitation does not work.

Therefore, reports should be seen as limited exercises, intended solely to help decide what should happen to an offender as a consequence of committing a particular offence. They should be aimed at negotiating the least restrictive sanction commensurate with the seriousness of the offence. They are aids to administering or managing the criminal justice system in relation to an individual offender. They do not cover everything in the offender's life and they do not cover all the considerations which the court may take into account, for example, harm to the public, the prevalence of a particular offence, local reaction and so on.

Report writers were decreasingly being trusted as 'experts' and were increasingly being required to spell out both the process of their inquiries and the details of their recommendations. For example, they were required to state their sources at the beginning – where they got their information from and what steps they had taken to verify it. They were also required to spell out in the conclusion exactly what a probation order would involve and why it was seen to be suitable. In other words, probation officers could no longer get away with saying 'in my opinion'. They had to produce the evidence to support their arguments and be prepared to defend it in court. They could no longer hide behind their professionalism.

It has been argued (Worrall 1990) that, in making sentencing recommendations, probation officers are faced with the dual dilemma of defining the appropriate 'moment of intervention' and defining the appropriate 'nature of intervention' in relation to any given potential client. That decision is made as a result of a professional assessment of the relationship between client need, agency resources and client motivation (that is, the extent to which the client's expressed desire to change is judged by the probation officer to be 'genuine' and the extent to which she is judged to have the capacity to benefit from the resources available). That assessment must then be translated into language that is acceptable to the court. The defendant must be presented in a form that is recognizable by solicitors, psychiatrists and, above all, sentencers.

Traditionally, probation officers have claimed authority for such reports on the grounds that they contain recommendations of 'expertly selected treatment based on scientific diagnosis' (Raynor 1985: 153). By the mid-1980s, however, probation officers were more modest in their claims:

> Any opinion expressed in the report about the appropriateness of some form of contractual sentencing ... should be offered to the court as a plausible alternative to the retributive tariff sentence ... The important issues are what the offender is prepared to do, whether and how far the social work agency is able to help him do it, and what assurances the court will require from both parties.
>
> (Raynor 1985: 153)

Pre-sentence reports and predicting risk

The increased focus on the offence rather than the offender culminated in the change of name to that of pre-sentence reports. As we have seen in Chapter 2, the underlying philosophy of the 1991 Act was one of 'just deserts' or the imposition of a sentence that is commensurate with the seriousness of the offence. The assessment of offence seriousness became one of two new skills required of probation officers in writing court reports – the other was risk assessment. The two are connected but they do not amount to the same thing. Probation officers have always been concerned with assessing risk in the sense of preventing, reducing or deterring recidivism. They have been less concerned with assessing the seriousness of an offence, preferring to see that as a moral rather than professional task and, therefore, as the job of the court. They have always sought to 'second guess' the court's view of the seriousness of an offence and have taken that into account, but they have not seen it as something for which they themselves have a direct responsibility.

The requirement that probation officers should now contribute to (or, some might say, collude with) an assessment of the *seriousness* or an offence subtly removed one area of potential conflict within the court. Probation officers are required not just to take account of how they think an offence might be perceived by others (which is fair enough); they were now required to enter that moral debate directly and take responsibility for making a moral judgement, based not on any professional knowledge but on sheer common sense. In fact, the moral question was quickly reduced to an administrative one and Gilyeat (1993) soon provided a handy *Companion Guide to Offence Seriousness*, with scales and diagrams to help the report writer calculate the number of applicable mitigating and aggravating factors and thus locate the offence in the right classification: 'less serious' (recommend discharge), 'serious enough' (recommend community sentence) or 'so serious' (abandon hope).

The task of *risk* assessment has proved more complex and more elaborate mechanisms have been devised for the purpose. The first explicit use of the term in relation to social inquiry reports was by Curnock and Hardiker (1979) who, coming from a mainstream social work tradition, argued that social inquiry reports require the writer to balance the *risk* posed by the offender with their *needs* and with the *resources* available to them (that is, personal, social and professional resources). Bottoms and Stelman (1988) elaborated further on the concept of risk, arguing that the report writer should distinguish between the risk of reoffending and the risk of the damage caused by reoffending to the offender and their family and friends. They dismissed a third distinction – that of risk to potential victims – as being a matter for the court and not the report writer. They went on to outline two sets of hazards that together might constitute a risk assessment. *Predisposing hazards,* based on research, suggest that reoffending is most likely to occur among young men whose first conviction was at an early age, who have a large number of previous convictions with no recent break in the pattern, who have previous experience of institutions and who commit offences alone. By contrast, the least likely to reoffend are older women with late first convictions, few previous convictions with a long gap since the last conviction, who have no previous experience of institutions and who commit offences in company. The seriousness of the current offence appears to have no direct bearing on the likelihood of reoffending. *Situational hazards* refer to factors specific to the individual offender and the circumstances surrounding the commission of the offence. Are the circumstances which gave rise to the offence likely to recur? Does the offender have a particular personal or social characteristic that makes them vulnerable (for example, an uncontrollable temper, a drink problem, debt)?

The process described here might be termed 'soft' risk assessment, since it is based on the subjective professional opinion of the probation officer, using their knowledge and skills to 'paint a picture' of the offender in their environment. Such an approach became less and less acceptable both to the probation service and the courts.

One of the earliest attempts to assess risk more 'objectively' was the Cambridgeshire Risk of Custody (ROC) Scale devised by David Bale (1987). The ROC scale consisted of a form which sought to quantify all the factors which courts might be expected to take into account (such as offence gravity, criminal history, age, gender and so on) and which would then provide a percentage likelihood of an offender receiving a custodial sentence (the risk score). This would then guide the probation officer in making their recommendation. Unfortunately, it was never made clear whether the scale was intended to be predictive (that is, what the court *would* do) or normative (what the court *should* do). Nor was it clear whether its purpose was to enable the probation officer to 'second guess' the court more successfully or to influence the court away from its most likely disposal (Raynor, Smith and Vanstone 1994). In the end, most officers used this and other versions of ROC scales as aids, which gave them an indication of the relative likelihood of custody for different groups of offenders. Bale himself conceded that 'the best probation officers will always out-perform a fixed scale, even if I have demonstrated that the scale can out-perform the average officer' (1987: 127).

It might be argued that risk of custody is not the same thing as the risk of reoffending, which in turn is different from the risk of harm. Probation officers' inability to separate these different issues has led to a great deal of 'fuzzy thinking' (Kemshall 1995, 1996; Webb 1996). In her research on risk assessment in pre-sentence reports, Kemshall found that officers were using a range of criteria that might well be challenged by a critical outsider as being little more than 'common sense'. Notions of risk were based on perceptions of 'unpredictable' behaviour, attitude to the offence, offender characteristics, motivation to change and so on. The only situation in which officers seemed willing to apply rigid procedures was in the case of sex offenders, but this, Kemshall suggests, was more to cover themselves than to protect potential victims. In most other cases, because the risk was diffuse, it was also more difficult to calculate and to grasp.

Kemshall concluded that there is no easy route to risk assessment and that 'fuzzy thinking' is not necessarily dangerous, for 'risk itself is fuzzy, changing constantly with differing probabilities and differing impacts for different people' (1996: 7). Although the term 'fuzzy' is one that most academics would balk at, the idea that risk in this context cannot be quantified actuarially is not exactly novel and it is telling that the probation service needed to be reminded of that. Risk-taking is now a well-recognized motivation for criminal activity (Katz 1988; Beck 1992) and unless that can be incorporated in probation officers' and sentencers' understandings, there is little hope of accurately calculating the risk of reoffending or the risk of harm. But discussion of 'risk-taking' as motivation is not acceptable in the discourse of pre-sentence reports – it is part of the 'social' that has been ejected from the exercise. 'Risk' is viewed as something that is wholly negative – to be assessed, quantified and managed (Robinson 2003).

Since the late 1990s, the issue of risk in probation practice has been developed to take account of risk of reconviction (rather than risk of custody), and the risk of harm to self and others, based on both actuarial and 'dynamic' factors. Systems were developed to help officers make objective assessments, and risk (likelihood of event) was separated from dangerousness (impact of the event). The question of dangerous offenders (particularly violent and sex offenders) was clarified when the Criminal Justice and Court Services Act of 2000 set up the working arrangements for Multi-Agency Public Protection Partnerships, MAPPPs, which commenced in April 2001 (see Chapter 9). Predictor scales such as OGRS (Offender Group Reconviction Score) used actuarial statistics to measure the static elements about an offender that do not change (age, gender, date of first conviction, etc.) and to plot these against offence statistics to produce a likelihood score. Assessment tools such as ACE (Assessment, Case management and Evaluation) focused on the dynamic factors in someone's life that are amenable to change. Their aim was to promote consistency and reliability, and they also encouraged the active participation of the offender in the supervision planning process.

The more sophisticated OASys system (common now to both prison and probation services, and operated electronically) looks at static, actuarial factors as well as dynamic factors that can and do change, such as behaviour and attitudes, drug and alcohol misuse, as well as the significant factor of relationships. In addition, this 'living document' (NPS 2002a) helps probation officers in their approach to supervision and sentence planning. Kemshall (2002) reminds us that the national and international approach to risk has changed. Not only are post-modern risks seen to be global and uncertain (as exemplified by the events of 11th September 2001), but in parallel, risk has become in-creasingly individualized:

> The risk society is peculiarly defensive, and is concerned with the distribution of risks, who produces them and why, and upon whom they fall.
>
> (Kemshall 2002: 97)

This is as true for offenders as it is for any other citizen, and hence the change in report-writing for sentencers. Probation officers now refer to the offender's awareness of the risk that they present to potential victims – an attempt at 'responsibilization'. Kemshall foresees an impact on justice:

> Justice ... will always be subject to prevailing views and notions of 'balance' – literally a weighing of public and victim safety against the rights of persons who are seen as dangerous, unworthy, imprudent and to a large extent responsible for their own predicament.
>
> (Kemshall 2002: 109)

The challenge for the probation officer writing the PSR is to convince the sentencer that their recommendation of sentence has considered the risks of reconviction and harm and can be seen as a defensible and realistic decision.

In writing Specific Sentence Reports (SSRs), a different approach is taken (Hoy 2002). SSRs are only written for offenders when a community sentence is being considered – custody must have been ruled out, and the offence must be serious enough for the community penalty. The SSRs are written by court officers (normally Probation Services Officers, not of probation officer grade) to a prescribed format. The sentencer must ask the officer to check on the defendant's suitability for a specific sentence (CRO, CPO or curfew order) and probation services have limits on the length of sentence confirmed by this method. If a more demanding sentence is required, say with conditions of attendance on a programme, then a full PSR will be required. A hand-written report of two pages is presented to the sentencers after about an hour. An abbreviated form of risk assessment will have been carried out, an interview regarding the offender's circumstances – work, health, etc., and reference made to colleague officers.

The advantages are expedience, both for the court, probation and the offender. If the offender has been on community orders before, then they will understand what is required of them, and will usually be pleased to have been sentenced that day (with no risk of custody from another, more punitive bench!). For probation services, the advantage is in scarce, specialist probation officer resources being used to write reports only on the most serious offenders who are guilty of the most serious offences. For courts, the need for no further delay in resolving a case is a great benefit to the managerialist cause. The dilemma, of course, is whether it is appropriate for PSOs to write these reports, and whether fuller risk assessment should be done. The latter may change as the ability to use the OASys risk assessment electronically becomes available. The former remains an issue. Hill (2002) explains that concerns expressed by probation services in Smith's (2001) survey were based on the skill levels of PSOs and the downgrading of the service by replacing probation officers in this role. However, she makes the point that 'the use of PSOs in this role depends on having the right tools, the right levels of training and the right levels of supervision' (Hill 2002: 93). The National Probation Service argues that PSOs have traditionally had some degree of contact with offenders, and their training in recent years under the NVQ system means that they should be able to work at this level.

Bold Steps (the annual plan for the NPS for 2004/05, before its amalgamation into the National Offender Management Service) (NPS 2004a) refers to the need to make Short Format Reports (SFRs), informed by OASys, the normal means of communicating appropriate disposals to sentencers. The new SFR will be adopted nationally in 2005/06. PSRs will only be used for the most dangerous offenders and those indicating the highest risk. Short Format Reports, like PSRs, will not require the sentencer to specify the anticipated sentence (as they currently do for SSRs). Using OASys to highlight needs to prevent reoffending, it will be up to probation officers to set out a programme that best addresses those needs. There is no further mention of SSRs, and these are likely to remain for 'sentencing on the day', but their future use is being reviewed (NPS 2004a).

The whole issue of report writing is very unclear at present and the names for the different types of report may well change. The new legislation provides for generic community orders, which become available in 2005 (CJA 2003). There is a requirement for more assessment to be made before sentence and this implies more intervention by probation officers at report stage, particularly in deciding which type of report to present to the court, as there will be limitations on which elements of the community order package will be assessed under which type of report. Such work puts the probation officer right at the heart of sentence design, as well as sentence planning. It will be their role to suggest the 'optimum package' for the individual offender, and gain sentencer support. Probation officer skills in report writing, offender and offence analysis and recommendation of the most appropriate sentence for the most serious and dangerous offenders will still be required, and necessitate a full PSR. Their role in the highly skilled job of engagement with such people and challenging their behaviour, will no doubt increase.

Conclusion

The content of reports is now heavily circumscribed by policy statements and National Standards and this, together with concerns about the potential dangers of discriminatory language, meant that pre-sentence reports were initially much more bland documents than social inquiry reports had been. That transformation of the 'case' into the human being was no longer obvious and one suspects that many reports could have been produced by computer software. They became part of the administration.

More recently, the requirement to engage the offender to consider culpability, victim impact and reparation within the offence analysis, their literacy and numeracy, substance misuse and offending patterns, and their own risk of harm and reoffending, etc., has made reports 'live' again, and should, therefore, become more useful to sentencers. The improvement in concordance (the match between the sentence given and the probation officer's recommendation) is encouraging. The NPS Performance Report Number 4 of June 2002 (www.probation.homeoffice.gov.uk) states that although overall concordance rates were static at 70 per cent, those for Accredited Programmes increased from 50 per cent to 70 per cent to the end of March 2002.

The probation service has always rightly seen reports as the public face of probation – as a skilled strategic document that encapsulates the ethos of the service. If recommendations have not been followed then the service has tended to blame its own lack of skills in communicating its message. But a message has a receiver as well as a sender and however sophisticated the sender may try to make the message, it will not be effective if it does not resonate with the receiver's own frame of reference – if the receiver is not prepared to listen. But the message is becoming more complicated, as Nash (2003) highlights. 'Pre-trial investigation' is no longer a matter for the National Probation Service in isolation. Increasingly, other agencies are involved in exchanging information, and risk assessment, in particular, is becoming a multi-agency function. Sentencers are also going to have to be aware of the recommendations of the Sentencing Guidelines Council, which, as a product of the Criminal Justice Act 2003, will have a mission of reducing imprisonment. In this context, it is possible, therefore, that community sentences will be recommended for a wider range of offences and that sentencers may finally be forced to listen to probation's message.

Chapter 7

Demanding but not degrading? The appeal of community punishment and electronic monitoring

Industrialist: We attach a lot of importance to your research on this product, you know.
Researcher: What happens if the research shows that the product is a winner?
Ind: We'll go ahead and introduce it quickly.
Res: What if the research shows it's a loser?
Ind: We wouldn't want to hold back on a good product like that on the basis of one little piece of research.

(Pease 1983: 78)

Whatever it is that drives the expansion of EM in Britain it is certainly not research into its proven effectiveness.

(Nellis 2003a: 253)

Introduction

From its introduction in 1973 the role of community service (now community punishment) has been ambiguous yet increasingly popular. Its chameleon-like ability to adapt its aims and objectives to fit almost every traditional justification of punishment has made it as versatile as the fine – indeed, it has been described as a 'fine on time'. But the incongruity of using unpaid supervised work schemes as a form of punishment at times of high unemployment in the community as a whole (as was the case in England and Wales in the first two decades of its existence) was never seriously questioned. Community service raised fundamental questions about our perceptions of both 'community' and 'service' – leading ultimately to its name change. In the first edition of this book, this chapter was devoted entirely to an examination of what had become, it was argued, the 'complacent face of punishment in the community'. Since then, community service has taken on a new identity as community punishment, and its role in the criminal justice system has become less ambiguous, though some of the core debates remain. In this edition, we have chosen to include in this chapter discussion of electronic monitoring and curfew orders, for reasons which may require some early explanation. The introduction of electronic monitoring in the late 1980s could be viewed as the *other* major penal innovation of the late twentieth century. Unlike community service, its appeal was not immediate and it was over a decade before it became established as a viable penal disposal in England and Wales; even now, its use is far more familiar as an adjunct to prison than as an alternative to it. Nevertheless, electronic monitoring, like community service/punishment, is a punishment *of the body,* and, as such, raises questions about the relationship between the legitimate *demands* of punishment and the *limits* that should be placed on punishment. Von Hirsch has asked the question 'What is the acceptable penal content of non-custodial sentences?' (1998: 195) and cautions against the fallacy that 'anything is better than prison'. By this he means the misguided belief that offenders are willing to put up with any deprivation, humiliation or imposition, provided it stops short of imprisonment and that we need not, therefore, concern ourselves overly with ethical constraints:

> Punishments should be of the kind that can be endured with self-possession by persons of reasonable fortitude. These individuals should be able to undergo the penalty (unpleasant as it inevitably is) with dignity, protesting their innocence if they feel they are innocent or acknowledging their guilt if they feel guilty – but acknowledging it *as a person,* not as a *slave,* would do. A person can endure deprivation of various goods and liberties with dignity, but it is hard to be dignified while having to carry out rituals of self-abasement, whether the lockstep, the stocks, or newer rituals.
> (von Hirsch 1998: 194)

So the purpose of this chapter is to examine the 'newer rituals' of punishment and to ask some of the 'old' questions about how punishments are justified and what, if any, are the limits to which we can punish in the name of 'public protection'.

The history of community service/punishment

Community service (as it was originally known) that requires offenders to undertake unpaid work is a relatively recent penal innovation, although its predecessor, hard labour, has a very long history. Since the 1960s, various forms of community service have developed in many countries, notably in America, Australia, Canada and New Zealand. It is interesting, however, that some countries have resisted it on grounds of principle and practice. In Spain, for instance, it was feared that rising unemployment would undermine its credibility and in Sweden it was felt that not only would it not reduce imprisonment but that work should be viewed as a privilege, not a punishment (McIvor 1992). Community punishment has been most popular in England, Wales and Scotland where it has been used for a wide variety of offenders. By contrast, it has been underused in America, where it tends to be used for white-collar offenders, juveniles and minor offenders only (McIvor 1992; Tonry and Hamilton 1995).

Community service emerged in Britain as a result of increasing concern about the rising prison population in the 1960s coupled with attacks on rehabilitative treatment. It was one of the recommendations of the Wootton Advisory Council on the Penal System in 1970 and was described as the 'most imaginative and hopeful' of its recommendations. It was incorporated into legislation in the 1972 Criminal Justice Act and six experimental pilot schemes were set up in 1973, under the responsibility of the probation service. It is no surprise that in the twenty-first century, when the prison population seems to be expanding exponentially, this sentence has been restructured to make it more attractive to sentencers in the hope, yet again, of reducing the prison population.

A community punishment order requires adult offenders to perform between 40 and 240 hours (increasing to 300 maximum with the generic community sentence legislated for in the Criminal Justice Act of 2003) of supervised unpaid work, normally to be completed within a year. Failure to complete the order satisfactorily results in a return to court and, possibly, a sentence of imprisonment. The 1982 Criminal Justice Act extended community service to 16-year-olds but reduced the maximum order for them, to 120 hours. The 1991 Criminal Justice Act abolished that limit. It is only available for imprisonable offences, but from the outset there was confusion about whether it was a direct alternative to custody or whether it could be used as a sentence in its own right. This confusion meant that there was concern among some in the probation service that it would be used too early in a criminal career and thus accelerate an offender's route into prison. It was seen as a gap-filling measure that was in danger of being a net-widening sentence. (Johnson and Rex [2002: 188] express concern that the sentence has indeed 'slipped quite steeply down-tariff'.) Some probation officers initially refused to co-operate or to recommend the sentence.

Although Home Office researchers evaluated the experiments (Pease *et al.* 1975), their concerns were largely disregarded in the government drive to extend provision throughout England and Wales by 1975. Pease was later to comment scathingly that:

> the realization that the community service research was not meant to inform the decision about whether community service orders should continue or should cease involved a reappraisal of what should be included in the research report.
>
> (Pease 1983: 78)

Fundamental questions were jettisoned in favour of administrative ones. Because of this and the lack of consensus about the purpose of community service, inconsistent practices developed across probation areas. The main inconsistencies were in relation to:

- what kind of offender was suitable
- what kind of work was suitable
- what standard of attendance and work was acceptable

In 1977 *Probation Journal* devoted a complete issue to reviewing the first five years of community service. The editorial asked the questions 'What exactly is the purpose of a community service order? What has the probation service made of this new provision?' There followed several heart-searching articles, all of which, though cautiously optimistic about community service, were conscious of its contradictory underlying penal philosophy and its challenge to traditional perceptions of the probation officer's job. For the first time, offenders were to be formally supervised by 'unqualified' community service officers, rather than by probation officers. Pease and McWilliams (1977) identified four ways in which community service differed from traditional probation work:

1 The need to view the offender as a giver rather than a consumer of help;

2 The specificity of the contract between court and offender (and implications for breach);

3 The degree of contact between the probation service and the community;

4 The way the service's performance is assessed by itself and by others.

The use of community service increased during the 1970s and levelled off in the 1980s at 7–8 per cent of sentences for indictable offences, compared with 10 per cent for probation orders and 14 per cent for immediate imprisonment. In absolute figures, there were 41,000 community service orders made in 1991, compared with 45,000 probation orders. From 1992 onwards, however, numbers of community service orders overtook those of probation orders, the former rising to 50,000 and the latter to 49,000 in 1994 (Home Office 1996b). However, while about 18 per cent of probation orders were made on women, only 5 per cent of community service orders were on women, comparing more closely with the proportion in prison at that time. The picture has changed in recent years. Community punishment order (CPO) starts were 52,409 in 2002 (a marginal increase since 2000), so a stable level seems to have been found. But with the recorded and convicted crime rate having fallen, this would suggest that net-widening has occurred and people are being punished more severely than in the 1990s. This is borne out by the reduction in the number of sentences that are fines, and the reduced number of cautions (Johnson *et al.* 2001). The gender balance has changed as well. The number of community service/ punishment orders made on women increased from 6 per cent of the total number in 1992 to 12 per cent in 2002 (Home Office 2004a), although 18 per cent of convicted offenders were women. But women are still deemed more suitable for community rehabilitation orders, as they accounted for 21 per cent of these in 2002. These facts bear out McIvor's study of the use of community service in Scotland (McIvor 1998), where she found that the women who were on community service orders were less likely to be those at risk of custody. She concluded, 'the potential for community service to divert women from short sentences of imprisonment is not being fully exploited' (McIvor 1998: 280).

The kind of work undertaken varies greatly but can be categorized in three ways:

- *Workshops:* manual work such as woodwork, metalwork or textiles, undertaken on probation premises, often to order for voluntary organizations and charities (much less favoured in later years);

- *Supervised teams:* primarily gardening and painting and decorating for elderly people, or renovation work for churches and other voluntary organizations, supervised by sessional supervisors;

- *Agency placements:* individual placements in nurseries, residential homes or any other voluntary organizations, such as charity shops, supervised by that agency.

National Standards and community punishment

In 1989, in an attempt to standardize practice, the government issued National Standards for community service. The purpose of these statutory rules was to make the order appear to be harsh punishment, to control offenders' choices, to impose greater structure on working arrangements and to enforce discipline and required standards of work (Vass 1990). In particular, they addressed the kind of work being undertaken. National Standards required the probation service to provide a range of placements, including 'at least one option providing hard manual work and consideration should be given to choosing placements which enhance public confidence in community service' (Home Office 1995e). Although the 1992 version of National Standards suggested that placements should also be 'personally fulfilling' (Home Office 1992b: 70) for the offender, the 1995 version exhorted probation services to 'ensure that the location and nature of any community service activity could not give the impression of providing a reward for offending' (Home Office 1995e: 35). A prohibition on placements abroad seemed to be a response to media criticism of a highly imaginative and altruistic project devised by Surrey probation service to undertake work in Romania in 1990 (Whitfield 1993). A similarly subtle shift of emphasis can be seen in the stated aims and objectives of community service. Both versions include 'reparation to the community' as an aim, but a comparison of the remainder of the relevant sections is illuminating:

> The main purpose of a CSO is to re-integrate the offender into the community through positive and demanding work, keeping to disciplined requirements.
>
> (Home Office 1992b: 67)

The main purpose of a CSO is to *prevent further offending* by reintegrating the offender into the community through *punishment*, by means of positive and demanding *unpaid* work, keeping to disciplined requirements.

(Home Office 1995e: 34, emphasis added)

By 2002, National Standards no longer specified the purpose of a CPO, but instead refer to all community sentences, saying that:

The purpose of a community sentence is to:

- provide a rigorous and effective punishment;
- reduce the likelihood of reoffending;
- rehabilitate the offender, where possible;
- enable reparation to be made to the community; and
- minimise the risk of harm to the public.

(Home Office 2002d: C7)

The requirement was no longer for hard manual work, but rather offenders have to be fully occupied and the placements must be physically, emotionally or mentally demanding. But the change of title to Community Punishment Order in 2001 was probably enough to signify that these orders should be tough enough to induce public confidence.

It had been anticipated that the Human Rights Act of 1998, which came into force in October 2000, would cause great disruption to the criminal justice system (Johnson and Rex 2002). Johnson and Rex describe how various Articles of the European Convention of Human Rights, which were adopted into domestic law in England and Wales by means of this Act, were expected to have an impact on the probation service's work with community service. In particular, there was a debate about whether community service orders could be deemed to be a form of slavery. However, the result was that it was shown that all probation practice, if carried out within the law and National Standards, should not be challengeable (Johnson and Rex 2002).

In October 2003, CPOs were changed again, in that additional elements were included in all orders – including the community punishment parts of CPROs. The new title was Enhanced Community Punishment (ECP). It is based on 'what works' principles (see Chapter 8) and includes a rehabilitative strand. Making use of the contact time that offenders have with their supervisors, the aim is to change attitudes and behaviours, and teach employment-related and problem-solving skills through 'modelling, reinforcement and guided learning' (NPS 2002b). This new sentence allows for several interdependent concurrent activities, which are based on the offender's individual needs for reintegration into their community. The five elements are integrated case management, pro-social modelling, problem solving at work, guided skills learning and placement quality standards. The upshot has been the requirement to develop and train many community punishment supervisors into their enhanced role, making their career development open to wider opportunities. The sentence has changed from being only about the work that the offender does for the community. The 'punishment' element remains, but the focus has been moved to the prevention of reoffending. Gelsthorpe and Rex (2004) have been involved in the research for ECP through their Pathfinder projects (pilots). There were many positive findings and the mix of skills accreditation with pro-social modelling seemed to be effective, ensuring the rapid adoption of ECP throughout England and Wales:

> But overall the offender questionnaire revealed a positive view from offenders both of how they were treated and what they gained from community service. There was a statistically significant association between both these elements (treatment and gains) and a positive impact on their skills, attitudes and behaviour (three quarters reporting that undertaking community service made them less likely to offend).
>
> (Gelsthorpe and Rex 2004: 242)

One of their most interesting findings is in comparing the reported perceptions (of an admittedly small sample) of women and of the men offenders. Women were more likely to report an impact on the way they see things whilst men reported an impact on their behaviour. Gelsthorpe and Rex suggest that recognizing these different pathways into offending and desistance could have value.

Whether reduced reconviction rates will be delivered has yet to be seen. It will also be interesting to see if sentencers recognize the rehabilitative strand to CPOs, and reduce the number of offenders sentenced to Community Punishment and Rehabilitation Orders when they feel that elements of reparation and rehabilitation are required, as well as a punitive sentence.

National Standards require recording of hours worked and state the procedures for breaching an offender in the event of failure to comply. Community service orders always had a higher rate of breach procedures than probation orders, rising from 11 per cent in 1985 to 18 per cent in 1991 (following the introduction of National Standards) and falling back to 15 per cent in 1994 (Home Office 1996b). Hine and Thomas (1995) suggest that this demonstrates an ethos in which breach proceedings are regarded as a 'first resort' rather than a 'last resort', with the expectation that courts will issue a warning and allow the order to continue, thus reinforcing its authority. The situation changed somewhat by 2002, when the breach level was down to 12 per cent. With this downward trend, it is not surprising that timely breach action for 90 per cent of cases became a service delivery agreement at the inception of the NPS in 2001. Perhaps the ethos had not changed as much as Hine and Thomas had earlier suggested. However, the introduction of targets has had an impact since 2001. Timely enforcement for all orders (not just CPOs) throughout the service for 2003/04 had increased to 77 per cent, having been 53 per cent two years before (NPS 2004c). Terminations of CPOs for reasons other than the completion of the order ran at 30 per cent in 2002. Mostly, the reasons for termination were a failure to comply with requirements of the order, or the conviction of a further offence (Home Office 2004a).

Vass (1990), however, questioned whether the increased structuring of community service may not be counter-productive in the long term since the success of community service depends on sophisticated negotiation between supervisor and offender, including a degree of tolerance of technical rule infraction. National Standards, he argued 'may well structure community service but they will not de-structure the prison' (Vass 1990: 131). Contemporary research supports this view. The Home Office Research Development and Statistics Directorate published research in 2004 showing that different enforcement strategies for non-compliance of community orders may not bring very different results (Home Office 2004f). The researchers found that:

> Offenders in areas with high rates of breach at court had reconviction rates which were not statistically significantly different from those in areas with low rates of breach at court. 'Strictness' of an area, therefore, appeared to have little impact on the overall reconviction rate.
>
> (Home Office 2004f: 3)

The conclusion of the report is that 'probation areas and policy makers should be realistic about what reductions in offending can be achieved in the short term through toughening up enforcement practices' (Home Office 2004f: 10).

The main change to community sentences introduced by the 1991 Criminal Justice Act was the combination order (now called Community Punishment and Rehabilitation Order – CPRO) which allows courts to combine a community rehabilitation order of between 12 months and three years, with between 40 and 100 hours of community punishment. Previously, the rationale behind the two sentences had been viewed as incompatible – an offender required *either* help and advice *or* to engage in reparation – and the two could not be used together at the same time. In practice, however, many offenders found themselves on both orders as a result of multiple court appearances, and the government sought to eliminate what it saw as an anomaly. In fact, it was introducing yet another net-widening disposal, destined to draw offenders nearer to custody (Moloney 1995). Combination orders quickly proved a popular disposal, their numbers rising from about 1,350 in 1992 to nearly 15,000 in 1995, rising to over 21,000 in 1998, but dropping back to about 15,500 in 2002. This drop may well be due to the increased incarceration rates at this time. In the early years of CPROs, about half included the maximum 100 hours of community service, but this has reduced to about 42 per cent of orders in 2002, possibly due to the requirement for courts to give credit for prompt guilty pleas (Home Office 1996b, 1996c, 2004a).

Penal philosophy and community punishment

The absence of a clear philosophy for community service/punishment has been both its strength and its weakness. Its weaknesses have already been outlined. Its strength is that it appeals to a wide variety of people, not least offenders themselves, for a wide variety of reasons. Duguid (1982) summarizes its attraction thus:

- *It involves punishment.* Regular attendance at placements deprives the offender of free use of his leisure time.

- *It has a rehabilitative element.* The offender must spend time helping others and this may help restore a sense of dignity and self-esteem, as well as improving the community's perceptions of the offender.

- *It contains an indirect element of reparation.* The work benefits the community in general and/or specific, often disadvantaged, sections of the community.

- *Unlike prison, it allows the offender to retain a job and to support a family.* If unemployed, it may help the offender to develop a work habit and to overcome social isolation.

- *It saves public resources and* is *arguably cheaper than prison.*

(Duguid 1982 cited in McIvor 1992: 9)

Now with ECP on stream, it may be possible to add to these attractions *the reduction in reconvictions* by means of the personal development of the offender learning new skills related to employability and problem-solving, and in adopting pro-social attitudes.

Curfew orders

Although curfew orders are not a part of probation staff's work, they represent a supervisory community penalty that is becoming increasingly popular with sentencers and increasingly embedded in the supervision experience of many offenders (Nellis 2003a; Bottomley et al. 2004). Court officers and probation officers are involved in writing SSRs and PSRs that address these sentences. The reports require a check to be made that the address given to the court is a suitable one, where the electronic monitoring equipment can be installed. Staff also have to check the impact that confining the offender to this address will have on other occupants – not always the best option for a young man with older relatives or one in an abusive relationship with a partner. Offenders on curfew orders may well be on other community orders and therefore managed by probation officers.

Curfew orders that can be monitored electronically were first legislated for in the Criminal Justice Act of 1991. However, they were not 'rolled out' nationally until December 1999 due to many problems with the efficacy of the equipment and a dispute between probation staff, NAPO and the Home Secretary of the time, Michael Howard, who was attempting to control probation professionals (Flynn 2002). The resistance was due, in part, to the fact that private security contractors are responsible for the operation of the system. The same systems and operators are used for home detention curfews as for those on early release from custody.

Curfew orders require the offender to remain at a given address in the stipulated hours, otherwise the electronic tag attached to their ankle will give a signal to the operator, who will alert the police for breach of the order. The maximum length of time of the order is six months and

12 hours per day. They can be set up by the operators to have different addresses for different days and different times on different days of the week, to take account of work patterns and domestic commitments. They can be ordered to run concurrently with another community order. Statistics show that there has been a steady growth in the number of curfew orders that are electronically tagged. In 1997, there were just 400 orders, but this rose to 6,300 in 2002 (Home Office 2003c). In 2002, breaches of electronically tagged curfew orders reduced to 19 per cent from 24 per cent in 2001. This may represent an improvement in the efficiency of the equipment, or perhaps more docile and compliant offenders!

Although first seen as a preventative measure to stop offenders being out at the times when they might commit further crime, efforts have been made to change their image to make them a punishment that restricts liberty and personal freedom. This was one of the issues of Human Rights legislation that caused dispute. Nellis (2003b) investigated the media and public reaction to electronic monitoring (EM) and found that 'there is no prevailing sense in the press of popular culture that EM constitutes a threat to them [civil liberties] (or, by implication, to us); it is simply not rigorous or invasive enough' (Nellis 2003b: 22).

There is no pretence that electronic monitoring has any rehabilitative, restorative or reintegrative value in itself, though some argue that it gives offenders an enforced 'breathing space' in which to reconsider the direction of their lives. It can be seen as a cheap method of incarceration that can help reduce prison numbers, and may have value in not disrupting people's lives, relationships and work opportunities.

The development of more sophisticated equipment has largely ruled out the concerns that were expressed earlier about the efficacy of the monitoring systems. Future developments will see satellite systems used to track offenders. Nellis (2003b) observes that, from some perspectives there is no problem with this in relation to offenders, as modern technology is used to track us all through pagers, mobile phones and credit card usage, for example, it can be proved where we have been. He cites the case of the positive use of EM in providing an alibi for an offender – he couldn't have done it, as his tag proved he was at home.

Research

Modern writers still refer to McIvor's (1992) significant research undertaken in Scotland. She undertook a comprehensive study over five years from 1986 to 1991, looking at the characteristics of offenders selected for community service, the nature of their work and progress, their attitudes to the experience and the attitudes of recipients.

McIvor found that offenders given community service were predominantly young, male, single and unemployed. They had settled living arrangements and had few problems related to alcohol or drugs. Their offences were mainly dishonesty, violence and public disorder. They had an average of five previous convictions and about one-third had been in prison. These findings accord largely with official criminal statistics.

Eighty-five per cent completed their order satisfactorily. Those breached had repeatedly failed to attend. They had more convictions than average and were more likely to have been on probation or sent to prison in the past. They were more likely to have been in group than in agency placements but that probably reflected the fact that riskier offenders would be allocated to groups anyway.

Offenders themselves had no clear preference for group or agency placements but unskilled practical work was viewed as the least rewarding. The most rewarding placements were those that brought the offender into contact with recipients, where new skills were developed and where the benefits to the recipient were apparent. Overall, offenders were very positive about community service.

There was a very similar picture from recipients, over 90 per cent of whom were satisfied with their experience of community service. There were a few complaints about unreliability, poor supervision and shoddy work but almost no problems related to the fact that those doing the work were offenders (for example, only one incident of theft from a recipient was reported).

A small sample of 134 offenders was followed for reconvictions for four years after completion of orders. After two years, 57 per cent had been reconvicted and after four years 66 per cent had been reconvicted. Reconviction rates tended to be slower than prior to the order and were for less serious offences. The most likely to be reconvicted were those with the most past offences and/or the most problems. Those who had particularly good experiences of community service appeared to be less likely to be reconvicted.

McIvor concluded:

The CS order may not have lived up to initial hopes that it would make a significant contribution to reducing the reliance of courts upon the use of custodial sentences. It is, however, a less costly option than imprisonment, one which many offenders find to be rewarding and worthwhile and one which appears to be no less effective than other court disposals in reducing recidivism. In most cases ... it is highly valued [by those] who have been the recipients of unpaid work.

(McIvor 1992: 188)

More recent figures from a sample (Home Office 2003c) show that the two year reconviction rates for those on CPOs that commenced in 1999 was at a rate of 60 per cent – showing a worsening in reconviction rates from McIvor's study, although a recent study in Scotland found that the reconviction rates for women following community service were very promising (McIvor 2004).

Women and community punishment

There is nothing in theory or in law to debar women from doing community punishment but sentencers have always had ambivalent feelings about giving such orders to women. It has always been viewed by courts as not quite appropriate. The chivalrous view is that it isn't quite nice for ladies to be doing such hard work and that probation is much better for all but the most hardened of them. The practicalities of availability have also historically always been an obstacle – the absence of acceptable child care facilities is the main problem – though the fact that it is a much greater problem if the woman goes to prison tends to be overlooked. Occasionally a magistrate will express a paradoxical view that is simultaneously enlightened and paternalistic:

> Community service is usually done in someone's spare time – women don't have any!
>
> (Magistrate quoted in Worrall 1990: 65)

It would be gratifying to think that this view was an expression of a deeper concern about the justice of requiring society's largest group of unpaid workers to perform even more 'voluntary' work as punishment (Dominelli 1984).

Within the probation service there are also concerns about finding appropriate work and supervision for such small numbers. What is meant by appropriate work? Should women be encouraged to broaden their horizons and do 'male' work or should they stick to what they know in order to ensure they get through the hours? Carlen and Worrall

(2004) cite an example from Western Australia, where one project enables women to collect large bags of old clothes from a central point and take them home to unpick all the buttons and zips. At first glance, this appears to be a soul-destroying and discriminatory project, but it allows women to do the work in their own homes at times of their own choosing and complete their hours with the least possible disruption to their normal lives.

Despite the increase in the number of orders being made on women in the late 1990s, the picture across the country, according to a Howard League report (1999) was one of women still being dealt with on a case-by-case basis and being regarded as 'anomalies'. The inception of the NPS in April 2001 changed much of that thinking. With its diversity agenda as one of its leading objectives, it was important for the service itself to provide placements for CPOs that could be filled by people from all backgrounds. So transport, child-minding and caring costs were covered by the service and care was taken to find appropriate placements. Convincing sentencers (and some defence solicitors) that a suitable placement would be found became another challenge.

Johnson and Rex (2002) claim that there is some scope for the greater use of CPOs as sentences for women. They cite better child care arrangements, an increase in the number of female CP supervisors, and the selection of work placements most suitable for women as pre-requisites for increasing the use of CP for women. CPOs are proving to be a popular sentence for younger women – in 1992, 7 per cent of 18–20 year olds sentenced for indictable offences received a CSO. By 2002, there were 9 per cent sentenced to CPOs. At the same time, young men of 18–20 were proportionately less likely to receive a CPO – reducing from 15 per cent in 1992 to 13 per cent in 2002 (Home Office 2003c). The same pattern emerges for those over 21 – an increase in CPOs for women (from 5 to 7 per cent) and a reduction for men (from 9 to 8 per cent). Barker's work (1993) showed that CS represented their first contact with the criminal justice system for a third of women on community service orders. Hine and Thomas (1995) also show concern about first-time women offenders receiving CSOs – 30 per cent in 1991 (as opposed to 13 per cent for men.) Worrall (2002b) points out that the figure rose to over 50 per cent by 1999 and claims that, recognizing the decline in fines on women, there seems to be a trend towards a greater used of community service for women who would previously have been fined or placed on probation, rather than sent to prison. So although the worst excesses of net-widening in relation to minor offending by women appear to have been curbed in the past decade, those who remain within the system are being propelled towards custody as fast as, if not faster than, ever (Worrall 2002b: 140).

Similar fears could be expressed regarding the use of electronic monitoring for women. In 2002, the total number of women found guilty at court increased by 9 per cent on the previous year (which is thought in part to reflect an increase in convictions for TV licence evasion) (Home Office 2003c). Sentencing statistics show that 600 curfew orders were made on women – 9.5 per cent of the total number. As with men, the most common offences that attracted this sentence were theft and handling, and offences of violence (Home Office 2003c). It is possible that future sentencing patterns will show that women can be dealt with successfully by electronic monitoring, and this could reduce the need to sentence them to the more rigorous community penalties which may not be as compatible with family life.

With increasing numbers of women being sentenced to CPOs there could be a case to be made for having women-only work groups, which might help to improve their compliance. This was a call made by the Howard League in 1999, but without much response. The Pathfinder projects for the new ECP did not include one exclusively for women. Through its diversity agenda, the aim of the NPS is to mainstream women and to change attitudes by challenging the behaviour of supervisors and male offenders on orders that could be deemed to be discriminatory. Nevertheless, after piloting in three Areas, in 2004, the Accreditation Panel approved the Women's Programme to be undertaken by those on community rehabilitation orders, so the day may therefore come when 'women-only' work teams are formed.

Restorative justice or punishment of the body?

The relationship between work and punishment is highly complex. The position of community punishment within that discourse remains under theorized. Indeed, the silence could be described as wilful, since any serious attempt to theorize the role of community punishment would almost certainly unearth some very uncomfortable explanations for its popularity and persistence. Far better to leave well alone, it might be argued, than to unsettle the foundations of one of the few penal success stories of the latter part of the twentieth century.

That was undoubtedly the tone adopted in *Paying Back: Twenty Years of Community Service* (Whitfield and Scott 1993). Pease and McWilliams' (1977) indicators of change had been absorbed into the culture of community service and the picture presented in the book is predominantly one of a visionary penal innovation founded and developed on the theory of restorative justice. The potential for reconciliation between the offender and the community is the book's unifying theme. The collection is unashamedly celebratory and includes nine pages of sunny photographs of schemes, offenders and recipients. One has to search for critical perspectives, but Oldfield's chapter on 'lost opportunities' strikes a more sombre note. He reminds us that community service made little impact on the use of imprisonment by courts, encouraged net-widening and may even have 'enabled a smoother transition towards the "justice" model ... with the emphasis in future likely to be on creating more punitively interventive disposals' (Whitfield and Scott 1993: 30). Community service, he argued, had become an *accompaniment* to imprisonment, not an alternative to it.

Foucault (1977) has established in our consciousness the recognition of a distinction between (historical) state punishment as the deliberate infliction of pain on the human body and (modern) disciplinary state punishment, where the object of penality is 'the soul' – the thoughts, will and inclinations – of the criminal. As such, the soul is susceptible to 'scientific knowledge' – to a whole set of assessments, diagnoses and normative judgements made by psychiatric, pedagogic and social work experts. The purpose of the project is to produce docile, obedient bodies by focusing attention on the 'mind' of the offender. The introduction of electronic monitoring might be seen as incarcerating offenders at home, and giving them the time and opportunity to reflect on their crimes, and thereby change their 'minds' about future offending. There is no evidence for this as yet. The battle for the mind of the offender, as we shall see in Chapter 8, has been fought primarily between those experts who base their knowledge claims on psychoanalysis and psycho-therapy, and those who are collectively termed cognitive behaviourists. Whichever school we subscribe to, Foucault has forever re-ordered our understanding of the development of penal analysis into that of the relationship between power, knowledge and the body (Smart 1983).

But what is the knowledge that underpins community punishment as a penal intervention? What 'expert' assessment and classification is required in order socially to construct an offender as 'suitable' to be punished by work? What model or theory of offending is invoked to support a recommendation that an offender should be 'sentenced to serve' (McIvor 1992)? The whole point about assessment for suitability for community punishment is that it is based on the criteria of 'fitness to work'. We know that those most likely to be placed on community punishment are fit young men and, since most criminals are fit young men, that is perhaps what we would expect. But all other forms of punishment either take no account of youth and fitness (for example, fines and conditional discharges) or they are imposed despite youth and fitness (as with prison and probation) because other factors are considered more important (for example, the offender's dangerousness or personal problems). Community punishment is the only sentence specifically designed for fit young men. All other offenders are judged suitable only to the extent that they display the same characteristics as fit young men. Those who do not meet the criteria are not always excluded but they are always seen as requiring 'special' provision, as being Other than a 'proper' community punishment offender. Thus women and those with health problems or disabilities have to be treated differently and always represent the compromise, the concession – not the authentic article. The response of the NPS to this claim would be that, whilst being on incapacity benefit is a contra-indication for a community punishment order, new types of place-ments and an inclusive view of disability should have allowed for a more flexible approach to assessing suitability in recent years. Only offenders are in a position to tell us whether this has been successful.

The authentic article, then, is he who can and, therefore, should work to regain his citizenship. This may be all very well in times of full employment, when it is only the sick or the criminal who do not work. In such times, the symbolic and practical value of community punish-ment is clear. The three R's – reparation, restoration and reintegration – may succeed in dignifying the voluntary efforts of the offender. There is no need to worry too much about the degree of pain inflicted on the body. 'Honest sweat' is the lot of every worker – there is nothing essentially different about work done by an offender.

But what happens in times of recession and high unemployment? When honest work is at a premium, how do we make sense of work as punishment? When working for nothing ceases to be exculpatory of itself and is seen instead as a reward for wrong-doing, it makes only limited sense to talk of reparation, and no sense at all to talk of restoration and reintegration. Teaching offenders to be disciplined, skilled workers in times of unemployment is not merely irrelevant but may even present a threat to the honest unemployed. The spectre of 'less eligibility' looms again, especially with ECP, where personal skill development is a key objective. The fortunes of community punish-ment as a mechanism of rehabilitation and reintegration (Johnson and Rex 2002) may well be related more to fluctuations in employment rates than to criminal justice policy. Were there to be a return to high levels of unemployment in England and Wales, attitudes to 'work as punishment' might well revert to something more visceral.

It could be argued, therefore, that the lasting appeal of community punishment has very little to do with civilized notions of restorative justice, rehabilitation or reintegration. It has far more to do with a return to Foucault's punishment of the body:

> But a punishment like forced labour or even imprisonment – mere loss of liberty – has never functioned without a certain additional element of punishment that certainly concerns the body itself: rationing of food, sexual deprivation, corporal punishment, solitary confinement.
>
> (Foucault 1977: 15–16)

That is not a recognizable description of community punishment, though we only have to look to the reintroduction of the chain gang in Alabama to see how easily it could become so. Suggestions are made regularly that offenders should wear emblazoned tabards and that most placements should involve hard physical work. There is little concern here with the 'soul' of the offender, nor yet with the production of Foucault's docile obedient bodies. What lurks here is the desire for spectacle. Prison keeps the really dangerous offender out of sight and our new millennium sensibilities require us to turn away in embarrassment from inadequate or mentally disordered offenders receiving their treatment. But watching healthy, fit young men being physically humiliated, or confined by electronic 'tags', may be the nearest we will get to the hanging, drawing and quartering of Foucault's shocking opening pages (1977).

Conclusion

The chameleon-like nature of community punishment has been viewed by many commentators as its strength but it remains a punishment without a knowledge base. It has no philosophy, because it is 'an undisguised attempt to curry favour with everybody' (Wootton cited in Pease 1983: 76). Compared with prison, it will always be viewed as a 'soft option' by those on the political right. Liberals will continue to cherish notions of reconciliation and restorative justice, while pragmatists will see it as a mechanism for damage limitation and the management of criminal careers – the forestalling or delaying of eventual incarceration. After the first few years of resistance and moral agonising, the quiet revolution of the gradual expansion of electronic monitoring (with little complaint from offenders themselves) has established yet another 'truck on the punishment train' (Broad 1991) and one to which probation officers must adjust. Even if they are not directly involved in its implementation, it has become 'integral to the very concept of supervising offenders in the community' (Nellis 2003a: 252).

In the first edition of this book, this chapter concluded as follows:

> Community service, it seems, just *is*. It requires no justification, no case to be made out for its legitimacy. It can be whatever we want it to be. It is the complacent face of Punishment in the Community.

This will no longer do. The legitimacy of community punishment and electronic monitoring have been explored by a number of writers and, in both cases, it has become clear that what makes these punishments of the body acceptable – to offenders (and consequently to those who think that offenders are more likely to stop offending if some notice is taken of their views on these matters) – is the *fairness* of their administration (Tyler 1990; Bottoms 2001; Weyell 2003; Nellis 2003a). Tyler's argument is that offenders will respond to punishment more on the basis of their experience of the *process* than the nature or *content* of the punishment. If they perceive themselves to have been treated fairly by the system in general and (for example) probation officers in particular, they are more likely to comply in the short term and stop offending in the longer term. Hence, even in situations where punishment is physically restrictive and formal consent is no longer required, legitimation is dependent on at least tacit consent and where that is absent, restriction alone achieves little. So the 'newer rituals' (von Hirsch 1998) of community punishment and electronic monitoring will only succeed not, in the end, by ever greater power of the state over the body of the offender but – if administered *fairly* – by ever more sophisticated ways of harnessing, controlling and changing the *mind* of the offender.

Chapter 8

From counselling to instruction: the development of 'help' in probation discourse

I am probably not alone in wondering what I was doing as a probation officer for 20 years ... Had I really gone to work every day believing that nothing worked?

(Schofield 1998: 13)

Introduction

Much work with offenders, both individually and in groups, is now based on cognitive behavioural approaches. Such approaches have in common a foundation in social learning theory, which stresses the importance of the link between how people think and how they behave:

It [social learning theory] assumes that offenders are shaped by their environment and have failed to acquire certain cognitive skills or have learned inappropriate ways of behaving. Their thinking may be impulsive and egocentric and their attitudes, values and beliefs may support antisocial behaviour. Advocates of this approach believe that, by drawing on a range of well-established cognitive and behavioural techniques, offenders can be helped to face up to the consequences of their actions, to understand their motives, and to develop new ways of controlling their behaviour.

(Vennard and Hedderman 1998: 101)

Cognitive-behavioural approaches proceed from the premise that people can be taught to access, understand and alter their own negative thinking processes and thus change their behaviour with assistance from psychologists or prison/probation officers who have received focused training themselves. Proponents of cognitive-behavioural approaches do not deny the contribution to offending behaviour of social factors such as poverty and lack of opportunities, but they argue that, in terms of *intervention* with offenders, there is very little evidence to suggest that attempts to resolve social problems alone reduce recidivism. By contrast, it is argued that there is now extensive cumulative evidence to suggest that cognitive-behavioural interventions have a positive and significant impact on rates of reoffending (Harding and Worrall 2004).

Thus, 'advise, assist and befriend' has given way to 'confront, control and monitor' offending behaviour. Changing the whole personality through insight-giving, or changing the offender's environment through welfare assistance are no longer seen as feasible goals. Instead, the focus is much narrower, less ambitious. What needs to be changed are particular pieces of unacceptable behaviour – no more and no less. And, ironically, this is seen as being less intrusive, more respectful of the offender 'as a whole person'. From McGuire and Priestley's ground-breaking book *Offending Behaviour: Skills and Strategems for Going Straight* (1985) to Ross and Fabiano's *Reasoning and Rehabilitation* programme (1989) the battle is now on for the 'mind' of the offender – or, at least, for those bits of the minds of particular (young, unemployed, male) offenders that most frighten respectable citizens.

The aim of this chapter is to examine the changing theoretical underpinnings of the 'help' offered by the probation service, the move away from psychotherapeutic approaches towards behavioural approaches and the resulting political and ethical dilemmas. In order to do this, the chapter is divided into three sections. The first considers the development of the physical settings in which 'help' has been offered; the second explores the changing nature of the 'help'; in the third we discuss other aspects of probation practice that fall into the broad category of 'help' and that demonstrate the multiplicity of demands made of contemporary probation officers.

The first section will begin by considering the development of probation centres that provided programmes of normalizing instruction to compulsorily attending groups of offenders in increasingly lavish purpose-built buildings as the visible representation of punishment in the community in the 1980s and 1990s. The partial restriction of liberty involved in these programmes provided an ideal 'last resort' sentence before imprisonment for serious and recidivist offenders. As the 'What Works' philosophy has underpinned the work of the service (see below), the use of probation centres has been supplanted. At the same time, probation hostels, which have a less glamorous tradition, continue to be regarded as the 'Cinderella' of service provision (White 1984), despite their ability to cater for some of the most basic needs of offenders.

The history of probation day centres

The emergence of probation day centres is usually associated with the prison crisis of the early 1980s, the search for tough alternatives to custody and the drift towards greater surveillance and control of offenders. The demise of the rehabilitative ideal in its classical individualized form stimulated a search among liberal and radical probation officers for alternative forms of therapeutic work. The 1970s saw an increased interest in groupwork of various kinds, ranging from prisoners' wives groups to groups for juveniles and groups for those unemployed or homeless offenders who tended to 'camp' in probation office reception areas. Provided participation was voluntary, group- work was viewed by many as a means of reducing the stigma of individualized work, facilitating self-help and mutual aid and redressing the unequal power relationship of 'one-to-one' work. In short, it was seen as a more democratic way of working with offenders (Senior 1985).

But groupwork presented a very practical problem to probation officers – space. Few probation offices had rooms large enough to cater for a group (which would be a minimum of six to eight people) in any comfort. Some had meeting rooms or staff rooms but these were viewed as 'no go' areas for clients and conflicts arose when some probation officers tried to negotiate for their use by groups. Some use was made of local community facilities but this involved fees to hire rooms and the inconvenience of transporting equipment and people. Groupwork was not for the faint-hearted and, since it tended to be regarded by management as an optional extra, only the most com- mitted and enthusiastic became involved. And when key personnel left or transferred to other offices, groups folded very quickly, thus losing much of their credibility with staff and clients alike. All this resulted in what Mair has called the 'garden gnome' syndrome (1995).

Summarized less humorously than in the original paper, this syndrome occurs when a probation officer wakes up one morning, decides she wants a new challenge and recalls that there have been a disproportionate number of garden-gnome thefts in the locality recently. She decides to set up a group for garden-gnome thieves and becomes an expert. Word gets around and soon every area is 'discovering' a need for groups for garden-gnome thieves. By the time the Home Office gets to hear, such groups are springing up all over the place, with a variety of different approaches, presenting a problem of co-ordination. The point of the fable is that such *ad hoc* developments demonstrate 'uncontrolled discretion, lack of accountability, reinvention of the wheel, flavour-of-the-monthism ... inefficiency and ineffectiveness' (Mair 1995: 254).

One way to establish the centrality and legitimacy of groupwork in relation to service resources was to raise its profile with sentencers. Making attendance at groups a condition of a probation order would ensure an appropriate allocation of resources and would enable such work to be taken more seriously by courts and the service itself. During the late 1970s, such conditions were included increasingly on an *ad hoc* basis but proved controversial on grounds of civil liberties. By 1982 the practice was successfully challenged in the Court of Appeal in the *Cullen* v. *Rogers* case. Subsequently, provision was added to the 1982 Criminal Justice Act in Schedule XI, making it legal for attendance conditions of up to 60 days to be included in probation orders. There were technical differences between Schedule XI 4(A) and 4(B) conditions, the former being rather more flexible in their application than the latter, but these distinctions need not trouble a present-day reader too much.

What actually went on in day centres?

What actually went on in day centres was viewed with suspicion from the outset. This is partly because it was never entirely clear what purpose they served. In a succinct and enlightening article written in 1982, Anne Howe and her colleagues posed the kind of questions that many were asking about this new sentencing 'toy':

> consider whether you are doing things *to* offenders, *for* them, or *with* them ... Are day centres about meeting client need or about changing Probation practice? With self-referral, people attend because they want to, because day centres are welcoming places

and users can see their personal problems responded to. They also keep people off the streets and overcome loneliness. Day centres are complex systems, organic and changing. Structure irons out uncertainties but it may discriminate against some users.

(Howe *et al.* 1982: 60–61)

The debate about voluntarism and compulsion continued throughout the 1980s (e.g. McLoone, Oulds and Morris 1987; Scarborough, Geraghty and Loffhagen 1987; Owen and Morris-Jones 1988) and represented the focusing of a wider and more fundamental debate about care versus control on to a particular (and literally) concrete setting. The debate also affected the content of day centre programmes. Achieving a balance between structured activities aimed directly at addressing offending behaviour and those aimed more at enhancing self-esteem and developing personal and social skills was not easy. It also became apparent that there were limits on the levels of participation that could be required of someone whose attendance was compulsory. Offenders could be compelled to attend and sit in a room with an instructor or trainer. But they could not be compelled to talk about themselves and certainly not to discuss any problems or behaviour which they might consider intimate or confidential. That could only be done voluntarily, whatever the court might say. So any notion of 'therapy' or 'treatment' had to be ejected from day centre discourse and programmes tended to fall into three broad categories:

1 *Educational* programmes, such as alcohol education, health education, literacy and numeracy, victim awareness, drugs education, jobseekers' clubs, debt management and so on;

2 *Leisure-control* programmes, designed to develop new constructive leisure skills, such as art, drama, sport and so on;

3 *Cognitive-behaviour* programmes, designed to enable offenders to identify and modify visible behaviour which was seen to cause problems to other people and which may or may not cause problems to the offender.

Each of these categories presented ethical dilemmas, though relatively minor ones in the first two instances. Anything described as 'educational' immediately poses the problem of 'how people learn' and it was apparent that, in the early years, enthusiastic probation officers with no training as teachers sometimes became disheartened by the lack of response among their 'pupils', especially those young adults who could not tolerate anything that reminded them of school. The spectre of 'less eligibility' also raised its head. Why should offenders have special education and extra help in finding jobs and accommodation when law-abiding folk cannot get such help? A similar criticism was levelled at 'leisure' activities. Arguments about self-esteem and the constructive use of time were not well received by a public having to pay more and more for their own leisure activities.

But by far the most difficult ethical minefield was the third category of activity. In order to compel participation in behaviour modification without invoking cries of 'treatment without consent!' probation officers had to construct the behaviour in question within a specific discourse in order to establish legitimacy for the programmes concerned. This will be considered in greater detail later in this chapter, but suffice to say at present that the behaviour had to be constructed as being:

- specific and bounded – not some generalised personality trait
- illegal and not just anti-social
- victim-creating or potentially victim-creating and not just a problem to the offender
- controllable by the offender and therefore a matter of choice
- capable of being corrected without recourse to medical or psychological expertise

Consequently, such programmes became known as 'offending behaviour groups' or 'offence-focused groups' to make clear that no attempt was being made to change either the personality of the offender or their social circumstances. On the one hand, it could be argued that this offered some protection to the offender against overly intrusive therapeutic intervention. On the other, however, it allowed probation officers to abrogate responsibility for treating the offender as a 'whole person' in a social context.

Probation centres and discrimination

Probation centres (known as day centres until 1992) have always been male-dominated environments. Mair's national survey (1988) found that 95 per cent of those attending were male. This means that, as with community service, a vicious circle of male-orientated provision existed whereby probation officers were reluctant to recommend such orders because of the poor provision and those working in centres blamed the absence of recommendations for the inadequate provision (Armstrong 1990). The picture was further complicated, as we saw in Chapter 6, by officers' fears that they may have been colluding with discrimination if they recommended for a probation centre order a woman who seemed to have an insufficiently hefty criminal record to warrant it (Dunkley 1992).

Women, of course, were not excluded from centres and there were many laudable examples of women-only groups (Mistry 1989; Carlen 1990; Buchanan, Collett and McMullan 1991; Jones *et al.* 1991). All too often, however, women have had to fit in with existing male-dominated groups. Including a lone woman in a male group, for example, on alcohol education, highlights the problem. Images of drunken women are very different from images of drunken men (McConville 1983) and stereotyped judgements (including those from other group members) may prove particularly intimidating for a woman in that situation. Not only is she unlikely to benefit from the experience of the group but she may well be rendered more vulnerable to breach proceedings if she feels she cannot face the situation. Such arguments are well-understood within the probation service but the practice persisted nevertheless. Provision for black and other minority ethnic offenders in centres was even more inadequate, except in a few notable areas such as the Black Groups Initiative in the Inner London Probation Service (Lawrence 1995; Powis and Walmsley 2002; Durrance and Williams 2004). The discussion on What Works (see below) will show that this has been addressed to some extent in recent years by the use of mentors in supporting minorities.

Probation hostels/approved premises

The probation service has a long history of partnership with charities and voluntary organizations in the provision of accommodation for young boys and girls (Le Mesurier 1935) but approved hostels for adults have only existed since 1973 (White 1984). Their development coincided with a broader concern about the impact of homelessness or poor accommodation on recidivism. Their aim was to provide probation clients with stable accommodation and sufficient support to complete their probation orders without reoffending. It was assumed that most would be employed or could be helped to find a job with the appropriate support and encouragement. Liaison with local housing departments often meant that permanent accommodation could be found after about 12 months in a hostel.

By the 1980s, however, the situation had changed considerably (HM Inspectorate of Probation 1993). There was a shortage of traditionally 'suitable' hostel residents and under-occupancy became a problem. In 1991 the average rate of occupancy was just under 75 per cent. With high levels of unemployment and the demand for provision to keep more serious offenders out of prison, especially while on remand between court appearances, the probation hostel became less of a roof over one's head and more of a house of correction in its own right. National Standards 2002 make clear that approved premises are for bailees, those subject to community sentences with a condition of residence in the approved premises, and for post custody licencees (Home Office 2002c). An occupancy rate target of 90 per cent is set for all hostels in England and Wales.

The hostel experience of the 1990s has been very much about providing 'a high restriction of liberty … in a structured and supervised setting' (HMI 1993: 13). Thurston (2002) suggests that this is due to the emerging role of probation services as contributors to public protection. As approved premises are now taking many more high-risk ex-prisoners (who include a high proportion of sex offenders requiring the hostel regime in order to monitor their behaviour), the places available to bailees and those serving community sentences are fewer. The result is more stable populations, as high-risk ex-prisoners need longer-term support before being moved on to other accommodation. Thurston claims that the strategic importance of finding such accommodation needs to be recognized.

There is a requirement that whilst supervised in approved premises, residents address and reduce offending behaviour, often by means of 'programmes designed according to the principles of effective practice' (Home Office 2002c: F7). Strict rules are applied prohibiting disruptive or offensive language, as well as violent or abusive behaviour. All this is quite reasonable in theory, and one would hope that most residents could be helped to reach such a standard of civilized conduct through the hostel experience. But it has meant that those most in need of the support provided by hostels are increasingly excluded because of the high standards they are required to reach *before* admission.

Hostels have also suffered from a lack of status within the probation service. Although wardens are qualified probation officers, the remaining staff are not, many being probation services officers. Indeed, working as an assistant warden is recognized as a stepping-stone for those wishing to enter training. Consequently, many stay in one hostel for only a year or so, in order to gain the minimum required experience.

Despite these concerns, it could be argued that the probation service – or rather NAPO – shot itself in the foot in relation to hostels. Following the 1991 Criminal Justice Act, the Home Office announced plans to increase the number of bail hostel places (admittedly with a view to privatizing some of the provision) in line with the Act's stated intention of reducing the remand population in prison. In response, NAPO began industrial action in 1992 against 'unsafe' staffing levels in many hostels (NAPO 1992). Although the dispute was settled in the same year, the additional NIMBY factor (Not In My Back Yard) meant that the planned expansion met with much local resistance and much of the money allocated by the Home Office remained unspent (NAPO 1993). Hostels, it seemed, were becoming too troublesome an issue. The estate now stands at 100 hostels, with 2,238 places (NPS 2003a) but problems continue. By 2003, NAPO was reporting a catalogue of complaints about the privatization of hostel cooks, cleaners and maintenance staff, ranging from the 'staggering 60 per cent increase in costs' to the plight of a project worker who fell and broke her ankle because light bulbs had not been replaced (NAPO 2003/4). Attempts to apply the What Works philosophy to hostel work through Pathfinder projects are being evaluated in 2004/5, though concerns have been expressed about the feasibility of such projects, given the staffing levels, daily crises and throughput experienced in hostels (NAPO 2003/4).

Probation hostels and discrimination

In 1991, a total of 878 offenders received probation orders with conditions of residence (HMI 1993). By 2002, this had reduced to 486, including those on CPROs (Home Office 2004a), reflecting the shift in population from bailees and those serving community sentences, to released prisoners.

Hostel provision for women is woefully inadequate, providing a total of 221 female beds, with only five all-women hostels in the country – in London, West Midlands, Merseyside, Greater Manchester and Thames Valley. Twenty-eight other hostels make some provision for women but this often amounts to three or four beds in an otherwise male-dominated hostel (Home Office 2003a). In such situations it is recognized that it is difficult 'to create a sense of safety and privacy for women without simultaneously suggesting a feeling of entrapment' (HMI 1993: 45; Wincup 1996).

It is no longer possible for hostels to accept women with young children, as rules state that residents must be over 18 years. However, the NPD acknowledges that there may be exceptional circumstances when a woman with a young child needs to be accommodated in approved premises. There could be human rights issues about not assessing her case individually (NPS 2002c; Scott 2002). The high-risk offenders that hostels are now taking will often present a serious threat to women residents. Consequently, some services find it difficult to accommodate women in an appropriate environment. A regional approach for women's accommodation has been tried but the number of available places overall has been reduced and this results in women travelling long distances away from their home areas. In these circumstances, it is perhaps not surprising that 'demand' for female hostel places appears low, while the female prison population continues to rise. Woolf and Tumim's recommendation (1991) for small-unit community prisons for women, allowing greater access to community provision, was derided by women's campaigners at the time, but, in the present penal climate, it now looks like a missed opportunity to improve the overall stock of supervised accommodation for women (Hayman 1996). Worrall (2002b) suggests that the Australian and European 'transitional' arrangements for women could be emulated.

Hostel provision for black and other minority ethnic offenders is also inadequate but for slightly different reasons. The Commission for Racial Equality has argued against separate provision for black people (HMI 1993) but hostels are still seen as 'white institutions'. As in other areas of anti-discriminatory practice, hostel staff are cautious about making any claims that they are successfully catering for minority ethnic residents. Nevertheless, this laudable introspection results in more and more such offenders being sent to prison. A solution to the hostel problem was found in West Yorkshire by 'celebrating diversity in a pro-active way' (Thurston 2002: 214). Employing a support worker, researching best practice, developing the confidence and skills of staff, and making some of the provision semi-specialist minority ethnic facilities, were all seen to be key features.

Having examined those physical settings, outside the traditional office, in which 'help' is offered by the probation service, we now turn to an examination of the nature of that 'help'.

The development of counselling in probation

The role of counselling in probation has always been ambiguous. Historically, the exhortation to 'advise, assist and befriend' was more closely associated with the duties of citizenship than with professional skills and knowledge. Probation officers in the early part of the century were viewed as being somewhat avuncular – upright citizens offering wayward youths the benefit of their experience within a relationship of benevolent authority.

Such work fitted well with Edwin Sutherland's theory of differential association (Taylor, Walton and Young 1972). Crime, like all social behaviour, is learned from those with whom one associates most closely. The extent and nature of the influence of a relationship will depend on its duration, its intensity and its importance to the person concerned. In the same way, law-abiding behaviour can be learned from wholesome relationships. As Le Mesurier says:

> The probationer may come to look on his probation officer in a new light, respect ripen into friendship, and the foundations be laid for a lasting relationship, the nature and influence of which will be evident after personal contact is no longer possible.
>
> (Le Mesurier 1935: 129)

Unfortunately, Le Mesurier spoils this warm picture by reminding the probation officer that it is difficult to cultivate such relationships when 10 or 20 probationers are reporting in one evening!

After the Second World War, however, much greater emphasis was placed on psychodynamic and, later, Rogerian approaches to counselling (Williams 1996), which required probation officers to develop particular interviewing skills and to work within a framework of social work values.

Psychodynamic approaches are, broadly speaking, concerned with what is 'hidden' and in particular with conflict that is hidden. Behaviour is viewed as a manifestation, expression or symptom of an underlying unresolved conflict. That unconscious conflict causes conscious anxiety that is managed through defence mechanisms such as repression, projection, splitting, denial, reaction formation and so on. Such mechanisms serve to bolster and protect a fragile and falsely positive self-image. At the root of the conflict are relationships between individuals and significant others, between the past and the present, between inner and outer reality. A key theme is that of *transference*, whereby an individual behaves towards another individual as though they were someone else in their life. An example might be the offender who treats their probation officer as though they were a parent or a son or daughter, thus engaging in inappropriate interaction. Related to that is the notion of *counter-transference* – for example, the similarly inappropriate feelings which an offender may invoke in the worker. The resolution of conflict comes through its conscious acknowledgement and acceptance, and the task of the worker as expert is to identify the source of the conflict and make that knowledge accessible to the client (Coulshed 1988; Lishman 1991).

Probably the most well-known articulation of these skills and values can be found in a book called *The Casework Relationship* by Felix Biestek (1961), which set out seven principles of 'casework':

Individualization is the recognition and understanding of each client's unique qualities and the differential use of principles and methods in assisting each toward a better adjustment. Individualization is based upon the right of human beings to be individuals and to be treated not just as *a* human being but as *this* human being with his personal differences. (p.25)

Purposeful expression of feelings is the recognition of the client's need to express his feelings freely, especially his negative feelings. The caseworker listens purposefully, neither discouraging nor condemning the expression of these feelings, sometimes even actively stimulating and encouraging them when they are therapeutically useful as a part of the casework service. (p.35)

The controlled emotional involvement is the caseworker's sensitivity to the client's feelings, an understanding of their meaning, and a purposeful response to the client's feelings. (p.50)

Acceptance is a principle of action wherein the caseworker perceives and deals with the client as he really is, including his strengths and weaknesses, his congenial and uncongenial qualities, his positive and negative feelings, his constructive and destructive attitudes and behaviour, maintaining all the while a sense of the client's innate dignity and personal worth. (p.72)

The non-judgmental attitude is a quality of the casework relationship; it is based on a conviction that the casework function excludes assigning guilt or innocence, or degree of client responsibility for the causation of the problems or needs, but does include making evaluative judgments about the attitudes, standards or actions of the client. (p.90)

The principle of client self-determination is the practical recognition of the right and need of clients to freedom in making their own choices and decisions in the casework process. Caseworkers have a corresponding duty to respect that right, recognize that need, stimulate and help to activate that potential for self-direction by helping the client to see and use the available and appropriate resources of the community and of his own personality. The client's right to self-determination, however, is limited by the client's capacity for positive and constructive decision-making, by the framework of civil and moral law and by the function of the agency. (p.103)

Confidentiality is the preservation of secret information concerning the client which is disclosed in the professional relationship. Confidentiality is based upon a basic right of the client; it is an ethical obligation of the caseworker and is necessary for effective casework service. The client's right, however, is not absolute. (p.121)

These principles have been set out at length because they are often wilfully misunderstood by those who wish to decry 'casework'. Although some of the language is dated, there is little here to which most probation officers could take exception in the routine of their work. The feasibility of casework within a probation setting has always been questioned, however, because of the authority vested in probation officers to return offenders to court (Walker and Beaumont 1981). The problem may not be quite as acute as in America:

Usually, the counselor [*sic*] carries a badge that enables him or her to arrest and incarcerate offenders. The counselor may carry handcuffs, leg and body chains, electronic surveillance bracelets, and even firearms ... [S]ome authorities are of the opinion that effective counseling relationships cannot be developed under such conditions.

(Masters 1994: 13)

Nevertheless, the likelihood of achieving genuine changes of attitude and behaviour in an offender under these conditions is justifiably viewed with some scepticism. By the 1970s, many probation officers saw traditional counselling as patronising and oppressive, designed to encourage clients to accept their place in the community and their lot in life (Raynor 1978).

The demise of the rehabilitative ideal outlined in previous chapters resulted in radical approaches to counselling which focused on the potential of groups to raise client consciousness of common problems and their social, rather than individual, causes. Groups were seen to provide mutual aid and self-help, and to redress the balance of power in the professional-client relationship. But they offered no immediate evidence of reducing recidivism and, as such, gained little credibility with management and the courts, who demanded more visible evidence of success.

Behavioural approaches to the 'treatment' of offenders had been of only peripheral interest to probation officers, mainly because of the levels of medical expertise required but also because of the ethical dilemmas posed by methods that were apparently applied without the informed consent of the offender/patient.

Behaviour modification is based on the belief that behaviour is learned through a process of stimulus and response. This may be done in one of two ways. Respondent (Pavlovian) conditioning is concerned with behaviour over which we may have little control, such as physical reflexes, sexual arousal, anxiety, fear and anger. It is relevant when considering specific inappropriate learned behaviours such as phobias, addictions or violent sexual behaviour. Here the key to understanding is that the client has made an inappropriate connection or association between a stimulus and a response. In a mild form, this is the basis on which advertising works. For example, a man may be sexually aroused by a picture of a scantily clad woman sitting on a sports car. Subsequently, driving fast cars may become a sexually arousing activity. There is no need for a Freudian explanation – the behaviour has been learned through association. In order to change the behaviour, it is necessary to break the connection – in working with phobic conditions techniques of *desensitization* (introducing the patient gradually to the feared experience) or *flooding* (overwhelming them in such a way that their fear reaction fails to function) may be employed to help a client control a fear reaction; in working with addictions (including sex offending) *aversion* techniques may be used so that the association becomes unpleasant rather than pleasurable. But such work tends to be specialized and is not often appropriate for probation officers unless it is very closely supervised in institutions by psychiatrists or psychologists.

Of more use on a day-to-day basis is operant (Skinnerian) conditioning which emphasises the importance of *consequences* as reinforcers of behaviour. Much use is made of the ABC model:

A = Antecedents   = Stimulus
B = Behaviour   = Response
C = Consequences = New Stimulus

In operant conditioning the initial response (B) may be random or experimental: for example, a child throwing her first tantrum when refused sweets or a teenager committing his first theft. Whether or not that response becomes a learned piece of behaviour will depend on the consequences (does the mother give in and provide sweets? Is the teenager caught?). Patterns of behaviour depend not so much on the original stimulus (lost in the mists of time) but on how present consequences reinforce present responses (Coulshed 1988; Lishman 1991).

In order to change (or shape) behaviour, the aim is to change the consequences by either increasing or decreasing the positive reinforcers (or rewards), depending on whether the behaviour is to be encouraged or discouraged. This might be done through modelling (behaving in the desired way to show the client the good consequences), contracts (agreeing rewards for behaviour changes), points systems or time out (physical removal from the source of reward) – or simply by praising and withholding praise. It is important to note here that punishment (the infliction of physical or emotional pain) should have no part in this form of behaviour modification for at least three reasons:

1 It doesn't help the person to learn new good behaviour;
2 It can have serious side-effects of depression or copying (negative modelling);
3 People learn to tolerate punishment.

Cognitive behavioural work has developed from operant conditioning but accepts that, unlike animals, humans are not just creatures of physical response. We are 'reflexive'. Intervening between stimulus and response is our perception of a situation. Our responses are shaped by our beliefs and thoughts about reality. Those beliefs and thoughts may be considered distorted when viewed objectively by other people (for example, a sex offender may *believe* that a five-year-old child is being seductive) but they have real influence in shaping our response to a stimulus. Changing our thought processes – the way we assess situations mentally – will change our responses in the same way as more physical or emotional rewards.

Cognitive behavioural approaches have become very popular within the probation service for all the reasons outlined earlier in this chapter. They have also provided the rhetorical link between discourses of 'help' and managerialism, or, as Oldfield describes it, 'the conjuncture of managerialism with a psychologically dominated discourse of effectiveness' (2002: 69). We can now turn to the ways in which the concept of 'effectiveness' has been incorporated into the helping project through the use of cognitive behavioural work.

What works? The effectiveness debate

The traditional measure of effectiveness in the probation service had been the correlation between report recommendations and sentencing decisions (known as concordance). As Raynor, Smith and Vanstone (1994) have said, when probation officers talked about effectiveness they tended to refer to their success in diverting offenders from custody. (We will see that ten years on, the term 'effectiveness' will have a different resonance for probation officers.) Reconviction rates were never of great interest, especially after the court order had ended. Probation officers felt that they could not be held responsible if an offender reoffended 12 months after a probation order had finished. If an offender navigated the order itself without reoffending, then that was considered sufficient success. Currently the national service has targets for reconviction rates after a two-year period following a community sentence, so staff certainly now have reconviction in their sights.

But Raynor, Smith and Vanstone suggested that it ought to be possible to steer a middle course, which identifies indicators of effectiveness other than crude reconviction rates but which nevertheless allows probation officers to assess their effectiveness in helping an offender to reform. These 'broader measures of success' (1994: 78–84) are:

- anti-poverty strategies, which establish networks of information and support to help offenders deal more successfully with official agencies concerned with benefits and employment;

- anti-oppressive practice, which ensures equality of treatment for black people and women and equality of access to appropriate provision inside and outside the probation service;

- drug misuse and harm reduction work;

- accommodation strategies;

- reduction of harm caused by the criminal justice system, by continuing to influence sentencers and seeking to divert as many offenders as possible from custody;

- reduction of harm caused to victims of crime, by assisting victim support schemes and increasing victim awareness among offenders.

There is no 'quick fix' to make people stop committing crime. Nothing can guarantee reform but all these measures will affect offenders' attitudes and behaviour, making it more likely and thus offering the greatest hope of long-term protection for the public. Any or all of these topics are likely to be addressed by a probation officer or probation services officer in their day-to-day work in 'case-managing' offenders. However, since the turn of the twenty-first century, this work has been 'supported' by the selection of certain offenders to attend accredited programmes that address their particular offending behaviour.

We saw in Chapter 2 that Robert Martinson's (1974) pronouncement that 'nothing works' helped to accelerate the loss of confidence in rehabilitative measures, and although he made a partial retraction in 1979, the legacy of disillusion persisted. In the late 1980s and early 1990s, however, a new mood of optimism accompanied the 'discovery' of cognitive behavioural approaches and a series of conferences entitled What Works? were held to encourage evaluative research and its dissemination. In the forefront of this movement was James McGuire, who gave new impetus to the probation service to experiment in its work with offenders. This was especially important at this time, for Michael Howard was appointed as Home Secretary in 1993, and his mantra of 'prison works' was beginning to find favour with the public who had law and order at the top of their public policy agenda (Mair 2004). Practitioners in England noted the success of the Canadian 'Reasoning and Rehabilitation' programme and based 'Straight Thinking on Probation' (STOP) on that (Raynor 1992; Raynor and Vanstone 1994; Knott 1995). The 'Reasoning and Rehabilitation' programme lasts for 35 half-day sessions and employs cognitive skills training; it aims to develop offenders' thinking skills and thus increase their range of problem-solving options. Central to the effective delivery of the programme is the concept of 'programme integrity'. This is assessed by videoing each session to check on the trainer's delivery. The STOP programme was evaluated by Peter Raynor and Maurice Vanstone and appeared to indicate a favourable reconviction rate for those who completed the programme in comparison with those dealt with in other ways by the courts. Raynor and Vanstone were the first to point out the tentative nature of the figures, and refer to the quality and quantity of contact with probation officers, as well as programme content, in offenders' assessments of their behavioural change (Raynor 1992). We will see that this hesitancy and lack of sound evidence still pervades 'What Works' programmes some ten years on (and for a detailed discussion of cognitive skills training, see Harding and Worrall 2004).

In 1998, Underdown's inspection report, *Strategies for Effective Supervision*, did much to 'kick-start' the 'What Works' agenda in the probation service. It has become the underlying approach for the newly created National Probation Service. Underdown's recommendations included an Agenda for Development, in which he identified service and programme design, targeting and assessment, delivery, case management, evaluation and developing the organization, as key (Underdown 1998). His list of Principles for Effectiveness emphasised the need for evidence-based practice, consistency and the need to engage offenders by using cognitive and behavioural perspectives. Mair (2004) suggests that a civil servant – the Head of Research and Statistics at the Home Office – and the Chief Inspector of Probation had roles in promoting the idea of 'What Works'.

What is also most significant is that 1997 saw the first Labour government for 18 years, with a burning desire to reform and modernize public services. New Labour were pushing evidence-based practice as a justification for change and funding in many areas of public service, such as health. Early legislation for the creation of the National Probation Service (NPS) in 2001 led to a sense of urgency to bring 'What Works' into the national picture. As Mair points out, 'What Works' could only work on a national scale, but he cites Robinson's (2001) argument that it was a catalyst to the creation of the NPS. So it could be said that this was a symbiotic relationship; giving the new national service a new way of working, to define it and distinguish it from all that had gone before.

However, it wasn't quite as simple as this. Spencer and Deakin (2004) claim that the 'What Works' agenda demanded changes in the theoretical outlook in the service, as well as practical application. (Changing the culture of practice away from the welfare-orientated approach was assisted by the change in training arrangements away from those of social work.) Secondly, assessment and risk management became a key probation function in order to allow the delivery of accredited programmes (the programmes are accredited by the Correctional Services Accreditation Panel). Thirdly, case management has had to change – in order to show that punishment in the community is being managed properly, enforcement is being measured.

Critics have observed that there has been too much concentration on rigidly-presented programmes, which, it is argued, will not work unless

> delivered in the context of effective case management, based on a full risk and needs assessment which tackles the multiple criminogenic factors ... which characterize most supervised offenders.
>
> (HMIP 2002)

Raynor would maintain that some criticism is simplistic (Raynor 2003). He argues that the use of OASys as the keystone of assessment of risk ensures that social and environmental factors are taken into account, but recognizes that 'case management now needs to become a priority' (Raynor 2003: 339). His paper rebuts the idea of too many psychologists being involved in accreditation, with too great a concentration on cognitive-behavioural programmes. Raynor says that with the roll out of Enhanced Community Punishment, programmes that contain no cognitive-behavioural element are now expected to account for half of the accredited programme completions. An alternative view would be that the sizeable reduction in targets for accredited programme completions in 2002/03 to 12,000 (from 15,000 for 2003/04) (NPS 2004d) indicated a significant degree of 'attrition', or perhaps, poor initial assessment. Research by Davies et al. (2004) has suggested that for many offenders, the literacy demands of cognitive skills programmes exceed their literacy skills. Put simply, they cannot read, write, speak or listen sufficiently well to benefit from the programmes. NAPO (2004) reported that probation staff felt coerced and even bullied into referring offenders inappropriately to accredited programmes in order to meet NPD targets. They claimed that 'a good idea is being systematically undermined by the ... obsession with targets and the belief that cognitive behaviour therapy is the only way forward' (NAPO 2004: 5).

Raynor (2003) admits that the diversity issues have been to some extent marginalized in the early days of 'What Works', but is reassured that work is being done to reflect the programme needs for women and black and minority ethnic offenders. Probation Areas are required to address the needs of these groups when providing services – mentoring and individual support (which for language difficulties may mean an interpreter or one to one programme) as well as special groups, are all deemed suitable (NPS 2004e).

Raynor recognizes that there may well be no conclusive evidence about the effectiveness of every programme, but is pragmatic – the time taken to complete a two-year reconviction study would stagnate any action in this area. He is confident that evidence will be found to demonstrate the efficacy of community penalties using the 'What Works' methods. Merrington and Stanley argue that the latest two-year reconviction rates show reductions, but that it is 'impossible to relate progress to particular innovations' (2004: 14). Hence they reiterate the need to improve case management, and not rely too much on programmes. They claim that the evidence to date suggests that the impact of programmes may fade over time. For this reason 'booster' programmes are now offered to some offenders. In addition they call for good targeting, which seems to 'be linked with successful results' (2004: 18). They feel that more detailed research and evaluation is required, but that publishing the work done to date, fully and so that it can be scrutinized, will add weight to the 'What Works' argument.

Reconviction is currently the favoured method of measuring effectiveness. However, some researchers, such as Farrall (2004), approach the issue from the other perspective: what makes offenders desist from offending? By tracking offenders subjected to probation orders, the variables of social context, motivation and probation supervision were selected and the influence of these interrelated factors on the outcome of the probation order were measured. Farrall states that 'Experiments do *not* work well if one is evaluating complex, multi-causal and contingent processes' (2004: 202), and criticises the 'What Works' literature for being dependent on experiment. Cognitive reasoning programmes would have been of little value to Farrall's sample, very few of whom demonstrated poor thinking skills. For this reason he suggests that, while there may be a role for cognitive behaviouralism, there is an imbalance in the focus of current probation work. He feels that more probation work should be focused on supporting probationers in addressing existing family problems and employment – on forward-looking interventions.

The jury is still out on 'What Works'. The fact that more research, measurement and evaluation are continuing will facilitate future decisions about the direction of probation practice, bounded by evidence of effectiveness. What most commentators seem to agree on is that the concentrated focus on accredited programmes has been misplaced. The need is, as was always intended, to have a 'What Works' agenda that combines assessment, programmes, case management and enforcement.

Specialist probation functions

In this final section, we will discuss other aspects of current practice that occupy probation staff. Some are old, some new and some barely on the agenda: an indication of the constantly changing range of interventions that probation provides.

Money Payment Supervision Orders (MPSOs)

These have been 'additional requirements' to community rehabilitation orders for many years. The court can make it a condition of the order that the offender works with the probation staff to sort out their financial situation. This may include the help of other agencies and partners, such as debt counselling organizations, or liaison with court fines offices. Sentences with this order rose steadily between 1989 and 1995 and there was a year on year increase of 94 per cent in 1996. This is seen to reflect the High Court judgement given in 1996, that other methods should be explored before the use of prison for those defaulting on fines (Home Office 1999). With the number of MPSOs dropping to 3,000 in 1998 and just 2,200 in 1999, it seems that this judgement has been superseded. The numbers of MPSOs are no longer quoted in the statistics. However, this aspect of an offender's life should still be a part of the normal case management process (Raine *et al.* 2003).

Drug Treatment and Testing Orders (DTTOs)

DTTOs were introduced by the Crime and Disorder Act 1998, and were available to courts nationally from October 2000. This was a new concept in terms of sentencing – a therapeutic sentence, but with a tough compliance regimen, that would continue to be monitored monthly by the sentencing court (and the same personnel) throughout its life. Unell (2002) notes that the purpose of the order is not to treat the drug addict as such, but to stop them offending (committing drug offences and dishonesty offences in order to support their illegal drug habit). She questions the ethical justification of the 'marriage of drug treatment and the criminal justice system'(2002: 229). Rumgay (2003a) feels that drug treatment, in general, in the probation service has not been sufficiently focused on the multi-agency collaborative approach, due to internal pressures and the demands of the 'What Works' agenda. However, it is clear that the DTTO does require probation services to engage effectively in partnership working in order to carry out testing and treatment, while still maintaining the case-management element throughout the order.

The sentence requires a PSR to determine the offender's suitability, current illicit drug use and particularly to assess their willingness and motivation to receive treatment. DTTOs are expensive in cash and resource terms, and had a budget of £54m for the year 2003/04. This cost may be the reason for the planned introduction in 2005 of a less intensive treatment plan to match the needs of offenders who are more stable and 'have less extensive treatment needs, a lower risk of reoffending and who have committed a lower volume of offending' (2004e: 2).

The success of the DTTO is very difficult to gauge. The pilot studies (evaluated by Hedderman and Hough, 2004) showed that a high rate of revocation affects the reconviction rates (as well as vice versa) and this is supported by the more recent studies of Hearnden and Millie (2004). What is clear is that these orders have a very high rate of attrition. The National Audit Office assesses that 'only' 28 per cent completed their orders (www.nao.gov.uk). Considering the high risk of reconviction that these offenders must have before being deemed suitable for a DTTO, and considering the nature of addiction and its impact on the offender's ability to function in what might be called 'normal' day-to-day living, this figure, whilst not exemplary, shows a positive impact for individual offenders – and for society. The other key feature of the NAO's report is that, of those who *complete* the order, 53 per cent will be reconvicted in two years, compared with 80 per cent of all those who *commence* DTTOs. In response, Hedderman and Hough (2004) suggest that the way forward is to give people a better chance of being 'completers' by not breaching them too readily, using a variety of techniques to aid compliance, and thirdly to reward actively that compliance. Their suggestion that probation services should have targets for completions as well as for commencements on DTTOs has now become adopted practice from 2004/05.

The DTTO is an initiative that politicians should back to the hilt. It is bound to take a long time to bring results; sentencers needed convincing to begin with, and it is always bound to be an uphill struggle to rehabilitate addicts. But if 90 per cent of the target for 2003/04 of 9,000 commencements can be reached, that will mean 8,100 people starting on DTTOs. If 28 per cent of them complete the order (let us be positive and say 30 per cent in the future), that means 2,430 will do so, and if only 50 per cent of them are reconvicted in two years, that is 1,215 people who are not creating havoc in their community or constantly in court for shoplifting and burglary offences and are kept out of prison. The political dilemma, of course, is that there is a 'less eligibility' factor again – those who are criminals are able to access drug treatment, and perhaps go to the top of the list. But is it not a better political stance to keep this funding in the law and order budget (which the public seems to be prepared to fund to a great degree) rather than to put the funds into health? We need only imagine the response of some tabloids to spending on drug treatment, when compared with that for cancer treatment.

Prolific Offender Projects

Now known as Intensive Supervision and Monitoring Projects, these are being developed to try to prevent reoffending amongst the most persistent offenders (Worrall *et al.* 2003; Worrall and Mawby 2004). They are premised on the assumption that a small number of offenders are responsible for a large proportion of acquisitive (and some violent) crime and that resources should be targeted on intensively supervising and monitoring this group. As such, these projects have emerged from the convergence of intelligence-led policing and evidence-based probation practice and their impetus has been provided by the 1998 Crime and Disorder Act's emphasis on multi-agency working and information exchange. Their central feature has been the combination of intensive attention from both the police and probation services. The key innovation of the projects has been joint working between two criminal justice agencies that, traditionally, have been wary of each other's aims and methods.

The other characteristics of the projects derive from this central feature. The project is staffed by designated police and probation personnel, and located on either police or probation premises. Participants in the project are required to meet local criteria that categorize them as 'prolific' – that is, among the most persistent property offenders in the locality – and they are subject to formal court orders of supervision or post-custodial licence. Participants are subject to high levels of police monitoring and programmes of intensive probation supervision that seek to address their offending behaviour and other needs such as housing, substance misuse, leisure, education and employment. In order to achieve this, there has to be an agreed mechanism of information exchange between participating agencies. There is an agreed procedure for swift enforcement in the event of non-compliance or further offending.

Evaluations of the projects have produced mixed results. The statistical analyses provide some evidence that the participants reduced their levels of offending while they were actively engaged on the project, but that this progress was not always maintained during the post-project period. These statistics, combined with close observation of the operation of the project and interviews with staff, managers and participants, suggest that the project provided a valuable 'maintenance' function that was effective in the short-term and laid foundations for possible longer-term benefits (Worrall *et al.* 2003; Worrall and Mawby 2004).

Following on from these projects, which are designed for all adult offenders, the NPS has targeted 18 to 20-year-olds with a specific Intensive Control and Change Programme that has been piloted in 11 areas since April 2003. It is likely to be rolled out nationally in 2004/05. The key features of the programme are that offenders are curfewed by electronic tag, and have 25 hours of contact per week – 7 hours of community punishment and 18 hours spent on rehabilitative or educational programmes. Partnership working is a key to the operation of the programmes (e.g. using Connexions staff) and, additionally, a mentor is involved with the young person. Fines and compensation to victims are ordered where appropriate. The orders may be reviewed by the sentencing courts at three and six month stages, giving a chance for offenders to tell of their progress. Breach proceedings follow swiftly if there is any failure to comply. The purpose is to divert those who are on the brink of a custodial sentence of less than 12 months and judged to be at either medium or high risk of reoffending. As with all community sentences, assessment of the right offender for the right programme is essential. Keeping young people out of custody by having a rigorous 'tough enough' community sentence is the stated aim (NPS 2003b).

Work with victims

This has been an aspect of probation officers' work that has not always received adequate recognition. It is traditionally associated with the role of the resettlement officer – the probation officer who works with offenders on their release from custody – rather than with mainstream probation work. However, victim contact was a 'stretch objective' in *The New Choreography*, and timely victim contact is a National Standard and a statutory duty under the Criminal Justice and Court Services Act 2000. The development of victim-awareness in rehabilitation orders followed on from the success of restorative measures within the new arrangements for youth justice under the auspices of YOTs (Williams 2002). Within OASys, PSRs and the case management function in community rehabilitation orders, victim awareness has to be addressed. All cognitive behavioural accredited programmes require that the offender consider the impact on the victim, and developing victim empathy is a measure of success. Of course, many offenders, especially drug users, do not recognize that there is a victim connected with their offending. Others, such as sex offenders and domestic violence perpetrators, have a distorted view of the victim and their role in the offence. The victim-awareness work done on accredited programmes whilst on re-habilitation orders should, therefore, help to alleviate the problems of inconsistency of practice across the country that Williams describes. Garland (cited in Robinson and McNeill 2004: 294) prefigures aspects of the current ideology well:

> It is future victims who are now 'rescued' by rehabilitative work, rather than the offenders themselves.
>
> (Garland 1997)

Racially motivated offending

Work in this area is closely aligned to victim work. It was an issue highlighted in the diversity agenda of *The New Choreography* (stretch objective VII) (NPS and Home Office 2001). Sadly, it only warranted one line: the focus of the strategy was on building a diverse and representative organization and aspects of service delivery to offenders. This is particularly disappointing as before the inception of the national service in 2001, work in this area was being done and evaluated (Dixon and Okitikpi 1999; Edwards 1999; Kay *et al.* 1998; Ray *et al.* 2001). The work by Kay *et al.* was a training pack, called *From Murmur to Murder*, which provided a structured programme. This clearly has not met the standards of the Accreditation Panel – or perhaps other priorities for a national roll-out have been recognized as more urgent. It is also unlikely that all probation areas have developed effective partnerships with their local black and minority ethnic communities – an essential feature for such work as far as Williams (2002) is concerned. However, some practitioners continue to press for more work in this area (Dixon and Court 2003). This is despite a negative view from the NPD, who believe that the Accreditation Panel thinks there is no need for separate programmes and that they would:

be recommending a new approach to research around racially motivated offenders, which would include monitoring them through cognitive behavioural programmes.

(Dixon 2003: 64)

Conclusion

At present there is a great danger in thinking that the 'What Works' framework is *the* solution. In its early days, the phrase was accompanied by a question mark which befitted the tentative and investigative nature of its claims. The question mark has since been dropped and the claims have become more assertive. Advocates of accredited programmes emphasise the importance of programme integrity. This may seem a reasonable requirement if programmes are to be evaluated. But such rigidity smacks of mystification and imperialism. In a satirical article, Bale describes EBSST – Exceptionally Brief Simple Solution Therapy:

Offenders [are] … rapidly forced to confront their offending behaviour, speedily acknowledge their distorted thinking, instantly renounce all habit-forming substances and pledge undying commitment to an all-encompassing relapse prevention plan.

(Bale 2000: 130)

Change is a process that takes time and, as Pitts argues, 'effective rehabilitation ventures are reflexive rather than directive … successful interventions do not seem to travel well' (1992b: 144). The danger of resisting the pessimism of 'nothing works' is that it is replaced by equally hollow rhetoric. We know that 'something works' or that 'some things work', but the circumstances under which some things work, for some people, some of the time, need to be researched honestly and sensitively, without recourse to meaningless soundbites that serve only as feeble rejoinders to the dominant discourse – that of 'prison works'. There is a need to have a full range of solutions to match diverse needs. Continuing to develop, evaluate and accredit work such as that addressing racially motivated offending is a fine example of expanding the range of things that work. Regaining recognition of the importance of day-to-day case management as a major factor in 'What Works' is just as important – perhaps more so.

Chapter 9

Unacceptable crimes or unacceptable criminals? Sex offenders

Introduction

The following two chapters will illustrate the changing attitudes to offenders, using sex offenders and young offenders as case studies. These two categories of offenders are not usually put together but the juxtaposition here is deliberate. Both the sex offender and the young offender have undergone a significant reconstruction within official discourse on crime and disorder. Both have been demonized but both (albeit in very different ways) have epitomized the contradictions that result from policies based on an inadequate understanding of the complexities of the issues involved. Sex offenders are constructed simultaneously as 'strangers' and 'known', as 'monsters' and 'ordinary blokes', but always as lying and manipulative recidivists. Young offenders are constructed simultaneously as 'just boys being boys [*sic*]' and 'little monsters', as 'growing out of crime' and being 'persistent offenders' but always as (ir)responsible offenders against society rather than as victims of its failures. And there are young sex offenders. Between a quarter and a third of alleged sexual abuse is estimated to have been committed by young people (Coombes 2003) although the 'cycle of abuse' theory (that abusers have been victims of abuse themselves) has been challenged by a range of studies that indicate rates of victimization among abusers of between 30 and 70 per cent (Harris and Staunton 2000; Bailey and Boswell 2004). Other factors perceived to contribute to sexual offending by young people are drugs and alcohol misuse and the influence of a male youth culture in which forcing young women to have sex remains acceptable to a significant minority of young men (Harris and Staunton 2000). The HM Inspectorate of Probation Thematic Inspection (1998) observed that, unlike other adolescent offending, sex offending is something that adolescents, once they start, tend to 'grow into' rather than 'out of'. The same inspection report expressed concern about 'the largest and most worrying gap in provision' for adolescent sex offenders (HM Inspectorate of Probation 1998: 12).

Sex offenders – monsters or ordinary blokes?

The change of public and governmental attitude towards sex offenders has forced the probation service to examine the value base of its work. Under attack have been the key concepts of social work value discourse that have traditionally governed the attitudes of probation officers. It is no longer deemed appropriate to exhibit 'acceptance', 'empathy' or a 'non-judgemental attitude' in relation to sex offenders. Indeed, the sex offender is no longer regarded as the 'client':

> I, along with many probation officers, find myself helping to justify the use of confrontational methods by recasting my client to be a past and potential future victim rather than the perpetrator in front of me.
>
> (Gocke 1995: 175)

Work is based on the assumption that the offender is lying, that he has offended more frequently than he admits and that no mitigation (even his own past experience of abuse) can excuse or even account for his present behaviour. Ironically, feminist analysis has been far more eagerly embraced in work with sex offenders than it has in relation to the treatment of women offenders (Worrall 2002a)

Sex offenders have been increasingly a focus of attention by the criminal justice system over the past decade (Thomas 2000). During the 1980s the police and courts were criticized for failing to take a serious enough view of sexual assault and rape. Following a guideline judgement from the Appeal Court in 1986 (*R* v. *Billam*) custodial sentences increased in length. There was also increased public concern about child sexual abuse, culminating in the Butler-Schloss inquiry in Cleveland in 1987. More offenders were charged and convicted and more were sent to prison. In 1979 20 per cent of sex offenders received custodial sentences; by 1989 the proportion had increased to 33 per cent and ten years later it was 60 per cent (Home Office 2003c). The impact on the prison population was considerable. In 1979 4.7 per cent of the prison population were sex offenders, in 1989 the proportion was 7.5 per cent, and since the early 1990s it has been around 12 per cent (Home Office 2003b). The trend was accompanied by a reduction in the number of sex offenders being fined, from 39 per cent in 1982 to 17 per cent in 1992 and 6 per cent by 2002 (Home Office 2003c). The proportion receiving community sentences rose from 24 per cent in 1992 to 28 per cent in 2002, though the absolute numbers (around 1,200) remained stable, reflecting a reduction in the overall numbers sentenced from 5,000 in 1992 to 4,400 in 2002. (It is important to note that, with the exception of robbery and drug offences, the numbers sentenced for all serious offences have declined during this period.)

The Criminal Justice Act 1991, which originally attempted to reduce the prison population, made an exception in respect of violent and sexual offenders, who could be imprisoned for a longer term than might otherwise be justified in order to protect the public from serious harm. By 1996, attitudes had hardened further. In the White Paper *Protecting the Public* (Home Office 1996a), the Home Secretary proposed automatic life sentences for those who repeat serious sexual offences and also suggested the registration of sex offenders in the community, requiring them by law to notify the police of any changes of address and prohibiting them from seeking employment which involves access to children. The Sex Offenders Act 1997 introduced sex offender registration (Thomas 2000) and, by 2002, 18,500 sex offenders were registered (Bryan and Doyle 2003). These included offenders who had been cautioned as well as those with convictions (Cobley 2003). Marshall (1997) pointed out that, had the legislation been retrospective, the number on the register might have been as high as 125,000. The following year, the Crime and Disorder Act 1998 placed a duty on local authorities, police, probation and health authorities to work together to address local crime problems and introduced a civil Sex Offender Order that could restrict the movements of any cautioned or convicted sex offender in the community. The Crime (Sentences) Act 1997 gave courts the power to impose discretionary life sentences for second serious sexual offences and extended periods of supervision where offenders were still considered to be at risk of causing harm following release from prison. The Criminal Justice and Court Services Act 2000 consolidated existing multi-agency work in legislation and the Multi-Agency Public Protection Arrangements (MAPPA) and Panels (MAPPP) for the assessment and management of serious violent and sexual offenders were established (Bryan and Doyle 2003). The Sexual Offences Act 2003 extended control over sex offenders by criminalizing behaviour known as 'grooming'. As Cobley (2003: 65) explains, 'grooming involves a potential offender making contact with potential victims (who will usually be children) either directly or through internet chatrooms, with a view to building a relationship of trust which can subsequently be exploited.' 'Grooming' is a concept that is well-known to those working with sex offenders but has only recently entered public discourse. It covers a wide range of behaviour and it may be difficult to prove intent to 'groom', while at the same time ensuring that those with a legitimate reason for discussing sexual matters with children (such as teachers or nurses) are not caught up in the legislation (Cobley 2003).

Probation officers find themselves working with sex offenders in a number of different contexts. They may prepare pre-sentence reports in which they are required to make judgements about the risk to the public of not imprisoning the offender. Officers who are seconded to prisons may work jointly with prison officers and prison psychologists on the Sex Offender Treatment Programme, which is run in selected prisons. More often, they are responsible for the statutory supervision of sex offenders following their release from a prison sentence. Finally, they may provide treatment programmes in the community for offenders placed on probation. The numbers of sex offenders placed on community rehabilitation orders has remained consistently low; they represent one per cent of all offenders placed on probation (759 in 2002). Numbers placed on community punishment orders have been negligible (120 in 2002) (Home Office 2004a).

In all these contexts, probation officers are given a more specific responsibility in relation to the law-abiding community than is expected of them in relation to other offenders. It is officially acknowledged that in the work by probation services with sex offenders, 'protection of the public [is] unambiguously identified as its central purpose' (HM Inspectorate of Probation 1998: 9).

This is particularly true where the victim is a child and work is governed by the provisions of Schedule 1 of the Children and Young Person Act 1933 and, more recently, by MAPPA. In this case, probation officers share with social services, Youth Offending Teams, education services and the police a duty to monitor the offender if he begins (or returns) to live with a family or in a place where he has substantial access to children. Information about an offender, which would normally remain confidential, becomes multi-agency property in the name of protecting the public. MAPPA has four core functions: the identification of all MAPPA offenders (including violent as well as sexual offenders); the sharing of information among relevant agencies; assessing the risk of serious harm; and managing that risk (Bryan and Doyle 2003). In addition to monitoring and supervising the sex offender directly, MAPPA has responsibility for deciding what information should be disclosed outside of MAPPA and to whom.

Knowledge about sex offenders is increasingly being seen as a community's right (Hebenton and Thomas 1996; Kemshall and Maguire 2003; Power 2003). In America, arrangements for 'tracking' sex offenders are widespread and have repeatedly withstood legal challenges that they constitute cruel and unusual punishment. The murder of Megan Kanka by a neighbour known to the authorities to be a sex offender led to federal legislation permitting 'community notification' of the details of local paedophiles (Power 2003). In England, the issue gained momentum in early 1997, when a council official faced disciplinary action for allegedly alerting mothers on a Birmingham housing estate that a sex offender, recently released from prison, was moving on to the estate (*Independent*, 9 January 1997). One local authority, Middlesbrough, apparently announced that it was formally excluding sex offenders from its housing estates (Thomas 2000). In 1998 Robert Oliver and Sydney Cooke were outlawed by community after community when they were released from prison and they had to seek refuge in police stations (Thomas 2000). The debate gained intensity in the summer of 2000 following the murder of Sarah Payne by a 'registered' sex offender, Roy Whiting, leading to demands for 'Sarah's Law' to mirror 'Megan's Law' in the US. Tabloid campaigns to 'name and shame paedophiles' resulted in public disorder and indiscriminate vigilante action (Greer 2003; Kemshall and Maguire 2003). More measured voices have attempted to argue that this might not actually be the best way to protect children because (a) children are more likely to be abused by family and friends than by strangers; and (b) that if sex offenders are not rehoused, they are more likely to become nomadic in their habits, losing contact with supervisors and drifting back into crime (Hetherington 1999). So far, the UK government has resisted calls for routine community notification of the whereabouts of sex offenders and has, instead, placed its confidence in registration, local MAPPA and police checks designed to ensure that known sex offenders are not able to secure employment with children. The failure of this procedure in the case of Ian Huntley, a known sex offender who obtained employment as a school caretaker and murdered two schoolgirls in Soham in 2002, highlighted the constantly conflicting images of sex offenders as being *both* 'monsters' and 'ordinary blokes'.

Knowing about the activities of sex offenders is packaged as a prerequisite to preventing their reoffending and thereby protecting the community. But knowledge has become a matter of business, with consumers and producers. In reality it provides the opportunity to profile, classify and manage offenders in the name of risk assessment and the New Penology, while at the same time making concessions to populist punitiveness (Simon 1998). Because sex offences are, quite rightly, regarded as extremely serious, there appear to be no ethical constraints on the ways in which the very few sex offenders who are apprehended are allowed to be treated (Matravers 2003). As Hebenton and Thomas reflect, these ethical issues have not been subject to any scrutiny:

> Is compulsory self-accusation, where the offender effectively 'carries a sign in public' admitting to being a moral pariah appropriate?
>
> (Hebenton and Thomas 1996: 109)

Who are sex offenders?

A number of laws cover sexual offences and a distinction is usually made between offenders against adults and offenders against children. Offenders are usually categorized as intra-familial child abusers, extra-familial child abusers, rapists/indecent assaulters and indecent exposers. The latter are normally still considered to be pathetic rather than dangerous but some feminists argue that the impact of such offences on their victims remains underestimated (McNeill 1987). It is also now part of the received wisdom of sex offender work that those engaging in 'inappropriate' sexual behaviour (such as 'flashing') may progress to commit more serious offences unless checked. In recent years, the ease of accessing illegal internet pornography involving children has further blurred the boundary between the 'monster' and the 'ordinary bloke'. Operation Ore, a current police investigation of thousands of people accessing such sites, has uncovered a range of 'respectable' men, including police officers, teachers and judges, indulging indirectly in child sexual abuse (Grange 2003; Carr 2004). Established models of predicting risk would not have identified this 'new class' of offenders (Metcalf and Stenson 2004).

It is generally believed that most sex offenders are not mentally ill, in the sense of having a diagnosable, psychiatric illness. Many of those prosecuted are regarded as having personality disorders but victim surveys suggest that offenders come from all socio-economic groups and that many offences go unreported. The attrition rate for sexual offences (that is, the difference between the number reported to the police and those which result in conviction) is extraordinarily high (Sampson 1994; Harris and Grace 1999). Therefore, the public image of the sex offender tends to be based on what may be untypical cases. The emphasis on 'stranger danger' is misplaced for two reasons: first, because most victims know their attacker and second, because they are not 'strange' – they are very 'normal' people.

Most sexual offences are committed by men on women and girls but we must not forget that men and boys can be victims and that a small percentage of abusers are women – estimates are between 5 and 20 per cent (Hetherton 1999). Female sexual abuse of children is almost certainly underreported but at the same time is extremely difficult to define since mothers are socially permitted to be far more intimate with their children than are men (Welldon 1988; Motz 2001). There is very little research in this area, though some of the earliest work was done in Styal prison (Barnett, Corder and Jehu 1990). The limited research that is available suggests that some women offenders are coerced into abuse by male accomplices or that the women themselves have been abused as children by men (Welldon 1996). The debate about the extent of sexual abuse by women has been characterized by what Forbes (1992) has called 'the search for equivalence'. Forbes argues that the 'discovery' of female sexual abusers represents a reassertion of a 'gender-free' analysis of child sexual abuse, which deflects attention from the centrality of male oppression in physical and sexual abuse. The creation of a moral panic about women's participation and collusion in sexual abuse is just one more example of the ways in which women are blamed for the behaviour of men (Worrall 2002a). Even when absent from the scene of the crime and doing no more than misguidedly providing an alibi, as in the case of Maxine Carr (who perverted the course of justice in an attempt to protect Ian Huntley, who murdered Holly Wells and Jessica Chapman in Soham in 2002), the vilification of women associated in any way with sexual offending is disproportionate because of its perceived 'unnaturalness'. Motz's (2001) argument that we do women a disservice by denying their agency or volition to commit violent and sexual crimes is comfortably appropriated by a populist punitiveness that is every bit as visceral in reaction to Maxine Carr as it was in reaction to Myra Hindley and Rosemary West.

Images of sex offenders

Attitudes towards sex offenders are highly ambivalent. When a 13-year-old 'rape beast' was found to be too young to be sent to custody because of a legal loophole (closed by the 1994 Criminal Justice and Public Order Act), the newspapers were outraged, despite the less-than-convincing circumstances surrounding the conviction (*Daily Star*, 12 November 1994). The fact that the boy was 'half-caste' and 'lives with his mother' (*Today*, 12 November 1994) undoubtedly fuelled the hyperbole about sons of the underclass. By comparison, Austen Donnellan, a 21-year-old university student, who might be expected to know better, received nothing but sympathy and support from the papers when he was acquitted of rape. Date rape is, after all, a phenomenon which threatens us all – men and women – because it challenges the games and rituals we all use in our relationships with the opposite sex. It makes us realize how vulnerable we all are and how easy it is to misread signs and to make mistakes. But the particular issue which infuriated the papers in this case was the anonymity rule which allowed the alleged victim – but not the alleged perpetrator – to remain unnamed. 'Shouldn't she now be named?' screamed the *Daily Mail* (20 October 1993) in a bid to punish the woman who, as a consequence of the acquittal became retrospectively constructed as a false accuser. Similar indignation accompanied the acquittals in 1995 of Michael Seear, a policeman, Craig Charles, a well-known television actor and, more recently, John Leslie, a television presenter.

The same analysis can be applied to notorious child sexual abuse cases. Myths about peculiar practices on remote islands underpinned the press reporting of the Orkney case, but 'ordinary blokes' were falsely accused by an obsessive and irrational female doctor in Cleveland (Campbell 1988). In both cases, ultimately, the rights of children to protection (but from whom? their parents or the system?) were sacrificed to the fears of adults (Asquith 1993). Feelings of disgust and revulsion are mixed with the terror of the false accusation. Sex offenders have to be seen as 'not like us' – as monsters, beasts, perverts – definitely not 'ordinary blokes'.

The construction of the monster is also influenced by racism. Just under half of all adult male sex offenders are convicted of rape (as opposed to child sex abuse) but that figure masks a more alarming statistical comparison. Just over one-third of white sex offenders are rapists, while 80 per cent of black sex offenders are convicted of rape. The myth of the black rapist serves not only to sustain and legitimize racial oppression but also to hinder the theorizing of rape. On the one hand, reliance on official statistics suggests that rape is dis-proportionately committed by black men. On the other, working with black sex offenders in a way which is confrontative but not oppressive presents a dilemma for probation officers (Cowburn and Modi 1995). Challenging a black sex offender's denial of guilt exposes a worker to accusations of racism and there is very little research or guidance available on working specifically with sex offenders from minority ethnic groups.

What happens to those convicted?

Nearly two-thirds of all sex offenders go immediately to prison, with the highest custody rate being 99 per cent for offenders found guilty by jury (as opposed to pleading guilty) in the Crown Court for offences of rape (Home Office 2003c). Traditionally, sex offenders or 'nonces' are the lowest form of life in prison and are placed on Rule 45 or in segregation for their own protection (Thomas 2000). More recently, with increased numbers, special units called Vulnerable Prisoner Units have developed to allow a more constructive and humane regime away from other prisoners. Grendon Underwood Prison was traditionally the only prison actively to 'treat' sex offenders: the regime is based very much on the lines of a therapeutic community with a psycho-therapeutic approach (Genders and Player 1995). Specialist units in Whitemoor and Frankland prisons have been opened in 2003/4 to provide high security therapeutic intervention for Dangerous Severely Personality Disordered offenders (DSPD) under the joint initiative between the Department of Health, Home Office and Prison Service (www.dspdprogramme.gov.uk).

An alternative, which was used in the 1960s and more in America than Britain, was behavioural therapy that attempted in a direct and physical way to force offenders to unlearn deviant behaviour, through aversion therapy, covert sensitization and masturbatory re-conditioning. In Britain, the use of the penile plethysmograph (PPG) to monitor an offender's physical response to sexual stimuli was described by the Prison Reform Trust as 'a degrading breach of human rights' (Thomas 2000: 91). Apart from prompting the kind of ethical objections highlighted by the book and film *A Clockwork Orange* (Burgess 1962), the other concern about such techniques was their inability to address the motivation that activated and sustained sex offenders or to provide offenders with any insight into their behaviour (Barker 1995).

In recent years, however, a cognitive behavioural approach has become widespread both inside prisons and among probation officers who run treatment groups for sex offenders – either for those not sent to prison or those released from it. The basis of this work is to challenge offenders' distorted thoughts and reasoning in relation to their victims and to help them manage their impulses by providing alternative courses of action which they view as being more rewarding. The work is based on the belief that, in order to commit a sexual offence, the offender has to overcome both internal and external inhibitions as well as the victim's resistance. He therefore has to convince himself that he is doing no harm (or that the victim deserves it) or release his inhibitions through drink or drugs. He has to manipulate the environment to make the offence possible and he has to groom the victim in order to reduce his or her resistance. All this takes careful planning, hence the refusal by workers to accept the claim that the offence was committed on impulse. It is assumed that offenders have committed several offences before they are caught and that any denial is lying. The offender is not allowed to deny either the facts or the impact of his offending. Every attempt to justify or excuse his offence is challenged. He is not allowed to blame his victim in any way. Instead he is put deliberately under pressure to discuss the offence in detail and admit that it was a matter of choice – that other choices were possible. A well-established routine is followed, whereby the offender is helped to unlearn and relearn appropriate sexual behaviour by considering in detail the antecedents of the offence, the behaviour engaged in and the consequences for himself and the victim. The Sex Offender Treatment Programme (SOTP) is now an accredited programme, run in around 25 prisons in England and Wales as well as in the community. It comes in several versions – 'core' (standard), 'booster' (refresher), 'adapted' (for prisoners with learning disabilities), 'extended' (advanced) and 'rolling' (for lower risk offenders). There is also a programme designed for convicted offenders who deny their guilt.

The early evidence was that such programmes are effective to the extent that recidivism rates appear to be reduced among those treated as compared to those untreated or treated in other sorts of programmes (Barker 1995; Hedderman and Sugg 1996; Beech et al. 1998). It is necessary, however, to select offenders carefully. Child abusers appear to respond better than rapists, perhaps because the latter find it harder to accept full responsibility for their actions in our 'rape-supportive culture' (Burt 1980 cited in Gocke 1995). Longer programmes are, perhaps predictably, more effective than short ones and programmes which teach offenders techniques which they can utilize themselves, especially to prevent relapse, are also successful. Finally, the quality and management of the staff involved is crucial to the effectiveness of the programme. As Gocke, among many others, has pointed out, working with sex offenders is often a stressful and stigmatized activity in itself:

> For periods of time I operate apparently untouched by the horror and despair of the details of the offending and how it relates to my own male attitudes and values, concentrating instead on the process of intervention. However, at fairly regular intervals this is pierced by an issue or an instance which brings out the sheer awfulness of the situation, leaving me upset, angry, depressed and self-doubting.
>
> (Gocke 1995: 177)

Workers less sensitive and reflective (and qualified) than Gocke may not manage their personal feelings so well. Waite (1994) is scathing about the poor training given to prison and prison probation officers in preparation for becoming tutors on the Sex Offender Treatment Programmes in prisons. The way in which the treatment is conducted may amount to little more than 'legitimized nonce-bashing' (Sheath 1990). It may be a legitimate way for prison officers, psychologists and probation officers to 'have a go' at sex offenders by verbally humiliating them. This, in turn, may be counter-productive because it puts offenders on the defensive and they learn to give the required responses without genuinely exploring their feelings and problems.

Contrary to popular belief, reconviction rates for sex offenders are low, whether or not they have received treatment – less than 5 per cent within two years (Friendship et al. 2003). This is particularly true for intra-familial offences against children, where the risk of reconviction is routinely over-estimated by the Parole Board when considering such offenders for early release from prison (Hood et al. 2002). Against this background, later evaluations of the SOTP present a more complex picture than earlier studies (Falshaw et al. 2003; Friendship et al. 2003). The impact of treatment on reconviction for sexual offences within two years is not statistically significant. However, if reconvictions for offences of violence are included (and many of the more serious sex offenders also have convictions for violence), then treatment seems to have a more significant impact. Notwithstanding this mildly positive message, it is now suggested (Falshaw *et al.* 2003) that reconvictions are a particularly unreliable measure of relapse into sex offending. In line with the orthodoxy that sex offenders commit many more offences than are officially recorded against them, Falshaw's study suggests that self-reported recidivism among sex offenders is five times higher than their reconviction rate.

'Dangerization' and public protection

Despite our knowledge that sex offending is widespread and under-reported, official discourse constructs sex offenders in a very specific way, on the basis of those who are convicted in the courts. Such an offender typically has a history of (often undetected) minor sex offending which escalates to the more serious. Once established, that pattern of offending persists for years unless checked. The offending is rarely impulsive and involves planning and the manipulation of people. The offender is skilled at denying the seriousness of his offence and at manipulating others into colluding with his denial (Home Office 1996a). Any other attempt to describe or account for the life and behaviour of the offender is constructed as Other and excluded from legitimated discourse. Anyone who challenges this construction risks being accused of collusion, unless the alleged perpetrator is black, in which case it is acknowledged that there may be a lack of fit between anti-racist values and the values underpinning work with sex offenders (Cowburn and Modi 1995).

The debate on working with sex offenders in the community has been virtually foreclosed. The field of intervention has been exploited to its maximum but, despite cautious optimism about risk assessment and treatment programmes, official government discourse now rejects the language of rehabilitation in favour of the language of surveillance and control through information. To this extent, the sex offender constitutes an example of the shift in penal thinking from the 'old penology' to the 'new penology' (Simon 1998; Nash 1999). But the situation is more complex than this. As Simon argues, policies towards sex offenders are not based only on actuarial risk assessment but are overlaid with an accommodation of populist punitiveness that discredits and disregards any 'objective' risk assessment that does not accord with 'common sense' perceptions of danger. Lianos and Douglas (2002) have created the term 'dangerization' to describe this process:

Dangerization is the tendency to perceive and analyse the world through categories of menace. It leads to continuous detection of threats and assessment of adverse probabilities, to the prevalence of defensive perceptions over optimistic ones and to the dominance of fear and anxiety over ambition and desire.

(2002: 110–111)

Dangerization demands that institutions (such as the criminal justice system) exercise ever greater control over social organization and render it increasingly predictable and 'safe'. People, it is argued, no longer trust their own assessments of other people (either because they fear being accused of being discriminatory or because they have simply lost the ability and desire to process complex social information) and they have no faith in experts to make such assessments either. Instead, they demand social environments that are controlled but non-judgemental, where they can avoid negotiating with those whose behaviour they find unacceptable without feeling guilty about it (Lianos and Douglas 2002). In short, as many criminologists have pointed out, the search for causes and remedies has given way to the identification of risk and mechanisms for reducing or avoiding it (Metcalf and Stenson 2004).

While the language of risk and dangerousness may give the appearance of eliminating judgements based on discrimination, the process of dangerization does no more than *mask* prejudice and social division. As Kemshall and Maguire argue, those living in the deprived areas where sex offenders tend to resettle may

feel that they are bearing a grossly unequal share of the risk … that they have no say in these decisions … that the consequences of an offence against their children would be dire … and that there is no conceivable benefit to themselves in accepting this burden of risk.

(2003: 113)

The probation service has no alternative discourse with which to challenge *dangerization* because, at a general level, it has been powerless to resist what Metcalf and Stenson (2004: 9) call 'government Esperanto' and, specifically, it has itself accepted the official construction of the sex offender. It has sacrificed its better judgement about why people offend and what makes them stop, based on decades of accumulated wisdom, but has found that it no longer matters (to the public, the media or the government) whether or not it delivers in terms of reducing risk and preventing reoffending. As Thomas and Tuddenham suggest, probation officers find it increasingly difficult on a daily basis to build the 'social capital' needed to reintegrate sex offenders into the community and 'maintain hope with this extremely socially excluded offender group' (2001: 16). The sex offender has been constructed as morally, socially and politically irredeemable. It is no longer his crimes that are unacceptable; he himself is unacceptable as a member of the community. He is forever non-reintegratable.

Chapter 10

Unacceptable crimes or unacceptable criminals? Juvenile and youth justice

Introduction

The development of the 'growing out of crime' or 'systems management' approach to juvenile justice during the 1980s has been generally acknowledged to have been a penal success story. Traditional tensions between 'justice' and 'welfare' models lessened as a multi-agency approach attempted to combine the best of both worlds in order to reduce the numbers of young offenders being imprisoned at the same time as resisting net-widening among pre-delinquent youngsters. But the myth of the 'hard core' of dangerous and/or persistent young offenders was tenacious and the murder of James Bulger 'proved' that the 'stunted little man' – the prematurely worldly wise artful dodger identified by Matthew Davenport Hill in 1855 and cited in Pearson (1983) – was still dangerously alive and well in the 1990s. By the end of the century, the New Labour government was demanding that 'no more excuses' be made for young offenders and the Crime and Disorder Act 1998 was described by some as 'the biggest shake up for 50 years in tackling crime' (Muncie 2000: 14). This chapter will explore just how different the treatment of young offenders is at the start of the twenty-first century and how much continuity remains with past attitudes.

In his book *Hooligan: a History of Respectable Fears*, Pearson (1983) traces back, generation by generation, the fears that respectable middle- and upper-class people have had about the dangerousness of young people. The middle-aged and old are always bemoaning the behaviour of the young and harking back to a golden age – about 30 years ago – which, of course, never existed. Pearson shows how public fears have always been fuelled by the media and how the stereotyped explanations of juvenile crime have been remarkably similar throughout the generations.

Such explanations always start with a typification of the 'British' (or should it be English?) way of life as one of natural domestic peace. Disorder, it is argued, is alien to English life and can only be explained by foreign influence. Every generation has had its own particular form of racism whereby it has blamed youthful disorder on (currently) black people and previously, Americans (during and after the Second World War), Irish people (the original hooligans of the early twentieth century), Mediterranean people (the mid-Victorian garrotters) and Arabs (as in 'street arabs').

Additionally, youth crime is then attributed to any combination of the following:

- lack of authority in the home (weak fathers)
- lack of affection in the home (working mothers)
- lack of discipline and moral teaching in school
- popular entertainment (ranging from street festivals and the theatre to football and television)
- unbridled freedom and luxury (as a result of the perceived increasing affluence of every younger generation)

And all this is mirrored and reinforced by a system of law and justice which is too lenient.

It is against this backcloth of constant public fear about the uncontrolled independence of youth – and the reality that something like 40 per cent of all crime is committed by people under the age of 21 years (Muncie 1999) – that the development of the juvenile, and latterly youth, justice system in England has to be seen.

Three questions underlie all debates about youth crime. First, how far can young people be held responsible for their criminal actions? Second, in a civilized society, how far should the welfare of a young person take precedence over the requirement to punish? Third, how can we prevent this troublesome youth from growing into a dangerous adult? In attempting to answer these questions, the history of juvenile and youth justice has been one of a pendulum swinging between neo-classical ('justice') arguments and positivist ('welfare') arguments.

The history of juvenile justice

Until the middle of the nineteenth century both adults and children were subject to the same laws and penalties, including prison, hanging and flogging. It is true that, in law, children under 14 were presumed to be incapable of committing a crime (*doli incapax*) but for children over seven it was possible and usual to rebut that principle so that children as young as that could be, and were, hanged for trivial offences.

In the early and mid-nineteenth century there was increasing concern about the crime and disorder supposedly resulting from the industrialization and urbanization of a rising (and therefore predominantly young) population (Gillis 1974). Early capitalism favoured young people because it increased their earning power. But it also separated them from their homes and families, making them independent, affluent and undisciplined. To this was added a fear of the growing socialism and social protest in Europe (the Chartist movement in England). The mixture was seen as lethal.

Official discourse began to categorize the vulnerable poor as belonging to either the dangerous or the perishing classes – the former being actively dishonest and disobedient, the latter being feckless and susceptible to contamination by the former. The distinction is an important one because it has persisted throughout the history of juvenile justice in various forms: namely, the depraved and the deprived, the delinquent and the neglected, the child in need of care or protection and the child in need of control. (For further articles on the history of juvenile justice, see Muncie *et al.*'s excellent reader (2002).)

Saving some children

The treatment of juvenile offenders in the nineteenth century provides a case study of the development of criminological thought from classical theory, through neo-classical theory to positivism. Reducing harsh penalties on the young and improving the living conditions of the poor were compatible with neo-classical thought but the development of the *reformatory movement* and later the *child-saving movement* falls squarely into the terrain of positivism.

It was recognized that the appalling conditions of child labour and the breaking of family ties had contributed much to a premature ageing of children and that they needed to be rescued, separated and protected. Thus adolescence was discovered, or created.

The delinquent is a little stunted man already – he knows much and a great deal too much of what is called life – he can take care of his own immediate interests. He is self-reliant, he has so long directed or misdirected his own actions and has so little trust in those about him, that he submits to no control and asks for no protection. He has consequently much to unlearn – he has to be turned again into a child.

(Matthew Davenport Hill, 1855, 'Practical Suggestions to the Founders of Reformatory Schools' cited in Pearson 1983: 167)

The model for the reformatory movement was that of the public school and with it a middle-class ideology of childhood and adolescence which involved parents – or parental substitutes – in responsibility for and supervision of the activities of their children. Under the banner of democracy and classlessness the lifestyle and ideology of the middle classes was imposed on the 'honest working classes' as the norm. Those working-class parents who could not or would not supervise their children were required to give them up to the state. Delinquent children were sent to reformatory school while vagrant, begging or neglected children were sent to industrial schools. The reformatory system was based on the assumption that proper training can counteract the impositions of poor family life, a corrupt environment and poverty, while also toughening and preparing delinquents for the struggle ahead.

By the end of the nineteenth century, the reformatory movement had given way to what has been called the *child-saving* movement (which started in America but had its equivalents in this country) (Platt 1969). It was dominated by middle-class women advocating what have been termed 'maternal values' and seeking to re-establish the virtues of the home at a time when industrialization threatened this. The most important feature which distinguished this from earlier reforming movements was the increasing focus on *the whole child* and on *all children*. Significantly, the distinction between reformatory and industrial schools lapsed and children in trouble were consolidated into a single conceptual category: the depraved and the deprived were one and the same. 'Couched in the language of welfare and supported by an army of professionals, attention was continually diverted from what children *do* to what children *are*' (Morris *et al*. 1980). Adolescence became an object of scientific observation and clinical treatment. What began as an attempt to protect adolescents against the decadent world of adults ended in imposing a new conformity sanctioned by positivist social science and separating them from their civil and social rights.

Regulating all children

The assumption now underlying work with young people was that all children were potential delinquents. Crime appeared to be rising but much of that was because of the extension of the criminalization process. More and more borderline anti-social behaviour (such as gambling, loitering, begging, dangerous play, malicious mischief and 'care and protection' situations) was being brought before the courts. 'Every boy and girl ... had in them a bit of the street arab' (Gillis 1974: 174). Crime was no longer a matter of free will or moral voluntarism. Rather it was a matter of psychological determinism. So punishment had to be replaced by prevention and control – and the earlier the better. Signs of criminality could be picked up early enough but this required constant vigilance. So it was no longer only a matter of separating out and institutionalizing certain children, but rather of regulating all youthful activity, either indirectly through the parental authority of good parents assisted by the school and organized gender-appropriate youth clubs (like Scouts and Guides) or directly through the state's professional mothers – who later became social workers!

In the early twentieth century, the welfare approach to juvenile justice was predominant. Following the Gladstone Committee in 1895, an indeterminate, rehabilitative sentence of borstal was introduced in 1900 and a separate juvenile court was established in 1908. The Juvenile Court dealt with both deprived and depraved children and this philosophy was reinforced in the 1933 Children and Young Persons Act which stated that the welfare of the child must be the prime consideration. Magistrates in Juvenile Courts were required to have special interest in children and restrictions were introduced on reporting cases. The terms 'conviction' and 'sentence' were removed.

The turning tide

The Children and Young Persons Act 1969 was the culmination of the conflict between 'welfare' and 'justice' models of juvenile justice. It attempted to decriminalize and depoliticize juvenile justice. The philosophy of treatment was intended to remove the stigma of criminal proceedings from young offenders. The distinction between the delinquent and non-delinquent child in trouble was blurred and the most appropriate people to deal with both were the trained experts – the social workers. And that meant predominantly local authority Social Service departments rather than the probation service.

But the political tide had already turned and the Act was about five years too late. It was never fully implemented or resourced and the 1970s saw youth crime once again becoming a moral panic and being repoliticized. Cautioning increased as did preventive intermediate treatment schemes but so did custodial sentences, as more and more young people were drawn into the system and, as we saw in Chapter 5, magistrates refused to entrust them to the care of social workers.

As we saw in Chapter 2, during the 1970s, the optimism of the welfare or rehabilitative model, which was dependent on economic and social confidence, came under attack from a number of directions and this had particular implications for work with young offenders. The political right turned the economic recession into a moral crisis and those working with young offenders were increasingly required to demonstrate their ability to control rather than to help them. At the same time the political left accused social workers of unwarranted intrusion into the lives and liberties of young people. Social inquiry reports were seen as unsubstantiated character assassinations that labelled and stigmatized young offenders, making it more likely that they would adopt a deviant identity. Social workers themselves, especially juvenile justice workers, were seen as irresponsible and dangerous empire builders, likely to do more harm than good. Magistrates and lawyers began to argue that 'due process' and common sense offered greater protection to young offenders than did social workers. And all this was set against a background of damning research studies that appeared to show that 'nothing works' and that rehabilitation is unattainable through any formal intervention (Pitts 1990).

But the 1982 Criminal Justice Act was not entirely a backlash. Although it rationalized and strengthened youth custody provision and introduced the 'short, sharp shock' (three weeks to four months of a regimented regime in a detention centre) it also had to avoid overcrowding in prisons. So it invested a lot of money in intermediate treatment and diversion schemes as alternatives to custody. Consequently, the government attempted to deal with the welfare/justice conflict with a policy of 'bifurcation', making a distinction between the hard core, persistent minority of offenders and the majority who were a tolerable nuisance.

The successful decade

The key turning point came in 1983 when the Department of Health and Social Security issued a circular to local authority Social Service departments known as the LAC 83(3) Initiative which did three things. First, it moved intermediate treatment away from preventive provision to alternatives to care and custody, moving it up-tariff. Second, it established inter-agency liaison in intermediate treatment provision later to be known as 'partnership'. Third, it provided special finances to pump-prime new projects for three years (Nellis 1991).

Social work intervention began to be reserved for those already showing signs of being persistent offenders. Juvenile justice workers used their skills to persuade key decision-makers such as the police and magistrates to intervene as little as possible and impose the minimum possible sentence on young offenders. A feature of this attempt to manage the system was 'gatekeeping', or the monitoring of decisions and developing strategies and tactics to influence decisions. To do this, social workers had to offer an 'alternative tariff' of sentences which were seen to be as challenging as custody but less damaging and less expensive. Examples were 'tracking' or intensive surveillance and the use of the 'correctional curriculum'. The latter, based on theories of human motivation, comprised a set of techniques to enable the offender to identify the moments in the behavioural sequence that culminated in the delinquent act, when they might have acted differently. Role-play, cartooning and video feedback encouraged the offender to identify key triggers to offending. The programme then desensitized the offender to those stimuli and taught alternative non-criminal responses. It was not necessary in either tracking or the correctional curriculum to understand or help the young person – their welfare was not a central concern, but their offending behaviour was.

The emphasis in New Right politics was on the responsibility of the individual; woolly-minded work with groups and communities was no longer acceptable. Social and environmental problems were irrelevant; what mattered was individual behaviour. Behaviourism offered the possibility of a time-limited, highly focused intervention, which addressed behaviour which those with the power and authority to penalize wanted to change. It could be quantified and measured and justified to a court.

Facts and figures

So what happened to juvenile crime in the 1980s and what has happened since? Contrary to popular impression, the 1980s and early 1990s saw a sharp fall in the number of young offenders (those aged 10 to 17 years) known to be committing crime. The number of young offenders found guilty or cautioned for indictable offences declined by 34 per cent between 1984 and 1994, from 206,800 to 135,800 (NACRO 1996). That decline far outstripped the 16 per cent fall in the number of young people under 18 years of age in the general population and was largely consistent across age and gender. Overall, the proportion of crime known to be committed by young offenders declined from 36 per cent in 1984 to 26 per cent in 1994. The proportion declined further to 23 per cent by 2002 (Home Office 2003c).

Most of the crime committed by young offenders is not particularly serious. In 1994 sexual offences and robbery each accounted for only 1–2 per cent of cautions or convictions for males, with another 11–12 per cent being for crimes of violence. Of the remaining 86–87 per cent the vast majority related to property, more than half being for offences of theft and handling stolen goods. For females, about three-quarters of all offences were theft and handling. Violence accounted for a similar proportion to that for males but robbery and sexual offences were virtually non-existent (NACRO 1996).

Cautioning increased significantly in the 1980s: in 1979, 50 per cent of all juveniles were cautioned. By 1990 it was 75 per cent for males and 89 per cent for females. This varied with age (higher when younger) and geographical area (for example, 85 per cent in Surrey to 44 per cent in Durham). By 1995 the proportions had fallen slightly, especially after Home Office circular 18/1994, which restricted its use. Nevertheless, Home Office research showed that 85 per cent of offenders cautioned did not reoffend. Nor was there much evidence to suggest that large numbers were being repeatedly cautioned (Home Office Statistical Bulletin 16/1996). Under the Crime and Disorder Act 1998, cautions for young offenders under 18 were replaced by reprimands and final warnings, although statistics still refer to the 'cautioning rate'. By 2002, the cautioning rate for this group had fallen to 49 per cent for males and 71 per cent for females (Home Office 2003c).

The reduction in the cautioning rate has resulted in proportionately more juveniles being sent to court but by 2002, one fifth of them – those who pleaded guilty on their first court appearance – were made subject to a new sentence, the Referral Order, introduced by the Youth Justice and Criminal Evidence Act 1999 (Home Office 2003c). This means that they are referred to a panel of community volunteers attended also by parents and members of Youth Offending Teams (discussed more fully later), that negotiates a contract with them covering reparation and steps to tackle their offending behaviour. If a contract is agreed and carried out, no conviction is recorded; if not, the juvenile returns to court for an alternative sentence.

Custodial sentences fell dramatically from a peak of 12,000 in 1984 to 3,600 in 1994 (the figures for girls fluctuated between 50 and 100). The White Paper *Crime, Justice and Protecting the Public* argued that 'there is no evidence that the reduction in the use of custodial sentences has resulted in increases in juvenile crime' (Home Office 1990a: 45). It even questioned 'whether it is necessary to keep the sentence of detention in a young offender institution for girls under 18' (1990a: 45). By 2002, the picture was very different with 5,700 males and 500 females sentenced to immediate custody (Home Office 2003c), though a year later, the Youth Justice Board (2003) was claiming a significant reduction again as a result of the introduction of Intensive Supervision and Surveillance Programmes for juveniles (discussed below).

As we saw in Chapter 3, the replacing of the Juvenile Court by the Youth Court in the early 1990s was an attempt to reflect the age balance of young offenders brought to court, which was overwhelmingly in the 14 to 17 age group, while younger offenders were being successfully diverted from prosecution. At the same time, however, courts were given the 'flexibility' to impose adult sentences on 16- and 17-year-olds. In other words, the boundaries between youth and adulthood were being blurred, ostensibly to reflect the differing rates of development among adolescents.

A return to Victorian values

Such blurring both reflected and reinforced a perceived desire of public opinion to treat young criminals less and less differently from their adult counterparts. In this, a return to early Victorian values can be detected. Two emergent moral panics of the early 1990s were joined by a third, more recent, folk devil. 'Rat Boy', the elusive persistent offender who laughed at the system, was soon accompanied by the more awful spectre of 'Child Killer' and then both were joined by 'Tank Girl', the new breed of 'feminist' girl criminal.

The 'growing out of crime' school (Rutherford 1986) taught us that many young people experiment with offending but most desist as they mature. A smaller group persists to become young adult criminals and an even smaller group commits one very serious offence. By conflating these three distinct groups, the myth is now being created that increasing numbers of youths are persistently committing increasing amounts of very serious crime – and increasing numbers of them are girls! We will now examine these three stereotypically constructed juvenile delinquents in more detail.

The persistent young offender

From 1991 onwards, there was increasing concern that a small number of children were committing a disproportionate amount of not-so-trivial crime, especially burglary and criminal damage. Because of their age, they could not be given custodial sentences and the option of being taken into care under section 7(7) of the 1969 Children and Young Persons Act had been abolished by the 1989 Children Act. Thus was born the myth of the wild child beyond the control of any authority. Earl Ferrers gave examples to the House of Lords:

> There are reports of a 14-year-old from Tyneside who has 28 convictions and who has escaped 22 times from local authority accommodation. Another 14-year-old boy in south London has admitted taking part in more than 1000 burglaries of shops and homes in the past two years ... He has been arrested 40 times but is too young to be given a custodial sentence for the crimes he has committed. That is pretty hot stuff.
>
> (cited in Morton 1994: 2)

In response, in 1992 Michael Howard announced his intention to introduce secure training centres for 12 to 14-year-old persistent offenders who were unable or unwilling to respond to supervision in the community. His definition of 'persistent' was the commission of three or more imprisonable offences, one of which must have been committed while under supervision, and the offence under current consideration must be serious enough to warrant a secure training order. In fact, although such children undoubtedly existed, their numbers were far fewer than the government and the media would have the public believe (Hagell and Newburn 1994). Despite this, and despite the very strong professional opposition to his proposals for 'prep schools of crime' (Morton 1994), the Home Secretary proceeded to include this provision in the 1994 Criminal Justice and Public Order Act. The first secure training centre opened its doors in 1998 at Medway and there are now three STCs, run by private operators according to Home Office contracts. Secure Training Orders, however, were replaced by Detention and Training Orders under the Crime and Disorder Act 1998 and STCs are now one of three differently run custodial provisions for persistent and serious juvenile offenders, the others being local authority secure children's homes and Young Offender Institutions. Since 2000, the Youth Justice Board has had overall responsibility for the custodial placement of all such juveniles.

In an attempt to reduce the numbers of persistent young offenders being sent to custody, the Youth Justice Board introduced Intensive Supervision and Surveillance Programmes (ISSP) in 2001, initially funding 41 schemes covering 84 Youth Offending Teams in England and Wales at an annual cost of £15 million and with a target number of 2,500 starts a year (by December 2003 there had been 7,465 starts). In 2002 the Street Crime Initiative provided a further £6.5 million a year, which allowed the Board to fund a further ten schemes covering 34 additional Youth Offending Teams (Youth Justice Board 2003). From 2004, they are available to all sentencers in England and Wales. ISSP aims to achieve a 5 per cent reduction in frequency and seriousness of offending and an evaluation has been undertaken by Oxford University (Merrington and Stanley 2004; see also Moore 2004 for a discussion of the evidence base in relation to successful intensive projects for young offenders).

Intensive Supervision and Surveillance Programmes (ISSP) for young offenders share all the key characteristics of Intensive Supervision and Monitoring Projects for adult offenders (see Chapter 8), although the delivery is by Youth Offending Teams that are already multi-agency in nature and there is a greater emphasis on the reintegration of participants into mainstream educational provision. There is also a greater focus on cognitive skills groupwork. The structure of ISSP is, if anything, even more demanding of participants, with initial requirements of 25 hours supervision per week and twice-daily surveillance checks, often involving electronic monitoring. The Audit Commission (2004) report on youth justice warns of the potential difficulties arising from multiple requirements within ISSPs that may prove too demanding for some young people. As with adult offenders, young offenders may be selected for participation in ISSP either as an alternative to custody or as a condition of a Detention and Training Order (DTO) following release from the custodial portion of the order. The official definition of a 'persistent young offender' is now a young person aged 10–17 years inclusive who has been sentenced by any criminal court in the UK on three or more separate occasions and reoffends within three years of the last sentencing occasion. This very broad definition runs the risk of net-widening and labelling children as 'persistent' when they are not (Monaghan 2000).

The University of Oxford Centre for Criminological Studies' evaluation of ISSP was conducted over three years. Initial data suggested that the programmes are targeting persistent young offenders with serious educational and substance misuse problems. The main challenges appear to be finding suitable accommodation and substance misuse treatment for the young people on the programmes and securing reintegration into education. In line with evaluations on similar programmes for adults (Worrall *et al.* 2003; Worrall and Mawby 2004), the study found positive changes, including reductions in reoffending, while the participants were on the programmes. Longer term reoffending rates were disappointing, although those who completed the programmes were less likely (76 per cent) to reoffend after a year than those who did not complete (85 per cent) (Youth Justice Board 2004a).

While England and Wales have seen significant changes in the treatment of young offenders, Scotland retains its unique system of Children's Hearings, where the welfare of the child remains the paramount concern in decisions about children 'in trouble' under the age of 16 years. Nevertheless, in the mid 1990s, two intensive supervision (though, notably, not explicit surveillance) projects were set up by the Scottish Office – Cue Ten and Freagarrach. Evaluations of both projects (Lobley and Smith 1999; Lobley, Smith and Stern 2001) drew conclusions that were similar to evaluations of adult projects – that offenders responded with reduced reoffending at least in the short term but that the projects were resource-intensive and could be challenged in terms of cost-effectiveness. A broader discussion about developments in Scotland concerning persistent young offenders can be found in recent work by McNeill and Batchelor (2002; 2004). They emphasise the dangers of attempting to separate 'analyses of, and responses to, youth crime from analyses of, and responses to, social exclusion' (2002: 40).

Child killers

There has always been an equivalent to a life sentence for juveniles who commit extremely serious offences such as murder, manslaughter and rape. The provision was to be found in section 53 of the 1933 Children and Young Persons Act which allowed courts to hold juveniles in secure accommodation 'at Her Majesty's Pleasure' and to transfer them to prison when they were old enough. (This section was repealed in 2000 and the provisions were transferred to Sections 90/92 of the Powers of Criminal Courts (Sentencing) Act 2000.) The number of young people, most of them very disturbed youngsters, who have been detained in this way for murder or manslaughter has fluctuated between 20 and 40 a year for the past 25 years and of these, only a handful in the whole 25 years have been under 14 years of age (Boswell 1996; Cavadino 1996; Home Office 2003c).

What, then, was so very different about Jon Venables and Robert Thompson? Was it the fact that so many adults saw them dragging James Bulger to his death and did nothing? Was it the blurred images on the closed circuit TV? Was it the perceived influence of video nasties? Was it just the fact that they were the youngest children to have been convicted of murder? Something about this offence was uniquely postmodern and challenging to our claim to be a civilized society. The veneer of morality seemed to be so easily and publicly stripped away and, despite all the technology, we were still unable to protect a vulnerable toddler from the violence of boys only a few years older than him (Hay 1995). Ever since William Golding's (1960) *Lord of the Flies*, we have had to confront our own knowledge of the depths of depravity that unsupervised boys are capable of, yet the only way in which we seemed able to cope with James Bulger's murder was to pretend that Venables and Thompson had committed an *adult* offence and should therefore be treated like adults, subjected to the full weight of adult sentencing. 'Freaks of Nature' (*Daily Mirror*, 25 November 1993) and 'Evil, Brutal and Cunning' (*Daily Mail*, 25 November 1993) were just two of the screaming headlines that greeted the convictions for murder. The *Sun* asked its readers to fill in a coupon demanding that the Home Secretary increase the boys' sentence tariff (the minimum time they should spend in prison to satisfy the requirements of retribution and deterrence before the authorities consider their rehabilitation) from the eight years set by the trial judge and the subsequent 10 years set by the Lord Chief Justice. The Home Secretary obliged and set the tariff at 15 years. In 1996 the High Court ruled that this decision was unlawful. The Home Secretary had the right to intervene in setting tariffs for adults but not for children. Children who kill must have their cases regularly reviewed as their personalities develop and mature – something which is inconsistent with a 15-year minimum sentence. In 1999, the European Court of Human Rights at Strasbourg ruled that Venables and Thompson had not received a fair trial – that they should not have been tried in public in an adult court with press coverage, that the Home Secretary should not have set the tariff and that their cases should have been judicially reviewed regularly, which they were not (*Guardian*, 16 December 1999). The boys were eventually released with new identities in June 2001.

As a result of the James Bulger case, the vexing issue of the age of criminal responsibility was reopened. The four-year zone between 10 and 14 years, when the onus is on the prosecution to produce evidence that a child *knew* that they had committed a serious wrong, was swept away by a High Court ruling in March 1994. Although reinstated by the

Law Lords a year later (Penal Affairs Consortium 1995), it was finally abolished by the Crime and Disorder Act 1998 (see Bandalli 2000 for an examination of the increasing 'responsibilization' of younger and younger children).

Tank Girl: the trouble with young women

Crime is overwhelmingly a masculine activity and the history of juvenile justice and youth social work has been the history of interest in white, working-class young men by white, working- and middle-class men. The underlying philosophy has been dominated by ideals of respectable masculinity. The belief that most children grow out of crime if left alone is also based on assumptions about male adolescence: assumptions that crime is an irritating but bearable extension of normal adolescent masculinity – that 'boys will be boys'. But crime is emphatically not an extension of normal adolescent femininity: it epitomizes everything which challenges our expectations of the ways in which 'nice girls' behave. As Lees (1993) points out, the predominant feature of adolescent femininity is walking the tightrope of sexual reputation, avoiding being labelled as either a 'slag' or a 'drag'. It may be true that girls, like boys, will grow out of crime, but the possible damage to their reputations and future life prospects as respectable wives and mothers may be too great to risk radical non-intervention.

In 1994 Lisa Brinkworth wrote an article in the *Sunday Times* entitled 'Sugar and spice but not at all nice'. The article claimed to have discovered 'all-girl gangs menacing the streets' and 'cocky, feminist, aggressive' superheroines targeting vulnerable women and other girls. Moreover, this 'new breed' of criminal girl apparently 'knows' that the criminal justice system is lenient on her. She 'knows' how to work the system, dressing smartly for court and playing up to the magistrates. The illustration for the article was 'Tank Girl' – an American cartoon fantasy heroine who turns the tables violently (and frequently to their surprise) on repressive and sadistic men. The reasons for this supposed upsurge in young female crime are, however, confused. On the one hand, Brinkworth argues that women's liberation has raised women's expectations but has not delivered in terms of careers and wealth. Consequently, frustration and anger lead to street violence. On the other hand, women are supposedly sick of feeling unsafe in the home and are now fighting back. (But why then are the targets so often not men but other young women?) Either way, according to Brinkworth, the responsibility for all this lies with feminism. This is what happens when you loosen the controls on women. This is what happens when adolescent girls are allowed to think themselves equal or superior to boys. It is every mother's and father's nightmare – their daughter's sexuality rampant and violent.

Brinkworth, in both this and a subsequent article (1996), was in the business of creating a third 'moral panic' alongside those of 'rat boy' and 'child killer'. At the time there was no evidence at all to support her argument other than one or two celebrated 'nasty' incidents that were only newsworthy *because* of their rarity. Feminist analyses of violence by women had revealed that the overwhelming majority of 'violent' women were themselves victims of violence. 'Battered woman syndrome' – though a highly contentious concept – was slowly being accepted by courts as, at the least, a mitigating factor in domestic violence committed by women. Campaigning groups such as 'Women in Prison' demonstrated that violent young women (such as Josie O'Dwyer – see Carlen *et al.* 1985) had been abused by individual men and by the prison system from an early age. Yet this was not the kind of 'girl violence' that Brinkworth was talking about. She was clearly on a different mission – the 'search for equivalence'. Her concern was to demonstrate that 'girls do it too'. And in so doing, she set in train a particular media 'hunt' characterized by the oft-repeated themes – younger and younger girls becoming increasingly aggressive, mushrooming girl gangs, increased use of drugs and, especially, alcohol, and the wilful abandonment of gender role expectations (Worrall 2002a; Alder and Worrall 2004).

The abandonment (for all its acknowledged shortcomings) of the traditional welfare-oriented approach to girls' delinquency, throughout the English-speaking world, has been simultaneously caused by, and reflected in, an increasingly punitive desire to criminalize and lock up the 'nasty little madams' (Worrall 1999; 2000; 2004a). Because the 'welfarization' and 'soft policing' of young women's behaviour by both formal and informal social control mechanisms has now given way to the straightforward 'criminalization' of that same behaviour, we are seeing increasing numbers of young women being incarcerated, not on spuriously benevolent welfare grounds, but on spuriously equitable 'justice' grounds.

In the actuarial language of the New Penology that now dominates criminal justice, a group which hitherto has been assessed as too small and too low-risk to warrant attention is now being re-assessed and re-categorised. No longer 'at risk' and 'in moral danger' from the damaging behaviour of men, increasing numbers of young women are being assigned to the same categories as young men ('violent girls', 'drug-abusing girls', 'girl robbers', 'girl murderers' – 'girl rapists' even) and are being subjected to the same forms of management as young men. This process of reconstructing 'troublesome young women' as 'nasty little madams' has been barely perceptible. This is partly because the theorizing of adolescent femininity and its relationship to state intervention has a complex history with many twists and turns. But it is also because, in actuarial terms, gender is one of the most certain predictors of offending. Young women present a very low risk when it comes to predicting offending. It is therefore not easy to adjust to the realization that youth (another sound predictor), class and race (less reliable predictors) may be displacing gender in the categorization and management of offending. If you are young, 'underclass' and from a minority ethnic group, these factors may now be more relevant to your risk assessment than being female.

The history of juvenile justice has been a history of the conflict between 'justice' and 'welfare' concerns and girls have tended to experience both the advantages and disadvantages of 'welfarism' to a greater extent than boys, on the grounds that they are 'at risk', 'in moral danger' and 'in need of protection'. Feminist critiques of 'welfarism' in the 1980s resulted in moves towards 'just deserts' for girls, which promised much, but delivered greater criminalization and in-carceration in the 1990s. But, as Muncie points out (2000: 29) the political agenda for the New Youth Justice is no longer based on matters of just deserts, deterrence and rehabilitation, but on the actuarial principle of risk assessment and techniques of 'identifying, classifying and managing groups sorted by levels of dangerousness'. So while common sense (and official statistics) may tell us that girls – even violent ones – are neither high-risk (in terms of the predictability of their violence) or dangerous (in terms of the harm they cause), they must nevertheless be made 'auditable'. They have to be given a risk classification and be subjected to objectives and techniques of management.

Contrary to popular belief, the number of female juveniles found guilty or formally cautioned in England and Wales has not risen overall from 1994 to 2002 (Home Office 2003c). The figures relating to girls show falls from 1,500 to 700 for 10–11 year olds; 14,700 to 9,200 for 12–14 year olds; and 16,200 to 13,400 for 15–17 year olds. What *has* changed, though, are rates of cautioning: from 100 to 94 per cent for 10–11 year olds; from 94 to 84 per cent for 12–14 year olds; and from 77 to 62 per cent for 15–17 year olds. The fall in cautioning rates has led to an increase in the numbers of girls appearing in court and being sentenced. In addition to changes in cautioning, patterns of sentencing have also changed. The Referral Order has become the most used sentenced for girls, outstripping Absolute and Conditional Discharges and Community Rehabilitation Orders.

Of most concern, however, has been the increase in the use of immediate custody, which rose from 3 to 6 per cent in the 1990s. In 1999 approximately 400 girls under the age of 18 years were sentenced to immediate custody – double the number in 1994. Serious concerns were expressed about girls being held alongside adult women in breach of the UN Convention on the Rights of the Child and about the inadequacy of the training for prison staff to deal with such vulnerable and damaged girls (Howard League 1997; Worrall 1999). With the introduction of DTOs, however, the Youth Justice Board took responsibility for the placement of all children in custody and in 1999, the government announced its intention to remove all girls under the age of 18 from prison establishments. By December 2003, 15-year-old girls were no longer placed in prison and the numbers of 16-year-olds had reduced. However, girls aged 17 years continue to be placed in prison and at the end of 2003, 91 juvenile girls were in prison (Howard League 2004). In 2004, the Youth Justice Board announced its plans to build discrete units within the Prison Service estate for all 17-year-old girls – the first to be completed early in 2005 (Youth Justice Board 2004b).

Youth justice, New Labour and 'no excuses'

The 'adultification' (Grisso and Schwartz 2000: 13) of Anglo-American juvenile or youth justice has been a key feature of criminal justice policy at the close of the twentieth century. In England and Wales, the Criminal Justice Act 1991 created the Youth Court which claimed simultaneously to take account of the maturity and stage of development of a young offender and to give 'flexibility' to courts by allowing them to treat 16 and 17-year-olds as either juveniles or adults. In practice, this reform reinforced the process of blurring the boundaries between adolescence and adulthood in the criminal courts – a process that was confirmed in the public mind by the treatment of James Bulger's killers (even though they were dealt with under different and long-standing child legislation). The Audit Commission Report (1996), *Misspent Youth*, that described the Youth Justice system as uneconomic, inefficient and ineffective, brought a managerialist perspective to an area of criminal justice that had hitherto largely escaped this kind of scrutiny. New Labour's response (Home Office 1997), however, was more ambiguous than it might at first appear. On the one hand, it made clear that the welfare of young offenders would no longer be of paramount importance and that protecting the public, punishing offences and preventing offending would be. On the other, it argued that there was no conflict between being concerned for the welfare of the young offender and wanting them to stop offending (or was this a linguistic sleight of hand reminiscent of John Patten's 'punishment' speech in 1988?). Net-widening provisions in the Crime and Disorder Act 1998 have ensured earlier intervention in the lives of 'anti-social' children (through the use of Anti-Social Behaviour Orders and Child Curfew Orders) and the abolition of *doli incapax* (the transitional period between 10 and 14 years when the onus was on the prosecution to prove that the child understood the seriousness of their action) has buttressed political determination to 'responsibilize' young offenders and their parents. Goldson (1999: 23) describes this process as 'the shrill punitive and retributive demands of a "no excuses" agenda which has severed the policy-research link'. Muncie (2000: 32) characterizes the Act as being driven by an 'all-pervasive political pragmatism'.

The 1998 Act restructured the delivery of youth justice, creating a Youth Justice Board and multi-agency Youth Offending Teams that were designed to bring together all those with expertise in dealing with young people (police, probation, social services, education and health), in order to provide an holistic (as well as accountable) approach to youth offending. The reality of the development of YOTs has been a painful process (Souhami 2003) but it would be difficult to be wholly negative about some of the work that is now being carried out in the name of the Youth Justice Board. As Crawford and Newburn argue, 'New Labour's youth justice is somewhat more tricky to characterize than some commentators would have us believe' (2003. 11). The range of legislative provision for young offenders is now so wide and varied that it is possible to identify some more enlightened practices amid the more punitive ones. Amongst these, one might cite the Youth Inclusion Programmes for 'at risk' young teenagers and the school holiday Splash schemes. After an alarming rise in the numbers of young offenders being incarcerated as a result of the Detention and Training Orders introduced in 2000, there was, by 2004, an indication of a down-turn, possibly as a result of increased use of Intensive Supervision and Surveillance Programmes (ISSPs) (Youth Justice Board 2003, 2004b).

Young offenders and restorative justice

The ascendancy of the philosophy of *restorative justice* has also been most marked in relation to young offenders. The Youth Justice and Criminal Evidence Act 1999 introduced Referral Orders and Youth Offender Panels. Referral Orders are available to juveniles on their first conviction in court if they plead guilty. They are referred to a Youth Offender Panel, consisting of one YOT member and at least two lay community panel members. They may also be attended by the victim and their supporter, as well as an adult supporter for the young person. The proceedings are underpinned by the concept of restorative justice – or at least the New Labour version of it – 'restoration, reintegration and responsibility' (Home Office 1997). The outcome is a 'contract' of activity to be undertaken by the young person, aimed at preventing reoffending. Crawford and Newburn's study (2003) of pilot areas reported mixed success. As with many innovations, those involved in implementation were enthusiastic and embraced the principles of restorative justice. Offering real choices to victims, treating lay people as equal partners and administering panels creatively, however, presented challenges, and the coercive context of 'restorative justice as punishment' inevitably placed some ethical limitations on the work that could be done with young offenders.

Haines (2000) provides a more critical appraisal of the popular but, he argues, widely misunderstood adoption of the concept of restorative justice, as applied to children through the establishment of Youth Offender Panels. The absence of any consensual definition of the term means that restorative justice has few agreed principles or boundaries. Haines' concern is that it remains untested against the various international protocols that protect the rights of children and that we should not assume that problem-solving and family group conferencing approaches are necessarily – in practice – in the best interests of children. Restorative justice, Haines argues, places too much responsibility on young people to participate in a process over which they have little control, by reason of their immaturity, and within which they lack the procedural safeguards that are afforded them in court. Moreover, the re-integration of the young offender, following censure and reparation, is an adult responsibility – it is not something that a young person should be expected to achieve for themselves. There must be a 'way back' for the young person and that must be an adult and state responsibility.

Attendance centres

Of all non-custodial disposals, the Attendance Centre Order has been the most neglected in the literature and it has been difficult to know how to include it in this book. Attendance Centre Orders have been available for juvenile and young adult offenders since 1948 and retained their popularity with sentencers, with 15 per cent of juveniles being so sentenced in a study of the Youth Court (O'Mahony and Haines 1996). Originally intended to punish by deprivation of leisure time, the order's similarity with community service has been pointed out (Gelsthorpe and Tutt 1986). Like community service, its objectives are unclear and its flexibility is attractive. It is used across the range of offences (not just for 'football hooligans', as many believe) and appears to float up and down the sentencing 'tariff', being used as both an alternative to custody and to fines or supervision orders (Raine *et al.* 2003. It has the advantage of lacking any strong public image, but is generally regarded favourably because:

> it is run (indirectly) by the police; structured (hours and attendance), and carefully programmed (physical training and constructive hobbies); all these factors have greater appeal ... than the unstructured and less specific arrangements of a supervision order to a social worker.
>
> (Gelsthorpe and Tutt 1986: 151)

On the other hand, it has also been sensitively used when sentencers (usually magistrates) are concerned about 'contagion' of young and immature offenders by their more sophisticated fellow attendees. Since the reorganization of the Youth Court under the regimen of the Youth Justice Board in 1999 as legislated for in the Crime and Disorder Act of 1998, several new sentences have been made available for young people and the impact has been a reduction in the number of Attendance Centre Orders given from 8,100 in 1998 to just 4,000 in 2002 (Home Office 2003c).

Conclusion

Although it is true that young people have always been perceived as troublesome by their elders, the assumed relationship between youth and crime seems to be stronger than ever. As Ian Loader (1996) has argued, young people are assumed to be the perpetrators of crime and are rarely constructed as victims or as consumers of criminal justice services. Yet much of the attention paid to young 'trouble-makers' may be due to their inexperience and greater likelihood of detection or to the systematic bias of criminal statistics which emphasise visible and easily counted 'street crimes' rather than the hidden crimes of the workplace and the home (Pearson 1994). In both the latter cases, young people are more likely to be the victims (for example, of employer negligence, sexual assault or child abuse) than the perpetrators.

Young offenders and sex offenders have in common their experience of *exclusion* from the community. Respectable citizens and figures of authority are less and less willing to communicate with either group and are increasingly demanding that they be 'known about', watched and moved on.

Chapter 11

The future of Punishment in the Community

Introduction

In the first edition of this book, this chapter began by anticipating that nothing was going to prevent the rise in the prison population, as mandatory minimum sentences and automatic life sentences were introduced, and a punitive philosophy underpinned the government's programme. How right that prediction was. In late 1996, there were 58,000 in prison, and in the summer of 2004, the figure climbed to just under 77,000 (www.hmprisonservice.gov.uk).

What *did* change, however, was the government – the first Labour ('New Labour') government for 18 years was elected in May 1997. Whilst it has been as punitive as its Conservative predecessor, the financial constraints for the probation service that NAPO envisaged were not to come to pass (NAPO 1997) – at least, not immediately. The whole area of effective community supervision was to become a major part of the government's criminal justice policy. It had no choice – the prisons were full, despite a reduction in overall crime levels (Home Office 2003c).

In its two terms since 1997, the government has made not one, but two radical changes to the probation service in England and Wales. The first was the creation of the National Probation Service in 2001, which has been fully outlined in Chapter 5. Making a National Probation Service of 42 Areas from 54 autonomous predecessors was no easy task. The many issues relating to governance and accountability, as well as staff concerns about professionalism and bureaucracy had all to be addressed. Local working with other criminal justice agencies in coterminous Criminal Justice Boards only just got underway in 2004. There has been no independent evaluation of the effect of this major change, although the NPS did its own review (NPS 2004b). However, after just three years of this radical, structural change, accompanied by a profusion of practice changes such as 'What Works', OASys, MAPPA and YOTs, the probation service is about to change fundamentally again. The first steps commenced in June 2004, with the full operation due in 2005/06. With very little consultation, the Home Secretary announced what is effectively a merger of prison and probation practices – although it is stated that the two services are not to be combined, despite Martin Narey being Chief Executive of both! The NPS is to be subsumed by the elegantly termed National Offender Management Service (NOMS) and the key aim is to effect 'seamless sentences' whereby offenders going to prison do not lose touch with their probation officers. Another key tenet of the plan is for 'contestability' and a splitting of provider and commissioning functions of 'interventions'. (At the time of writing, interventions have not been specified, but probably include accredited programmes, Enhanced Community Punishment, Approved Premises and Basic Skills provision.) In line with government policy for devolution, the NOMS will be organized on a regional basis, although this has been resisted by many (Hansard 2004).

How has this all come about? Sentencing and court arrangements had been reviewed by Halliday and Auld in 2001. The resulting legislative changes were presented in the Criminal Justice Act 2003 (outlined in Chapter 4) and the Courts Act 2003, respectively. It was the Carter review of Correctional Services (2003) that promoted the new organization with a view to finding 'more effective ways of using scarce resources if we are further to reduce crime' (Home Office 2003d: 1). So it is safe to assume that this was a Treasury-driven reform to ensure that 'the different parts of the criminal justice system work closer together' (Home Office 2003d: 1). The government response to Carter (Home Office 2004d) accepted the recommendations, and then asked for comments from the various interested parties.

There then followed a Home Office Consultation on the NOMS Organizational Design – clearly showing Martin Narey's preferred organizational model, but not stating what other options had been considered. The focus was on regional working, for management, business (HR, IT, finance, etc.) and commissioning. The structure did not appear to have any strategic changes for the prison service, but had far-reaching implications for probation functions. The regional philosophy flew in the face of the efforts that had been made effectively to manage the criminal justice system based on coterminous areas. Consultation took place over the summer of 2004, and NAPO made some well-argued points based on the significant risks to the probation service as well as to the Carter objectives of reducing crime and maintaining public confidence (*A Risk Too Far*, NAPO 2004). NAPO identified risks in dismantling the NPS by splitting it into two parts – commissioning and interventions (or purchaser/provider); it foresaw problems in introducing contestability based on competition rather than co-operation; it saw risks in moving away from the local community, especially with regard to promoting and reflecting diversity; it perceived there to be a risk in introducing a confused governance model which may give rise to conflicts of interest; and finally it felt that the rushed and ill-prepared administrative change would impact on the implementation of the Criminal Justice Act 2003 and other outstanding matters with which NAPO has been engaged (such as workload measurement). NAPO particularly had concerns about:

- the lack of a Business Case for NOMS and the current lack of a Gateway Review;
- the lack of an opportunity for the 2001 NPS reforms and restructuring to be fully implemented and assessed;
- the continuing lack of parliamentary scrutiny and full and open consultation with stakeholders. (NAPO 2004)

Four specific questions were asked in the consultation:

1. Does the model provide a rational and cost-effective means of delivering the NOMS reforms, while reducing bureaucracy?
This was impossible to comment upon as no figures for costs were given. Ten regional boards were proposed to supplant the 42 probation boards, but some 'local' structure will surely still be required, if only to maintain those vital links and community partnerships that have been legislated for and welcomed.

2. Do Regional Offender Management Boards need a separately appointed chairman (sic)?
In the light of the success brought to the role by the 42 Board chairs it would seem appropriate to do this, especially in view of the governance role. It would be strange if the Audit Commission did not have a view on this.

*3. A name was requested that was more appropriate than Public Sector
Interventions for managing community penalties.*
It is unlikely that anyone will come up with a better name, understood
by all parties, but especially by offenders, than 'probation'.

4. What liaison arrangements are necessary below the regional tier?
The Area Boards set up just three years ago seem to have got this right,
so what was the case for not retaining them?

At the end of the consultation period, a remarkable thing transpired.
The minister, Paul Goggins, announced that note had been taken of the
400 responses received and that a delay in bringing about the changes,
particularly the structural ones, would enable local areas to continue to
manage offenders locally, whilst 'introducing the concept and practice
of end to end offender management' (Hansard 20.7.04: 17WS). A few
days later, Martin Narey announced that 'designing a new organisation
at this pace could severely impact on performance in the probation
service' (Home Office 2004g). An interim design and structure was set
out – with some significant changes to that consulted upon earlier in the
year. And yet, it did not seem to have been thought through fully – how
could it have been, in such a short time?

Regional Offender Managers (ROMs) were appointed in the autumn
of 2004, with the role of commissioning prison places on a
'contestability' basis, but developing contestability in probation
alongside having operational responsibility for probation areas –
managing their performance (Home Office 2004g). The idea of splitting
offender management from interventions did not go away, but was
given more time.

Whilst there appeared to be a dramatic turn around within a few
weeks (the consultation period closed on 11 June 2004) the four key
questions for which answers had been sought were not specifically
addressed. However, all have a place in the new framework, so civil
servants seem to have heard the messages from the respondents. It
must have been clear to the Home Office that respondents were not in
favour of a new regional structure for operationally managing prisons
and probation. The interim design has put paid to this, but it may well
re-emerge. The name 'probation' seems to remain (for the time being)
sitting alongside that of NOMS and ROMs. Keeping the 42 Boards
allows for local liaison arrangements. But this also has another,
worrying, purpose. The NOMS 'Update' of September 2004 (Home
Office 2004h) pushed contestability a bit further by suggesting that 'the
retention of the Boards also offers us the opportunity to consider

whether or not we should allow the private sector to compete to run a whole probation area'.

But perhaps the most important question was why this had to happen, only three years after the last fundamental change, and at the same time as the Carter proposals enshrined in the Criminal Justice Act 2003 were being implemented. Could not the reduction in the prison population and the cost-savings required be achieved without creating a whole new structure? Could not creative ways of working together, as is achieved in some areas and regions with the resettlement of offenders leaving prison, be a model of probation and prison collaboration? Could not sentencers and those who influence them (such as the Crown Prosecution Service, Justices' Clerks' Society and the media) be persuaded that sentencing is becoming more punitive, whilst crime is reducing? Could not better training convince them that community sentences can be more effective than can incarceration, in reducing reoffending? The Carter Report admits that the interplay between 'public perception, media, politicians and sentencers' has 'helped to drive up the severity of sentencing' (Home Office 2003d: 12).

The focus of the new NOMS arrangement is very much based on community sentences – offender managers are, in effect, going to be probation officers. Perhaps for the first time we are going to see community sentences as 'the default option' and custody at the extreme end of the scale. Community sentences will, as ever, be described by their advocates as 'alternatives to custody' while being dismissed by their opponents as 'soft options'. But have we regained a sense of graduated response using a range of measures which can be tailored to the needs of those 'middle-range' offenders whose pace of offending needs to be slowed down while they are helped to mature or to resolve the personal and social problems that underlie their offending behaviour? The new sentences and ways of working may help probation staff to work in this way again. The offender managers will, after all, be responsible for 'designing' the package of activities or 'interventions' for each offender sentenced to a community sentence. Having been seduced by the concept of 'bifurcation' (Bottoms 1983) and the language of 'seriousness' to view offences as either 'serious' or 'not serious', have we now remembered that most offences that come before the courts – and most offenders – lie somewhere in between? These are the people whose offences are 'serious enough' for a community penalty. (These distinctions, defined in the Criminal Justice Act 1991, are still used as a basis for sentencing (Magistrates' Association 1993, 2003).) And it is anticipated that they will continue to be the majority of offenders with whom offender managers engage. The new measures under the Criminal Justice Act 2003 include the conditional caution as a means of diversion for those offences deemed 'not serious'. Meanwhile, the service will also be responsible for managing the sentences of more serious offenders, by offering a tight and controlling package of measures that will mean that community sentences are no longer seen as 'soft options'.

Comparative probation

It is easy to become obsessed with the problems of criminal justice in England and Wales and this book has not pretended to provide any genuinely international perspective on the issues discussed. Nevertheless, it is perhaps important to set developments in England and Wales in the broader context of developments in other penal systems. Analyses have shown that the ambiguities related to 'alternatives to custody' have been experienced by other Western European countries, especially those with previous reputations for liberal penal systems (Sim, Ruggiero and Ryan 1995). Over-emphasis on bifurcation and the simplistic serious/not serious divide has led to a backlash in both Holland (van Swaaningen and de Jonge 1995) and Sweden (Leander 1995) where the public, as in England and Wales, have questioned the definition of 'not serious'. Non-incarcerative measures are increasingly concerned with the restriction of liberty, surveillance and monitoring, rather than with welfare and treatment. The use of 'pure' probation seems to be decreasing everywhere. The attempt to unhitch such measures from prison by making 'intermediate sanctions' sentences 'in their own right' has also had contradictory consequences. No longer seen as 'alternatives to custody' they have become alternatives to each other, thus widening the net of penal intervention – a familiar story.

In France, for example, TIG (the equivalent of community service) is frequently used for first-time car offenders (Gallo 1995) and in Germany alternatives are often used where charges would otherwise have to be dropped through insufficient evidence (Messner and Ruggiero 1995). There is also the danger that the very existence of 'alternatives' reinforces the belief that those in prison *must* be the 'hard core' of offenders and that prison regimes can therefore justifiably reflect this (Leander 1995). But, as van Swaaningen and de Jonge point out, too much criticism of this process serves only to 'vacate the political space to those forces who want to increase the retributive elements' in the non-incarcerative measures, while at the same time alienating probation officers who are struggling to prevent the expansion of the use of prison (1995: 39).

A more detailed and comprehensive study of probation around the world is provided by Hamai *et al.* (1995). Across the world, the concept of probation appears to imply four key elements: selection (that is, assessment as suitable); a conditional suspension of punishment (no longer the case in England and Wales); personal supervision and, finally, guidance or treatment (Hamai *et al.* 1995: 4). Beyond that basic definition, probation may mean many different things depending on the social and economic framework within which it has to function. Indeed, one of the authors argues that any attempt to reify or essentialize the concept should be discouraged (Harris 1995). Speaking at the NPS Conference in 2004, Marie Brossy-Patin of the National Federation of Welcome and Social Readaptation Associations in France, emphasised the need to add reintegration to this list. She explained that her organization's key words were 'sanction without exclusion'.

Comparing the use of probation in England and Wales with other countries, a number of conclusions can be drawn. First, the probation service is probably the largest and most professionalized, with service delivery probably the most coherent and accountable, in the world. In this respect it might still be regarded as 'the envy of the world', as the following example confirms:

> The NPS is one of the leaders in important areas such as risk assessment, equal opportunities, substance misuse and effective practice – PMS (Czech Probation and Mediation Service) is very appreciative of being able to benefit from such expertise and experience.
>
> (NPS 2004b: 3)

Despite this, or perhaps because of it, it also seems to be the least flexible and most angst-ridden service. Second, it makes less use of volunteers and community facilities than other countries. It seems more conscious of the ambiguities and tensions in the role of probation officer and more concerned about loss of autonomy and professional discretion. In some countries, such as Japan, Canada and the Philippines, volunteers are used extensively and systematically to supervise offenders – a practice which is wholly consistent with notions of reintegration of offenders into the community (Hamai and Ville 1995). In fact, in Japan for probation and parole work – the latter being 22 per cent of the caseload – barely over 1000 probation officers are employed, whilst there are nearly 50,000 volunteer probation officers, plus over 200,000 members of the Women's Association for

Rehabilitation Aid, and 6,000 'Big Brothers and Sisters'. Nationally there are over 5,000 'Co-operative Employers' who assist by offering stable employment for probationers and parolees. These figures, denoting high community support to offenders, are significant in a country where over half the caseload for the service is made up of juvenile probationers. Reintegration can only be aided by such work (www.moj.go.jp). Third, the export of a therapeutic model of probation (perceived to be 'British') to developing countries, such as India, has been particularly unsuccessful, partly because of its costliness and partly because of its inappropriateness to resolving the social and economic causes of crime in these countries (Hamai and Ville 1995). Similarly, Worrall (2004b) has argued the inappropriateness of imposing a western model of cognitive-behavioural work on Aboriginal people, whose civilization has been all but destroyed by British colonialism.

Seeing custody as the alternative

In the first edition of this book, we asked four concluding questions about the future of punishment in the community:

1 Is the 'punishment in the community' experience unique to England and Wales, or can we learn lessons from the experiences of other penal systems?

2 Is the search for an articulated set of 'values', which is disinctively associated (only) with the probation service, any longer a relevant or worthwhile venture?

3 Can the rhetoric of 'partnership', with its managerialist assumptions, yet be subverted to provide a genuinely wider range of services to a genuinely wider range of offenders?

4 Is there any hope that newly-deprofessionalized probation officers might yet resist being reconstructed as 'corrections officers' and opt instead to revive and invest in the modest objectives and effective skills of helping offenders to solve the personal and social problems which make it difficult for them to choose *not* to offend?

In revisiting these issues, it is clear that the questions themselves require modification before one can even begin to seek to answer them. In this edition, we rephrase these issues as questions of:

1 Globalization of (community) punishment talk
2 Probation values and human rights
3 Partnership in the post-Crime and Disorder Act world
4 Offender managers of the future.

Globalization of (community) punishment talk[i]

The English-speaking world of probation and community corrections has been pre-occupied with a model of focused, accountable, standardized intervention in the lives of offenders, based on the actuarial concept of risk assessment, the science of cognitive behavioural psychology, the morality of individual responsibility and the politics of restorative justice. At the same time, that world has seen a dramatic rise in the prison population and a blurring of the boundary between freedom and custody. Offenders increasingly receive sentencing packages that involve time spent under supervision both inside and outside prison, and technology now makes it possible for many of the restrictions of imprisonment to be visited on offenders in their own homes and communities. In addition, practitioners are often overloaded with the bureaucratic demands of 'programme integrity' and evaluation, finding themselves with less and less time to consider the underlying values and philosophy of their work and thus making themselves vulnerable to the vagaries of crisis-driven law and order policy. The globalization of punishment talk has provided comforting *prêt a manger* solutions in the form of an international trade in penal ideas, of which 'What Works' is but one – the fast food of punishment in the community. Little account, it seems, need be taken of regional, let alone local differences of demography, culture or economy.

So how do we make sense of these developments in the context of the globalization of crime and punishment discourses? How do we take advantage of the insights offered by global knowledge while at the same time taking account of national, regional and local differences? How can we learn from each other without being forced into adopting a bland and simplistic language which we *think* we all recognize but which may, in reality, mean very little to any of us? If the 'What Works' agenda is to be more than just a 'phase' in the treatment of offenders, then it needs to demonstrate that it has within it the seeds of its own development and adaptation to changing social, political and economic circumstances.

The question of *practice wisdom* involves national and international comparative research, in order to learn about approaches and programmes that are successful with particular types of offenders, in particular locations at particular times. Some will be cognitive-behavioural programmes that lend themselves to conventional forms of evaluation. But many more will have grown out of locally identified needs and resources, not the least of which will be enthusiastic and skilful individual workers. Not all will immediately reduce recidivism in any measurable way, but all will be aiming to influence offenders' attitudes, behaviour and circumstances, making them 'stop and think' before offending next time and thus offering the greatest hope of long-term protection for the public. In this search for practice wisdom, there is also a need to explore what *doesn't* work. It is part of the received wisdom of 'What Works' that intervention which focuses only on insight-giving or the therapeutic relationship and which does not include a problem-solving dimension is not successful with offenders. But what is less well publicised is that there is plenty of research on other things that don't work (Trotter 1999). These include approaches which focus on blame and punishment, those where the goals are set only by the worker rather than collaboratively, lack of clarity on the part of the worker about his or her role and authority, pessimism and a negative attitude by the worker and, finally, failing to see the offender in their family and social context.

The question of *political awareness* involves asking why the simple phrase 'What Works' has become so invested with meaning. Or is it precisely because it *lacks* meaning that it has become so ubiquitous? There are at least four interest groups whose purposes might be served by the 'What Works' agenda and whether those interests are to be viewed positively or negatively will depend entirely on one's standpoint:

- The interests of *governance* are served to the extent that the 'What Works' agenda demonstrates to a sceptical public that community sentences can be tough, demanding and based on scientific premises which can be tested and evaluated.

- The interests of *management* are served to the extent that the agenda demonstrates accountability – showing that resources are being used efficiently, effectively and, above all, economically – and giving managers confidence that they know exactly what their workers are doing and why.

- The interests of *professionalism* are served to the extent that the agenda reassures individual workers that they are doing something worthwhile with the minimum of risk to their own status – that the areas in which they have to exercise their own judgement are limited and consequently so is the potential for error, thus reducing the otherwise stressful nature of the job.

- Finally, the interests of *restorative justice* are served to the extent that the offender, victim and, possibly, the wider community believe that the agenda delivers on its promises. Whatever the content of any particular intervention, it can be argued that 'What Works' aims to instil in the offender a sense of responsibility towards the community in general and empathy for the victim in particular. But in return, the offender has the right to expect to be *reintegrated* into that community and unless that right is respected, 'What Works' becomes little more than a sophisticated form of the stocks – as indeed it is for many sex offenders who, no matter what programmes they have co-operated with, remain irredeemable and non-reintegratable in the eyes of the community.

Probation values and human rights

'Probation values' were first explicitly contested in the 1980s when, in response to the 'nothing works' assertion, the balance between 'care' and 'control' became the focus of debate for more than a decade. In the 1990s, the search for distinctly 'probation values' became more complex in the face of the government's managerialist agenda and increasing demands that the probation service work in partnership with other agencies.

Nellis (1995a,b) attempted to encapsulate these dilemmas in the more succinct agenda of 'community justice' but he met with considerable opposition. This was not because his proposed values of 'anti-custodialism', 'restorative justice' and 'community safety' were in themselves anathema to probation officers but because he linked them with a demand that the probation service should cease to view itself as a social work agency. He rightly made explicit that the route down which the service had allowed itself to be led removed it further and further from traditional social work values. In reply, James (1995) complained that Nellis continued to treat the probation service as though it had a future independent of the rest of the criminal justice system, neglecting the interdependent and corporatist nature of criminal justice agencies. The probation service, he argued, is part of a system that is increasingly well co-ordinated around a philosophy of 'crime control'. That philosophy is not inherently antipathetic to rehabilitation – provided rehabilitation is applied to the *right groups* of offenders. The problem is not, therefore, that the probation service is fighting a lone battle for the moral high ground, but that fewer and fewer offenders are deemed 'suitable' for rehabilitative measures. We might now wish to add that the rehabilitative measures themselves have to be the *right measures*. Ten years on, that prescient debate has proved all too relevant to an understanding of the role of 'values' in punishment in the community in the twenty-first century.

Nellis (2001a and b; Nellis and Gelsthorpe 2003) continued to lead the debate and to accuse the probation service of failing to face up to, and take advantage of, the changes that are being forced upon it. His argument is always complex and sophisticated. On the one hand, he despairs of the 'forced forgetting' and lack of appreciation of the service's past that seem to characterize government rhetoric. At the same time, he argues that maintaining the name 'probation' for something that bears little resemblance to the service's past, serves only to fuel the government's portrayal of the service as obsolete (2001: 34). More recently, with Gelsthorpe (2003), he calls for 'a more synthesised statement' of the values underpinning the NPS. He is pessimistic that this can be done if the probation and prison services are merged and wonders whether 'we may look back on the present as the point at which the possibility of distinct probation values began to fade' (2003: 228). While the discourse of human rights provides 'ground rules' and obligations for future engagement with offenders and victims, it does not of itself provide the value base for a future probation service any more so than does *A New Choreography*'s 'eclectic mix of moral commitments … scientific aspirations … and organisational imperatives' (Nellis and Gelsthorpe 2003: 230). Conceptualizing and articulating 'normative statements by which the service and its officers can stand' (2003: 241) remains a challenge.

Partnership in the post-Crime and Disorder Act world

Over the past decade, the probation service has been forced to recognize that it does not work in isolation in the criminal justice system and partnership has become a major feature of its activities (Nellis 1995c; Rumgay 2003b), especially since the Crime and Disorder Act 1998. Under New Labour, it is difficult to identify any aspect of the work of the service that is not done in collaboration or consultation with other agencies and organizations: Youth Offending Teams, Prolific Offender Projects, DTTOs, Multi-Agency Public

Protection Arrangements, local Criminal Justice Boards and Forums, Crime and Disorder Reduction Partnerships – and so the list goes on. Electronic Monitoring and Satellite Tracking may not yet involve probation officers directly in implementation but officers are dealing increasingly with offenders under such surveillance (Mair 2001). Yet training for partnership work is still neglected and the naïve assumption remains that all that is required is good will (Rumgay 2003). The creation of the NOMS clearly demonstrates that partnership is the future of punishment in the community, but the challenge will be to ensure that partnership provides a genuinely wider range of services for a genuinely wider range of offenders and is not pursued simply in the interests of bureaucracy and managerialism.

In the summer of 2004 the Home Office produced a National Action Plan called *Reducing Re-offending* (Home Office 2004i). It is significant in two ways. First, it brings together all agencies, government depart-ments and partners which carry any responsibility for offenders. Prisons and probation (and NOMS) are obviously included, but there are roles for local authorities, health trusts, job centres, the police and the Department for Education and Skills, amongst others. And the reason that this seemingly disparate group are given new respon-sibilities is its second notable feature. The emphasis is on the delivery of services – 'pathways' of intervention – rather than the pathologizing of individual offenders through the discourse of 'criminogenic needs'. In response to the Social Exclusion Unit's Report (2002), it appears to represent a radical and welcome shift of official rhetoric, with the focus on: accommodation; education, training and employment; mental and physical health; drugs and alcohol; finance, benefit and debt; the needs of children and families of offenders; as well as attitudes, thinking and behaviour. Of course, as a strategy document, it is full of worthy statements about Key Action Areas and who will have responsibility at national, regional and local level. At this stage, it has no targets and desired outcomes. But it is formidable in showing the number of working connections that already exist and the ministerial recognition that crime and offenders exist in a social context. Tackling social exclusion in this way may well see the reduction in crime and punitive sentencing that we desire.

Offender managers of the future

Referring to probation officers as being 'newly-deprofessionalized' has proved to be unfair. The Diploma in Probation Studies is demanding, both intellectually and professionally, and has produced a generation of enthusiastic and competent probation officers. But their work has become heavily circumscribed by the objectives and targets of Home Office policy, allowing little scope for individual autonomy or creativity. This is unlikely to change with the creation of NOMS.

In the same way that new practices emerged with the new NPS in 2001, such as MAPPA, OASys, etc., there are bound to be new demands on practitioners in their day-to-day work. One of the most clearly sign-posted is that case management will be carried out using a multi-skilled team – more so than it is at present. PSOs will be used to a greater extent, and the familiar problems of front-line staff lacking professional qualifications are likely to again be voiced by NAPO. This is unlikely to receive much attention when the prison service expects its recruits to be functioning effectively after an eight week training period (www.learndirect-advice.co.uk). But perhaps this closer working relationship with prison staff presents an opportunity for probation staff to manifest their professionalism and effectiveness in offender management.

One of the concerns that emerge from the proposed structure for NOMS is the way that 'interventions' are separated from case management, as if they are an 'add-on' to a sentence, managed by a different organization and authority line. History could provide some help to NOMS here. One of the major reasons for breach of orders where the condition of attendance on a programme such as Think First is stipulated, is the attrition that occurs before the programme is due to start (Roberts 2004). Helping the offender before the programme begins requires liaison between the programme manager or tutor, case manager and offender, in the form of pre-group sessions, providing support and encouragement. Roberts' research suggests that pre-group sessions may assist in improving attendance and programme completion, which in itself has benefits for the offender including a reduced reconviction rate. This work is indicative of how programmes and 'interventions' are integral to community orders, not 'bolt-ons'. How will this work be facilitated when separate organizations are running the two parts?

Probation officers of the future may also have concerns about their career structure. At present, working as a programme or treatment manager provides good experience for an ambitious officer seeking a senior officer post. These sideways moves may now require the officer to leave NOMS, working for a partnership organization, with an unclear route back in.

The proposed structure for NOMS seems to be an adaptation of the way in which prisons work, which is unlikely to fit comfortably with the structure and culture of probation areas and their work with their local communities. This is central to the whole issue. The culture of the probation service, as outlined in this book, has changed dramatically over the last 100 years. But to anticipate that it can change further and become more 'correctionalist' seems to cut against the grain of probation officers as 'compulsive understanders' (Fullwood 1996). Probation staff have responded to managerialist demands of them and their work, but must continue to engage with the social worlds that offenders inhabit.

Conclusion

In the summer of 2004 there are at least two different 'readings' of the future of punishment in the community. One reading is represented by Cohen's (2004) view, which likens NOMS to the 1994 film *Speed*, in which a police officer and a teacher are trapped on a school bus that has been rigged with a bomb. If they allow the bus's speed to slow to less than 50 mph, the bomb will explode. The accelerator must be held down at all times, regardless of the havoc wreaked, in order to prevent greater carnage. Cohen predicts that NOMS will become yet one more governmental disaster and a byword for Whitehall ineptitude.

An alternative reading is that we may finally have turned a corner – maybe not for the probation service itself, whose future may indeed be ineluctably hitched up to the future of imprisonment, but possibly for offenders, whose behaviour may at last be recognized to stem as much from social as from individual causes. Perhaps when we come to write the third edition of this book, NOMS will have produced the desired result – community sentences as the 'default option' for 'serious enough' offences, a reduction in reoffending and the prison population at much reduced levels. We can only hope so.

†Parts of this section are reproduced by kind permission of Willan Publishing from pp 327–8 and 338–41 of Mair, E. (ed) (2004) *What Matters in Probation*.

Recommended further reading

- An accessible introductory text that, amongst other things, provides a detailed history of the ideas and policies of probation is Raynor, P. and Vanstone, M. (2002) *Understanding Community Penalties.* Buckingham: Open University Press.

- An up-to-date summary of recent developments and the changing context of offender management in the community is provided by Chui, W.H. and Nellis, M. (eds) (2003) *Moving Probation Forward: Evidence, Arguments and Practice.* Harlow: Pearson Longman.

- For a very lively, critical and controversial examination of the 'What Works' agenda for offender rehabilitation, read Mair, G. (ed) (2004) *What Matters in Probation.* Cullompton: Willan Publishing.

- In Maguire, M., Morgan, R. and Reiner, R. (eds) (2002) *The Oxford Handbook of Criminology.* Oxford: Oxford University Press, you will find a comprehensive and balanced resumé of the key issues and debates surrounding community penalties in the chapter by Peter Raynor.

- For a book containing interesting chapters written by probation practitioners and managers as well as academics, read Ward, D., Scott, J. and Lacey, M. (eds) (2002) *Probation – Working for Justice* (2nd edition). Oxford: Oxford University Press.

- A range of more explicitly theoretically orientated essays can be found in Bottoms, A., Gelsthorpe, L. and Rex, S. (eds) (2001) *Community Penalties: Change and Challenges.* Cullompton: Willan Publishing.

- The Coulsfield Inquiry into Alternatives to Prison supported by the Esmée Fairbairn Foundation reported in November 2004. In addition to the formal report it also funded an edited book: Bottoms, A., Rex, S. and Robinson, G. (eds) (2004) *Alternatives to Prison: Options for an insecure society.* Cullompton: Willan Publishing.

References

Adler, F. (1975) *Sisters in Crime.* New York: McGraw-Hill.

Alder, C. and Worrall, A. (eds) (2004) *Girls' Violence: Myths and Realities.* New York: SUNY Press.

Allen, H. (1987) *Justice Unbalanced.* Milton Keynes: Open University Press.

Armstrong, S. (1990) *Alternatives to custody? Day centre and community service provision for women.* Occasional Paper 4, University of Keele: Centre for Criminology.

Asquith, S. (ed) (1993) *Protecting Children: Cleveland to Orkney: More Lessons to Learn?* Edinburgh: HMSO.

Audit Commission (1996) *Misspent Youth.* London: Audit Commission.

Audit Commission (2004) *Youth Justice: A review of the reformed youth justice system.* (www.audit-commission.gov.uk/reports/)

Bailey, R. and Boswell, G. (2004) *Sexually Abusive Adolescent Males – A Literature Review.* Community and Criminal Justice Monograph 4. Leicester: De Montfort University.

Baker, S. (1993) *The Rise and Fall of Unit Fines.* Unpublished dissertation, Keele: Keele University.

Bale, D. (1987) 'Using a risk of custody scale', *Probation Journal*, 34 (4): 127–31.

Bale, D. (2000) 'Pure fiction: an infallible guide to national standards', *Probation Journal*, 47 (2): 129–31.

Bandalli, S. (2000) 'Children, Responsibility and the New Youth Justice', in B. Goldson (ed) *The New Youth Justice.* Lyme Regis: Russell House Publishing.

Barker, M. (1993) *Community Service and Women Offenders.* London: Association of Chief Officers of Probation.

Barker, M. (1995) 'What works with sex offenders?', in G. McIvor (ed) *Working with Offenders*. Research Highlights in Social Work 26. London: Jessica Kingsley.

Barnett, S., Corder, F. and Jehu, D. (1990) 'Group treatment for women sex offenders against children', *Groupwork*, 3 (2): 191–203.

Beaumont, B. (1995) 'Managerialism and the Probation Service', in B. Williams (ed) *Probation Values*. Birmingham: Venture Press.

Beck, U. (1992) *Risk Society: Towards a New Modernity*. London: Sage.

Beech, A., Fisher, D., Beckett, R. and Scott-Fordham, A. (1998) *An evaluation of the prison sex offender treatment programme*, Research Findings 79. London: Home Office.

Biestek, F. (1961) *The Casework Relationship*. London: Unwin University Books.

Blagg, H. (1998) 'Restorative Visions and Restorative Justice Practices: Conferencing, Ceremony and Reconciliation in Australia', *Current Issues in Criminal Justice*, 10 (1): 5–15.

Boswell, G. (1996) *Young and Dangerous: the Background Careers of Section 53 Offenders*, Aldershot, Avebury.

Bottomley, K., Hucklesby, A., Mair, G. and Nellis, M. (eds) (2004) *Electronic Monitoring of Offenders: Key developments*. Issues in Community and Criminal Justice Monograph 5. London: NAP.

Bottoms, A. (1983) 'Neglected features of contemporary penal systems' in D. Garland and P. Young (eds) *The Power to Punish*. London: Heinemann.

Bottoms, A. (2001) 'Compliance and community penalties', in A. Bottoms, L. Gelsthorpe and S. Rex (eds) *Community Penalties: Change and Challenges*. Cullompton: Willan.

Bottoms, A. and McWilliams, W. (1979) 'A non-treatment paradigm for probation practice', *British Journal of Social Work*, 9 (2): 159–202.

Bottoms, A. and Stelman, A. (1988) *Social Inquiry Reports*. Aldershot: Wildwood House.

Bottoms, A., Rex, S. and Robinson, G. (eds) (2004) *Alternatives to Prison: Options for an insecure society*. Cullompton: Willan Publishing.

Braithwaite, J. (1989) *Crime, Shame and Reintegration*. Cambridge: Cambridge University Press.

Braithwaite, J. (1999) 'Restorative justice: Assessing optimistic and pessimistic accounts', in M. Tonry (ed) *Crime and Justice, A Review of Research*, 25: 1–126.

Brinkworth, L. (1994) 'Sugar and spice but not at all nice'. *The Sunday Times*, 27 November.

Brinkworth, L. (1996) 'Angry young women'. *Cosmopolitan*, February 1996.

Broad, B. (1991) *Punishment under Pressure*. London: Jessica Kingsley.

Brown, S. (1990) *Magistrates at Work*. Milton Keynes: Open University Press.

Brownlee, I. (1998) *Community Punishment, A critical introduction*. Harlow: Longman.

Bryan, T. and Doyle, P. (2003) 'Developing Multi-Agency Public Protection Arrangements', in A. Matravers (ed) *Sex Offenders in the Community: Managing and Reducing the Risks*. Cullompton: Willan.

Buchanan, J., Collett, S. and McMullan, P. (1991) 'Challenging practice or challenging women? Female offenders and illicit drug use', *Probation Journal*, 38 (2): 56–62.

Burgess, A. (1962) *A Clockwork Orange*. Harmondsworth: Penguin Books.

Byrne, J.M., Lurigio, A.J. and Petersilia, J. (1992) *Smart Sentencing: the Emergence of Intermediate Sanctions*. London: Sage.

Calverley, A., Cole, B., Kaure, G., Lewis, S., Raynor, P., Sadeghi, S., Smith, D., Vanstone, M. and Wardak, A. (2004) *Black and Asian Offenders on Probation*. Home Office Research Study 277. London: Home Office.

Campbell, B. (1988) *Unofficial Secrets*. London: Virago Press.

Campbell, B. (1993) *Goliath: Britain's Dangerous Places*. London: Methuen.

Carlen, P. (1976) *Magistrates' Justice*. London: Routledge Kegan Paul.

Carlen, P. (1988) *Women, Crime and Poverty*. Milton Keynes: Open University Press.

Carlen, P. (1989) 'Crime, inequality and sentencing', in P. Carlen, P. and D. Cook (eds) *Paying for Crime*. Milton Keynes: Open University Press.

Carlen, P. (1990) *Alternatives to women's imprisonment*. Buckingham: Open University Press.

Carlen, P., Hicks, J., O'Dwyer, J., Christina, D. and Tchaikovsky, C. (1985) *Criminal Women*. Oxford: Polity Press.

Carlen, P. and Powell, M. (1979) 'Professionals in the magistrates courts', in H. Parker (ed) *Social Work and the Courts*. London: Edward Arnold.

Carlen, P. and Worrall, A. (2004) *Analysing Women's Imprisonment*. Cullompton: Willan.

Carr, J. (2004) 'The role of the Internet in the commission of crime', *Criminal Justice Matters*, 55: 24–5.

Cavadino, M. and Dignan, J. (1997) *The Penal System: An Introduction*. London: Sage.

Cavadino, P. (ed) (1996) *Children Who Kill*. Winchester: Waterside Press.

Charles, N., Whittaker, C. and Ball, C. (1997) *Sentencing without a Pre-Sentence Report*. Home Office Research Findings 47. London: HMSO.

Chaudhuri, A. (2000) 'Twisted sisters', *Guardian*, 15 August 2000.

Chigwada, R. (1989) 'The criminalisation and imprisonment of black women', *Probation Journal*, 36 (3): 100–05.

Chigwada-Bailey, R. (2004) 'Black women and the criminal justice system', in G. McIvor (ed) *Women who Offend*. Research Highlights in Social Work 44. London: Jessica Kingsley Publishers.

Chouhan, K. (2002) 'Race Issues in Probation', in D. Ward, J. Scott and M. Lacey (eds) *Probation: Working for Justice* (2nd edition). Oxford: Oxford University Press.

Cobley, C. (2003) 'The legislative framework', in A. Matravers (ed) *Sex Offenders in the Community: Managing and Reducing the Risks*. Cullompton: Willan.

Cohen, S. (1979) 'The punitive city: notes on the dispersal of social control', *Contemporary Crises*, 3: 339–63.

Cohen, S. (1983) 'Social control talk: telling stories about correctional change', in D. Garland and P. Young (eds) *The Power to Punish*. London: Heinemann.

Cohen, S. (1985) *Visions of Social Control*. Cambridge: Polity Press.

Cohen, N. (2004) 'The end of the probation service', *New Statesman*. Vol 17, Issue 806.

Cook, D. (1997) *Poverty, crime and punishment*. London: Child Poverty Action Group.

Coombes, R. (2003) 'Adolescents who sexually abuse', in A. Matravers (ed) *Sex Offenders in the Community*. Cullompton: Willan.

Coulshed, V. (1988) *Social Work Practice: an Introduction*. London: Macmillan.

Cowburn, M. and Modi, P. (1995) 'Justice in an unjust context: implications for working with adult male sex offenders', in D. Ward and M. Lacey (eds) *Probation: Working for Justice*. London: Whiting & Birch.

Crawford, A. (1998) *Crime Prevention and Community Safety*. Harlow: Addison Wesley Longman.

Crawford, A. (2001) 'Joined-up but Fragmented': Contradiction, Ambiguity and Ambivalence at the Heart of New Labour's "Third Way"', in R. Matthews and J. Pitts (eds) *Crime, Community and Disorder*. London: Routledge.

Crawford, A. and Newburn, T. (2003) *Youth Offending and Restorative Justice*. Cullompton: Willan.

Curnock, K. and Hardiker, P. (1979) *Towards Practice Theory*. London: Routledge Kegan Paul.

Davies, K., Lewis, J., Byatt, J., Purvis, E. and Cole, B. (2004) *An Evaluation of the Literacy Demands of General Offending Behaviour Programmes*. Home Office Findings 233. London: Home Office.

Denney, D. (1992) *Racism and Anti-Racism in the Probation Service*. London: Routledge.

Department of Health/Home Office (1992) *Report of Health and Social Services for Mentally Disordered Offenders* (Reed Report) Cmnd. 2088. London: HMSO.

Department of Health (2000) *Children accommodated in Secure Units, Year ending 31 March 2000: England and Wales*. Statistical Bulletin 2000/15. London: Department of Health.

Dixon, L. (2003) 'Report of Hate Crime Conference', *Probation Journal*, 50 (1): 64–6.

Dixon, L. and Court, D. (2003) 'Developing good practice with racially motivated offenders', *Probation Journal*, 50 (2): 149–53.

Dixon, L. and Okitikpi, T. (1999) 'Working with racially motivated offenders: practice issues', *Probation Journal*, 46 (3): 157–63.

Dominelli, L. (1984) 'Differential justice: domestic labour, community service and female offenders', *Probation Journal*, 31 (3): 100–03.

Donzelot, J. (1980) *The Policing of Families*. London: Hutchinson.

Downes, D. (1997) 'What the next government should do about crime', *The Howard Journal of Criminal Justice*, 36 (1): 1–13.

Downes, D. (1998) 'Toughing it Out: From Labour Opposition to Labour Government', *Policy Studies* 19 (3–4): 191–98.

Drakeford, M. (1993) 'The probation service, breach and the Criminal Justice Act 1991', *The Howard Journal of Criminal Justice*. 32 (4): 291–303.

Drakeford, M. and McCarthy, K. (2000) 'Parents, responsibility and the New Youth Justice', in B. Goldson (ed) *The New Youth Justice*. Lyme Regis: Russell House Publishing.

Duguid, G. (1982) *Community Service in Scotland: The First Two Years*. Edinburgh: Scottish Office Central Research Unit.

Dunkley, C. (1992) *Groupwork with Women in Probation Day Centres*. University of Manchester: Department of Social Policy and Social Work.

Durrance, P. and Williams, P. (2004) 'Broadening the agenda around what works for black and Asian offenders', *Probation Journal*, 50 (3): 211–24.

Eaton, M. (1985) 'Documenting the defendant: placing women in social inquiry reports', in J. Brophy and C. Smart (eds) *Women in Law*. London: Routledge Kegan Paul.

Eaton, M. (1986) *Justice for Women?* Milton Keynes: Open University Press.

Edwards, R. (1999) 'Working with racially motivated offenders', *Probation Journal*, 46 (1): 37–9.

Falshaw, L., Friendship, C. and Bates, C. (2003) *Sexual offenders – measuring reconviction, reoffending and recidivism*. Findings, 183. London: Home Office.

Farrall, S. (2002) *Rethinking What Works with Offenders: Probation, Social Context and Desistance from Crime*. Cullompton: Willan.

Farrall, S. (2004) 'Supervision, motivation and social context', in G. Mair (ed) *What Matters in Probation*. Cullompton, Willan.

Fatic, A. (1995) *Punishment and Restorative Crime-Handling: a Social Theory of Trust*. Aldershot: Avebury.

Faulkner, D. (1993) 'All flaws and disorder', *Guardian*, 11 November 1993.

Faulkner, D. (1996) *Darkness and Light: Justice, Crime and Management for Today*. London: The Howard League for Penal Reform.

Feeley, M. and Simon, J. (1992) 'The new penology' in J. Muncie, E. McLaughlin and M. Langan (eds) (1996) *Criminological Perspectives, a Reader*. London: Sage.

Flynn, N. (2002) 'Organisation and Management: a Changing Agenda', in D. Ward, J. Scott and M. Lacey (eds) *Probation: Working for Justice*. Oxford: Oxford University Press.

Folkard, M.S., Smith, D.E. and Smith, D.D. (1976) *IMPACT: Intensive Matched Probation and After-Care Treatment*. Home Office Research Study 36. London: HMSO.

Forbes, J. (1992) 'Female sexual abusers: the contemporary search for equivalence', *Practice*, 6 (2): 102–11.

Foucault, M. (1977) *Discipline and Punish*. London: Allen Lane.

Fowler, R. (1999) 'When Girl Power packs a punch', *Guardian*, 12 July 1999.

Frazer, E. and Lacey, N. (1993) *The Politics of Community: A Feminist Critique of the Liberal-Communitarian Debate*. London: Harvester Wheatsheaf.

Friendship, C., Mann, R. and Beech, A. (2003) *The prison-based Sex Offender Treatment Programme – an evaluation*. Findings 205, London: Home Office.

Fullwood, C. (1996) 'The future of the probation service: the case for the compulsive understander', *Probation Journal*, 43 (3): 118–26.

Fullwood, C. (2002) 'The Social and Criminal Policy Context', in D. Ward, J. Scott and M. Lacey (eds) *Probation: Working for Justice*. Oxford: Oxford University Press.

Gallo, E. (1995) 'The penal system in France: from correctionalism to managerialism', in V. Ruggiero, M. Ryan and J. Sim (eds) *Western European Penal Systems: a Critical Anatomy*. London: Sage.

Gardiner, S. (1995) 'Criminal Justice Act 1991 – management of the underclass and the potentiality of community', in L. Noaks, M. Levi and M. Maguire (eds) *Contemporary Issues in Criminology*. Cardiff: University of Wales Press.

Garland, D. (1985) *Punishment and Welfare: A History of Penal Strategies*. Aldershot: Gower.

Garland, D. (1990) *Punishment and Modern Society*. Oxford: Oxford University Press.

Garland, D. (1995) 'Panopticon days', *Criminal Justice Matters*, No. 20, Summer, 3–4.

Gelsthorpe, L. (2004) 'Female Offending: A Theoretical Overview', in G. McIvor (ed) *Women who Offend*. Research Highlights in Social Work 44. London: Jessica Kingsley Publishers.

Gelsthorpe, L. and Rex, S. (2004) 'Community service as reintegration: exploring the potential', in G. Mair, (ed) *What Matters in Probation*. Cullompton: Willan.

Gelsthorpe, L. and Tutt, N. (1986) 'The Attendance Centre Order', *Criminal Law Review*, 146–53.

Genders, E. and Player, E. (1995) *Grendon: a Study of a Therapeutic Prison*. Oxford: Clarendon Press.

Gillis, J.G. (1974) *Youth and History*. New York: Academic Press.

Gilyeat, D. (1993) *A Companion Guide to Offence Seriousness*. Ilkley: Owen Wells Publisher.

Gocke, B. (1995) 'Working with people who have committed sexual offences', in B. Williams (ed) *Probation Values*. Birmingham: Venture Press.

Goffman, E. (1961) *Asylums*. Harmondsworth: Penguin Books.

Golding, W. (1960) *Lord of the Flies*. Harmondsworth: Penguin Books.

Goldson, B. (ed) (1999) *Youth Justice: Contemporary Policy and Practice*. Aldershot: Ashgate.

Goldson, B. (ed) (2000) *The New Youth Justice*. Lyme Regis: Russell House Publishing.

Gordon, C. (1979) 'Other inquisitions', *Ideology and Consciousness*, 6: 23–46.

Grange, T. (2003) 'Challenges for the police service', in A. Matravers (ed) *Sex Offenders in the Community: Managing and Reducing the Risks*. Cullompton: Willan.

Greer, C. (2003) *Sex Crime and the Media: Sex offending and the press in a divided society*. Cullompton: Willan.

Grisso, T. and Schwartz, R.G. (eds) (2000) *Youth on Trial: A Developmental Perspective on Juvenile Justice*. Chicago: The University of Chicago Press.

Groombridge, N. (1995) 'Candid cameras', *Criminal Justice Matters* No. 20, Summer, 9.

Hagan, J. (1994) *Crime and Disrepute*. Thousand Oaks: Pine Forge.

Hagell, A. and Newburn, T. (1994) *Persistent Young Offenders*. London: Policy Studies Institute.

Haines, K. (2000) 'Referral Orders and Youth Offender Panels: Restorative Approaches and the New Youth Justice', in B. Goldson (ed) *The New Youth Justice*. Lyme Regis: Russell House Publishing.

Hamai, F. and Ville, R. (1995) 'Volunteer probation personnel', in F. Hamai, R. Ville, M. Hough, R. Harris and U. Zveckic (eds) *Probation Around the World*. London: Routledge.

Hamai, F., Ville, R., Harris, R., Hough, M. and Zvekic, U. (eds) (1995) *Probation Around the World*. London: Routledge.

Hansard (2004) 19th May 2004 Column 271WH – Column 295 WH. London: House of Commons.

Hardiker, P. and Willis, A. (1989) 'Cloning probation officers: consumer research and implications for training', *The Howard Journal of Criminal Justice*, 28 (4): 323–9.

Harding, J. (2003) 'Which way probation? A correctional or community justice service?', *Probation Journal*, 50 (4): 369–73.

Harding, R. and Worrall, A. (2004) *Cognitive Skills Training in the Western Australian Prison System*. Report No 23. Perth, WA: Office of the Inspector of Custodial Services (www.custodialinspector.wa.gov.au).

Harradine, S., Kodz, J., Lemettl, F. and Jones, B. (2004) *Defining and measuring anti-social behaviour*. Home Office Development and Practice Report 26. London: Home Office.

Harris, J. and Grace, S. (1999) *A Question of Evidence: Investigating and Prosecuting Rape in the 1990s*. Home Office Research Study 196. London: Home Office.

Harris, R. (1980) 'A changing service: the case for separating care and control in probation practice', *British Journal of Social Work*, 10 (2): 163–84.

Harris, R. (1992) *Crime, Criminal Justice and the Probation Service*. London: Routledge.

Harris, R (1995) 'Studying probation: a comparative approach' and 'Reflections on comparative probation', in F. Hamai, R. Ville, M. Hough, R. Harris and U. Zveckic (eds) *Probation Around the World*. London: Routledge.

Harris, V. and Staunton, C. (2000) 'The antecedents of young male sex offenders', in G. Boswell (ed) *Violent Children and Adolescents: Asking the Question Why*. London: Whurr Publishers.

Haxby, D. (1978) *Probation: a Changing Service*. London: Constable.

Hay, C. (1995) 'Mobilization through interpellation: James Bulger, juvenile crime and the construction of a moral panic', *Social and Legal Studies*, 4 (2): 197–223.

Hayman, S. (1996) *Community Prisons for Women*. London: Prison Reform Trust.

Hearnden, I. and Millie, A. (2004) 'Does tougher enforcement lead to lower reconviction?', *Probation Journal*, 51 (1): 48–58.

Hebenton, B. and Thomas, T. (1996) 'Tracking sex offenders', *The Howard Journal of Criminal Justice*, 35 (2): 97–112.

Hedderman, C. (2003) 'Enforcing supervision and encouraging compliance', in W.H. Chui and M. Nellis (eds) *Moving Probation Forward: Evidence, Arguments and Practice*. Harlow: Pearson Longman.

Hedderman, C. (2004) 'Why are more women being Sentenced to Custody?', in G. McIvor (ed) *Women who Offend*. Research Highlights in Social Work 44. London: Jessica Kingsley Publishers.

Hedderman, C. and Hough, M. (1994) *Does the Criminal Justice System Treat Men and Women Differently?* Home Office Research Findings 10. London: HMSO.

Hedderman, C. and Sugg, D. (1996) *Does Treating Sex Offenders Reduce Reoffending?* Home Office Research Findings 45. London: HMSO.

Hedderman, C. and Hough, M. (2004) 'Getting Tough or being Effective: What Matters?', in G. Mair (ed) *What Matters in Probation*. Cullompton: Willan Publishing.

Heidensohn, F. (1985) *Women and Crime*. Basingstoke: Macmillan.

Hetherington, P. (1999) 'The Invisibles', *Guardian*, 13 October 1999.

Hetherton, J. (1999) 'The idealisation of women: its role in the minimization of child sexual abuse by women', *Child Abuse and Neglect*, 23 (2): 161–64.

HM Inspectorate of Probation (1993) *Approved Probation and Bail Hostels: Report of a Thematic Inspection*. London: Home Office.

HM Inspectorate of Probation (1998) *Exercising constant vigilance: the role of the Probation Service in protecting the public from sex offenders*. London: Home Office.

HM Inspectorate of Probation (2000) *Towards Race Equality, Thematic Inspection*. London: Home Office.

HM Inspectorate of Probation (2002) *Annual Report 2001–02*. London: Home Office.

Hill, L. (2002) 'Working in the Courts' in D. Ward, J. Scott and M. Lacey (eds) *Probation, Working for Justice*. Oxford: Oxford University Press.

Hine, J. and Thomas, N. (1995) 'Evaluating Work with Offenders: Community Service Orders', in G. McIvor (ed) *Working with Offenders*. Research Highlights in Social Work 26. London: Jessica Kingsley.

Home Office (1988) *Punishment, Custody and the Community*, Cmnd. 424. London: HMSO.

Home Office (1990a) *Crime, Justice and Protecting the Public*, Cmnd. 965. London: HMSO.

Home Office (1990b) *Supervision and Punishment in the Community*, Cmnd. 966. London: HMSO.

Home Office (1990c) *Partnership in Dealing with Offenders in the Community*. London: HMSO.

Home Office (1991) *Organising Supervision and Punishment in the Community: a Decision Document*. London: HMSO.

Home Office (1992b) *National Standards for the Supervision of Offenders in the Community*. London: Home Office.

Home Office (1995c) *Strengthening Punishment in the Community*, Cmnd. 2780. London: HMSO.

Home Office (1995e) *National Standards for the Supervision of Offenders in the Community*. London: Home Office.

Home Office (1996a) *Protecting the Public*, Cmnd. 3190. London: HMSO.

Home Office (1996b) *Probation Statistics England and Wales 1994*. London: Home Office.

Home Office (1997) *No More Excuses – A New Approach to Tackling Youth Crime in England and Wales*. Cm 3809. London: Home Office.

Home Office (1998) *Joining Forces to Protect the Public*. London: Home Office.

Home Office (1999) *Probation Statistics 1999*. London: Home Office.

Home Office (2002a) *Statistics on Mentally Disordered Offenders, England and Wales, Statistical Bulletin 13/0*. London: Home Office.

Home Office (2002b) *Criminal Statistics England and Wales, 2001*. London: Home Office.

Home Office (2002c) *Justice for All, Summary*. London: Home Office.

Home Office (2002d) *National Standards for the supervision of offenders in the community 2002*, revised 2002. London: Home Office.

Home Office (2003a) *Annual Report 2002/2003*. Her Majesty's Inspectorate of Probation, London: Home Office.

Home Office (2003b) *Prison Statistics England and Wales 2002*, Cm 5996. London: Home Office.

Home Office (2003c) *Criminal Statistics England and Wales, 2002, Cm 6054*. London: Home Office.

Home Office (2003d) *Managing Offenders, Reducing Crime* – Correctional Services Review, Patrick Carter. London: Home Office.

Home Office (2004a) *Probation Statistics England and Wales 2002*. London: Home Office.

Home Office (2004b) *Section 95: Gender and the Criminal Justice System*. London: Home Office.

Home Office (2004c) *Statistics on Race and the Criminal Justice System 2003*. London: Home Office.

Home Office (2004d) *Reducing Crime – Changing Lives*. London: Home Office.

Home Office (2004e) *Towards Race Equality, Follow-up Inspection Report*, Her Majesty's Inspectorate of Probation. London: Home Office.

Home Office (2004f) *Investigating links between probation, reinforcement and reconviction*, Report 41/03, RDS. London: Home Office.

Home Office (2004g) *National Offender Management Service Update, Issue 3*. London: Home Office.

Home Office (2004h) *National Offender Management Service Update, Issue 4*. London: Home Office.

Home Office (2004i) *Reducing Re-offending, National Action Plan*. London: Home Office.

Hood, R. (1992) *Race and Sentencing*. Oxford: Clarendon Press.

Hood, R., Shute, S., Feilzer, M. and Wilcox, A. (2002) 'Sex offenders emerging from long-term imprisonment: a study of their long-term reconviction rates and of Parole Board members' judgements of their risk', *British Journal of Criminology*, 42: 371–94.

Horn, R. and Evans, M. (2000) 'The effect of gender on pre-sentence reports', *Howard Journal*, 39(2): 184–204.

Howard League (1997) *Lost Inside: the imprisonment of teenage girls*. London: Howard League for Penal Reform.

Howard League (1999) *Do Women Paint Fences Too? Women's Experience of Community Service*. London: Howard League for Penal Reform.

Howard League (2004) *Advice, understanding and underwear: working with girls in prison*. London: Howard League for Penal Reform.

Howe, A., Johnson, B., Purser, B. and Read, G. (1982) 'Establishing day centres', *Probation Journal*, 29 (2): 60–61.

Hoy, C. (2002) *An Investigation into the Changes in Sentencing Patterns of Certain Community Sentences at Warrington Magistrates' Court between 1996 and 2001*. Unpublished MA Dissertation. Keele: Keele University

Hudson, B. (1987) *Justice Through Punishment*. Basingstoke: Macmillan.

Hudson, B. (2001) 'Human Rights, Public Safety and the Probation Service: Defending Justice in the Risk Society', *The Howard Journal of Criminal Justice*, 40 (2): 103–13.

Humphrey, C. (1991) 'Calling on the experts', *The Howard Journal of Criminal Justice*, 30 (1): 1–18.

Humphrey, C. and Pease, K. (1992) 'Effectiveness measurement in the Probation Service: a view from the troops', *The Howard Journal of Criminal Justice*, 31 (1): 31–52.

Hutton, W. (1995) *The State We're In*. London: Jonathan Cape.

Ireland, P. (1995) 'Reflections on a rampage through the barriers of shame: law, community and the new conservatism', *Journal of Law and Society*, 22 (2): 189–211.

Jackson, H. and Smith, L. (1987) *Female Offenders: an Analysis of Social Inquiry Reports*. Home Office Research Bulletin 23. London: HMSO.

James, A.L. (1995) 'Probation values for the 1990s – and beyond?', *The Howard Journal of Criminal Justice*, 34 (4): 326–43.

Johnson, K. *et al.* (2001) *Cautions, Court Proceedings and Sentencing, England and Wales, 2000*. Home Office Statistical Bulletin. London: Home Office.

Johnson, C. and Rex, S. (2002) 'Community Service: Rediscovering Reintegration' in D. Ward, J. Scott and M. Lacey, (eds) *Probation: Working for Justice*. Oxford: Oxford University Press.

Jones, M., Mordecai, M., Rutter, F. and Thomas, L. (1991) 'The Miskin Model of groupwork with women offenders', *Groupwork*, 4 (3): 215–30.

Jordan, B. (2004) 'Criminal justice, social exclusion and the social contract', *Probation Journal*, 50 (3): 198–210.

Katz, J. (1988) *Seductions of Crime: Moral and Sensual Attractions in Doing Evil*. New York: Basic Books.

Kay, J., Gast, L., Clarke, P., Mason, G., Mayer, J., Sisodia, B., and Squires, S. (1998) *From Murmur to Murder: working with racially motivated and racist offenders*. Birmingham: Midlands Probation Training Consortium.

Kemshall, H. (1995) 'Risk in probation practice', *Probation Journal* 42 (2): 67–72.

Kemshall, H. (1996) 'Risk assessment: fuzzy thinking or decisions in action?', *Probation Journal*, 43 (1): 2–7.

Kemshall, H. (2002) 'Risk, Public Protection and Justice', in D. Ward, J. Scott, and M. Lacey, (eds) *Probation, working for justice*. Oxford: Oxford University Press.

Kemshall, H. and Maguire, M. (2003) 'Sex offenders, risk, penality and the problem of disclosure to the community', in A. Matravers (ed) *Sex Offenders in the Community: Managing and Reducing the Risks*. Cullompton: Willan

Knight, C. (2002) 'Training for a modern service' in D. Ward, J. Scott and M. Lacey (eds) *Probation: working for Justice* (2nd edition). Oxford: Oxford University Press.

Knott, C. (1995) 'The STOP programme: reasoning and habilitation in a British setting', in J. McGuire (ed) *What Works: Reducing Reoffending*. Chichester: John Wiley

Knowsley, J. (1996) 'Girl gangs rival boys to rule the streets', *Sunday Telegraph*, 6 May 1996.

Kosh, M. and Williams, B. (1995) *The Probation Service and Victims of Crime: a Pilot Study*. Keele: Keele University Press.

Lacey, M. (1984) 'Intermediate treatment: a theory for practice', *Probation Journal*, 31 (3): 104–7.

Lawrence, D. (1995) 'Race, culture and the probation service', in G. McIvor (ed) *Working with Offenders*. Research Highlights in Social Work 26. London: Jessica Kingsley.

Lawson, C. (1978) *The Probation Officer as Prosecutor*. Cambridge: Institute of Criminology, University of Cambridge.

Lea, J. and Young, J. (1984) *What Is to be Done about Law and Order?* Harmondsworth: Penguin Books.

Leander, K. (1995) 'The normalization of Swedish prisons', in V. Ruggiero, M. Ryan and J. Sim (eds) *Western European Penal Systems: a Critical Anatomy.* London: Sage.

Lees, S. (1993) *Sugar and Spice.* Harmondsworth: Penguin Books.

Le Mesurier, L. (1935) *A Handbook of Probation.* London: NAPO.

Lianos, M. and Douglas, M. (2002) 'Dangerization and the end of deviance: the institutional environment', in D. Garland and R. Sparks (eds) *Criminology and Social Theory.* Oxford: Clarendon Studies in Criminology.

Liddle, M. (2001) 'Community penalties in the context of contemporary social change', in A. Bottoms, L. Gelsthorpe and S. Rex (eds) *Community Penalties: Change and Challenges.* Cullompton: Willan.

Lishman, J. (1991) *Handbook of Theory for Practice Teachers in Social Work.* London: Jessica Kingsley.

Loader, I. (1996) *Youth, Policing and Democracy.* London: Macmillan.

Lobley, D. and Smith, D. (1999) *Working with Persistent Juvenile Offenders: An Evaluation of the APEX Cue Ten Project.* Edinburgh: The Scottish Office Central Research Unit.

Lobley, D., Smith, D. and Stern, C. (2001) *Freagarrach: An Evaluation of a Project for Persistent Juvenile Offenders.* Edinburgh: The Scottish Office Central Research Unit.

McConville, B. (1983) *Women under the Influence.* London: Virago.

McCue, J. (2003) 'Anonymity laws may not be enough', *Guardian Unlimited*, 4 August 2003. (http://media.guardian.co.uk/broadcast/story/)

McGuire, J. and Priestley, P. (1985) *Offending Behaviour: Skills and Stratagems for Going Straight.* London: Batsford.

McIvor, G. (1992) *Sentenced to Serve.* Aldershot: Avebury.

McIvor, G. (1998) 'Jobs for the boys? Gender differences in referral for community service', *Howard Journal*, 37 (3): 280–91.

McIvor, G. (2004) 'Service with a smile? Women and Community "Punishment"', in G. McIvor (ed) *Women who Offend.* Research Highlights in Social Work 44. London: Jessica Kingsley Publishing.

McLoone, P., Oulds, G. and Morris, J. (1987) 'Alcohol education groups: compulsion v. voluntarism', *Probation Journal*, 34 (1): 25.

McNeill, S. (1987) 'Flashing: its effects on women', in J. Hanmer and M. Maynard (eds) *Women, Violence and Social Control.* Basingstoke: Macmillan.

McNeill, F. and Batchelor, S. (2002) 'Chaos, containment and change: responding to persistent offending by young people', *Youth Justice*, 2 (1): 27–43.

McNeill, F. and Batchelor, S. (2004) *Persistent Offending by Young People: Developing Practice.* ICCJ Monograph 3. London: NAPO.

McWilliams, W. (1990) 'Probation practice and the management ideal', *Probation Journal*, 37 (2): 60–7.

McWilliams, W. (1992) 'The rise and development of management thought in the English probation system', in R. Statham and P. Whitehead (eds) *Managing the Probation Service: Issues for the 1990s*. Harlow: Longman.

MacPherson, Sir W. of Cluny, (1999) *The Stephen Lawrence Inquiry*. London: HMSO.

Magistrates' Association (1993) 'Sentencing guidelines', in B. Gibson *et al.* (1994) *Criminal Justice in Transition*. Winchester: Waterside Press.

Magistrates' Association (2003) *Sentencing Guidelines*. London: Magistrates' Association.

Mair, G. (1988) *Probation Day Centres*. Home Office Research Study 100. London: HMSO.

Mair, G. (1995) 'Specialist activities in probation: confusion worse confounded?', in L. Noaks, M. Levi and M. Maguire (eds) *Issues in Contemporary Criminology*. Cardiff: University of Wales Press.

Mair, G. (2001) 'Technology and the future of community penalties', in A. Bottoms, L. Gelsthorpe and S. Rex (eds) *Community Penalties: Change and Challenges*. Cullompton: Willan.

Mair, G. (2004) 'The origins of What Works in England and Wales: a house built on sand?' in G. Mair (ed) *What Matters in Probation*. Cullompton: Willan.

Mair, G. and Brockington, N. (1988) 'Female offenders and the probation service', *The Howard Journal of Criminal Justice*, 27 (2): 117–26.

Malloch, M. (2004) 'Women, drug use and the criminal justice system,' in G. McIvor (ed) *Women who Offend*. Research Highlights in Social Work 44. London: Jessica Kingsley Publishers.

Marshall, P. (1997) *The prevalence of convictions for sexual offending*. Home Office Research Findings No 55. London: Home Office.

Marshall, T.F. (1999) *Restorative Justice: An Overview*. London: Home Office.

Martinson, R. (1974) 'What works? Questions and answers about prison reform', *The Public Interest*, 35: 22–54.

Maruna, S. (2001) *Making Good: How Ex-Convicts Reform and Rebuild their Lives*. Washington, D.C. : American Psychological Association.

Masters, R.E. (1994) *Counseling Criminal Justice Offenders*. Thousand Oaks, CA: Sage.

Mathiesen, T. (1983) 'The future of control systems', in D. Garland, and P. Young (eds) *The Power to Punish*. London: Heinemann.

Matravers, A. (2003) 'Setting some boundaries: rethinking responses to sex offenders', in A. Matravers (ed) *Sex Offenders in the Community: Managing and Reducing the Risks*. Cullompton: Willan.

Matthews, R. (1990) 'New directions in the privatization debate?', *Probation Journal*, 37 (2): 50–9.

Mawby, R. and Walklate, S. (1994) *Critical Victimology*. London: Sage.

May, T. (1991) *Probation: Politics, Policy and Practice*. Buckingham: Open University Press.

May, T. (1994) 'Transformative power: a study in a human service organization', *The Sociological Review*, 42 (2): 618–38.

Merrington, S. and Stanley, S. (2004) ' "What Works?": Revisiting the evidence in England and Wales', *Probation Journal*, 51 (1): 7–20.

Messner, C. and Ruggiero, V. (1995) 'Germany: the penal system between past and future' in V. Ruggiero, M. Ryan and J. Sim (eds) *Western European Penal Systems: a Critical Anatomy*. London: Sage.

Metcalf, C. and Stenson, K. (2004) 'Managing risk and the causes of crime', *Criminal Justice Matters*, 55: 8–9 and 42.

Millard, D. (1982) 'Keeping the probation service whole: the case for discretion', *British Journal of Social Work*, 12: 291–301.

Mistry, T. (1989) 'Establishing a feminist model of groupwork in the probation service', *Groupwork*, 2: 145–58.

Moloney, N. (1995) *Combination Orders: their History, Use and Impact*. Social Work Monograph 137. Norwich: University of East Anglia.

Moore, R. (2004) 'Intensive supervision and surveillance programmes for young offenders: the evidence base so far' in R. Burnett and C. Roberts (eds) *What Works in Probation and Youth Justice: Developing evidence-based practice*. Cullompton: Willan Publishing.

Monaghan, G. (2000) 'The Courts and the New Youth Justice', in B. Goldson (ed) *The New Youth Justice*. Lyme Regis: Russell House Publishing.

Morris, A. (1987) *Women, Crime and Criminal Justice*. Oxford: Basil Blackwell.

Morris, A., Giller, H., Szwed, E. and Geach, H. (1980) *Justice for Children*. London: Macmillan.

Morton, J. (1994) *A Guide to the Criminal Justice and Public Order Act 1994*. London: Butterworths.

Motz, A. (2001) *The Psychology of Female Violence: Crimes Against the Body*. Hove: Brunner-Routledge.

Moxon, D. (1995) 'England abandons unit fines', in M. Tonry and K. Hamilton (eds) *Intermediate Sanctions in Overcrowded Times*. Boston: Northeastern University Press.

Muncie, J. (1999) *Youth and Crime: A Critical Introduction*. London: Sage.

Muncie, J. (2000) 'Pragmatic realism? Searching for Criminology in the New Youth Justice', in B. Goldson (ed) *The New Youth Justice*. Lyme Regis: Russell House Publishing.

Muncie, J., Hughes, G. and McLaughlin, E. (eds) (2002) *Youth Justice: Critical Readings*. London: Sage.

Murray, C. (1990) 'Underclass' in *The Emerging British Underclass*. London: Institute of Economic Affairs.

NACRO (2001) *Girls in the Youth Justice System*, Youth Crime Briefing. London: NACRO.

NAPO (1992) *NAPO News*, March.

NAPO (1993a) *NAPO News*, February.

NAPO (1997) *NAPO News*, January.

NAPO (1998) *NAPO News*, July.

NAPO (1999) *NAPO News*, December.

NAPO (2000a) *NAPO News*, March.

NAPO (2000b) *NAPO News*, April.

NAPO (2003) *NAPO News*, September.

NAPO (2003/4) *NAPO News*, December/January.

NAPO (2004a) *NAPO News*, February.

NAPO (2004b) *NAPO News*, July.

Nash, M. (1999) *Police, Probation and Protecting the Public*. London: Blackstone Press.

Nash, M. (2003) 'Pre-trial investigation', in W.H. Chui and M. Nellis (eds) *Moving Probation Forward: Evidence, Arguments and Practice*. Harlow: Pearson Longman.

National Probation Service and Home Office (2001) *A New Choreography, Strategic Framework 2001–2004*. London: National Probation Service.

National Probation Service (2002a) *Briefing*, Issue 2. March 2002.

National Probation Service (2002b) *Briefing*, Issue 8. December 2002.

National Probation Service (2002c) *Approved Premises Handbook*. April 2002.

National Probation Service (2003a) *Probation Circular 72/2003*. December 2003.

National Probation Service (2003b) *Briefing*, Issue 12 April 2003.

National Probation Service (2004a) *Bold Steps: Objectives and Targets 2004/5 Annual Plan* for the National Probation Service. London: National Probation Directorate.

National Probation Service (2004b) *Setting the Pace – how the National Probation Service has delivered A New Choreography*. London: National Probation Directorate.

National Probation Service (2004c) *Annual Report 2003/04*. London: National Probation Directorate.

National Probation Service (2004d) *Performance Report 11*. February 2004.

National Probation Service (2004e) *What Works News, Issue 16*. February 2004.

Nellis, M. (1989) 'Keeping tags on the underclass', *Social Work Today*, 20 (37). 18–19.

Nellis, M. (1991) 'The last days of juvenile justice', in P. Carter, T. Jeffs and M. Smith (eds) *Social Work and Social Welfare Yearbook* 3. Buckingham: Open University Press.

Nellis, M. (1995a) 'Probation values for the 1990s', *The Howard Journal of Criminal Justice*, 34, (1): 19–44.

Nellis, M. (1995b) 'The "third way" for probation: a reply to Spencer and James', *The Howard Journal of Criminal Justice*, 34 (3): 350–3.

Nellis, M. (1995c) 'Partnership, punishment and justice', in D. Ward and M. Lacey, (eds) *Probation: Working for Justice*. London: Whiting & Birch.

Nellis, M. (2000) 'The new probation training', *Criminal Justice Matters*, 39: 22–23.

Nellis, M. (2001) 'Community penalties in historical perspective', in A. Bottoms, L. Gelsthorpe and S. Rex (eds) *Community Penalties: Change and Challenges*. Cullompton: Willan.

Nellis, M. (2002) 'Probation, partnership and civil society' in D. Ward, J. Scott and M. Lacey (eds) *Probation: Working for Justice*. Oxford: Oxford University Press.

Nellis, M. (2003a) 'Electronic monitoring and the future of probation', in W.H. Chui and M. Nellis (eds) *Moving Probation Forward: Evidence, Arguments and Practice*. Harlow: Pearson Longman.

Nellis, M. (2003b) 'News Media, Popular Culture and the Electronic Monitoring of Offenders in England and Wales', in *Howard Journal of Criminal Justice*, 42 (1): 1–31.

Nellis, M. and Gelsthorpe, L. (2003) 'Human Rights and the Probation Values Debate', in W.H. Chui and M. Nellis (eds) *Moving Probation Forward: Evidence, Arguments and Practice*. Harlow: Pearson Longman.

Newburn, T. (2003) *Crime and Criminal Justice Policy* (2nd edition). London: Longman.

Oldfield, M. (1993) 'Assessing the impact of community service: lost opportunities and the politics of punishment', in D. Whitfield and D. Scott (eds) *Paying Back: Twenty Years of Community Service*. Winchester: Waterside Press.

Oldfield, M. (2002) *From Welfare to Risk: Discourse, Power and Politics in the Probation Service*. Issues in Community and Criminal Justice Monograph 1. London: NAPO.

O'Mahony, D. and Haines, K. (1996) *An Evaluation of the Introduction and Operation of the Youth Court*, Home Office Research Study 152. London: HMSO.

Orwell. G. (1949) *Nineteen Eighty Four*. Harmondsworth: Penguin Books.

Owen, L. and Morris-Jones, R. (1988) 'They don't come voluntarily, do they?', *Probation Journal*, 35 (1): 30–31.

Parker, H. (1988) 'Greenpapering over the cracks', Paper presented to Management Study Day, Greater Manchester Probation Service, 4 October 1988.

Patten, J. (1988) 'Punishment, the Probation Service and the Community', Speech to Association of Chief Officers of Probation, Home Office, 15 September 1988.

Pearson, G. (1983) *Hooligan: A History of Respectable Fears*. London: Macmillan.

Pearson, G. (1994) 'Youth, crime and society', in M. Maguire, R. Morgan and R. Reiner (eds) *The Oxford Handbook of Criminology*. Oxford: Clarendon Press.

Pease, K. (1983) 'Penal innovations', in J. Lishman (ed) *Social Work with Adult Offender*. Research Highlights No 5. Aberdeen: University of Aberdeen.

Pease, K. and Bottomley, K. (1986) *Crime and Punishment: Interpreting the Data*. Milton Keynes: Open University.

Pease, K. and McWilliams, W. (1977) 'Assessing community service schemes: pitfalls for the unwary', *Probation Journal*, 24 (4): 137–9.

Pease, K. *et al.* (1975) *Community Service Orders*, Home Office Research Study 29. London: HMSO.

Perry, F. (1979) *Reports for Criminal Courts*. Ilkley: Owen Wells.

Phillpotts, G. and Lancucki, L.B. (1979) *Previous Convictions, Sentence and Reconvictions*. Home Office Research Study 53. London: HMSO.

Pitts, J. (1986) 'Black young people and juvenile crime: some unanswered questions', in R. Matthews and J. Young (eds) *Confronting Crime*. London: Sage.

Pitts, J. (1990) *Working with Young Offenders*. London: Macmillan.

Pitts, J. (1992a) 'Juvenile justice policy in England and Wales', in J.C. Coleman and C. Warren-Adamson (eds) *Youth Policy in the 1990s*. London: Routledge.

Pitts, J. (1992b) 'The end of an era', *The Howard Journal of Criminal Justice*, 31 (2): 133–49.

Pitts, J. (1993) 'Theorotyping: anti-racism, criminology and black young people', in D. Cook and B. Hudson (eds) *Racism and Criminology*. London: Sage.

Platt, A. (1969) *The Child Savers*. Chicago: University of Chicago Press.

Power, H. (2003) 'Disclosing information on sex offenders: the human rights implications', in A. Matravers (ed) *Sex Offenders in the Community: Managing and Reducing the Risks*. Cullompton: Willan.

Powis, B. and Walmsley, R.K. (2002) *Programmes for Black and Asian offenders on Probation: Lessons for Developing Practice*. Home Office Research Study 250. London: Home Office.

Prison Reform Trust (2000) *Justice for Women: The Need for Reform* (The Wedderburn Report). London: Prison Reform Trust.

Raine, J. (2002) 'Modernisation and Criminal Justice', in D. Ward, J. Scott and M. Lacey (eds) *Probation: Working for Justice* (2nd edition). Oxford: Oxford University Press.

Raine, J., Dunstan, E. and Mackie, A. (2003) 'Financial penalties as a sentence of the court', *Criminal Justice* 3 (2): 181–97.

Ray, L., Smith, D. and Wastell, L. (2001) 'Racist violence and probation practice', *Probation Journal*, 49(1): 3–9.

Raynor, P. (1978) 'Compulsory persuasion: a problem for correctional social work', *British Journal of Social Work*, 8 (4): 411–24.

Raynor, P. (1985) *Social Work, Justice and Control*. Oxford: Basil Blackwell.

Raynor, P. (1992) *Straight Thinking on Probation: One Year On*. Bridgend: Mid-Glamorgan Probation Service.

Raynor, P. (2001) 'Community penalties and social integration: "community" as solution and as problem', in A.Bottoms, L. Gelsthorpe and S. Rex (eds) *Community Penalties: Change and Challenges*. Cullompton: Willan.

Raynor, P. (2003) 'Evidence-based probation and its critics', *Probation Journal*, 50 (4): 334–45.

Raynor, P. and Vanstone, M. (1994) *Straight Thinking on Probation: Third Interim Evaluation Report*. Bridgend: Mid-Glamorgan Probation Service.

Raynor, P., Smith, D. and Vanstone, M. (1994) *Effective Probation Practice*. London: Macmillan.

Raynor, P. and Vanstone, M. (2002) *Understanding Community Penalties: Probation, policy and social change*. Buckingham: Open University Press.

Reiner, R. (1989) 'Race and criminal justice', *New Community*, 16 (1): 5–21.

Rex, S., Gelsthorpe, L., Roberts, C. and Jordan, P. (2004) *What's promising in community service: implementaion of seven Pathfinder projects*. Home Office Findings 231. London: Home Office.

Roberts, C. (2004) 'An Early Evaluation of a Cognitive Offending Behaviour Programme ('Think First') in Probation Areas', *Vista*, 8 (3): 130–36.

Robinson, G. (2001) 'Power, knowledge and "What Works" in probation', *Howard Journal*, 40: 235–54.

Robinson, G. (2003) 'Risk and risk assessment' in W.H. Chui and M. Nellis (eds) *Moving Probation Forward: Evidence, Arguments and Practice*. Harlow: Pearson Longman.

Robinson, G. and McNeill, F. (2004) 'Purposes matter: examining the "ends" of probation', in G. Mair (ed) *What Matters in Probation*. Cullompton: Willan.

Ross, R. and Fabiano, E. (1989) *Reasoning and Rehabilitation: a Handbook for Teaching Cognitive Skills*. Ottawa: The Cognitive Centre.

Rumgay, J. (2003a) 'Drug treatment and offender rehabilitation: Reflections on evidence, effectiveness and exclusion', *Probation Journal*, 50 (1): 41–51.

Rumgay, J. (2003b) 'Partnerships in the Probation Service', in W.H. Chui and M. Nellis (eds) *Moving Probation Forward: Evidence, Arguments and Practice*. Harlow: Pearson Longman.

Rutherford, A. (1986) *Growing out of Crime*. Harmondsworth: Penguin Books.

Sampson, A. (1994) *Acts of Abuse*. London: Routledge.

Sanders, A. and Senior, P. (eds) (1994) *Jarvis' Probation Service Manual* (5th edition). Sheffield: PAVIC Publications.

Scarborough, J., Geraghty, J. and Loffhagen, J. (1987) 'Day centres and voluntarism', *Probation Journal*, 34 (2): 47–50.

Scarman Centre National CCTV Evaluation Team (2003) *National evaluation of CCTV: early findings on scheme implementation – effective practice guide*. Home Office Development and Practice Report. London: Home Office.

Schofield, H. (1998) 'What works? Effectiveness led practice into the millenium', *NAPO News*, Issue 101: 13–14.

Schofield, H. (1999) 'Probation training: late modernism or post-modernism?', *Probation Journal*, 46 (4): 256–58.

Scott, J. (2002) 'Human Rights: a Challenge to Culture and Practice' in D. Ward, J. Scott and M. Lacey (eds) *Probation: Working for Justice*. Oxford: Oxford University Press.

Scull, A. (1977/1984) *Decarceration: Community Treatment and the Deviant*. Cambridge: Polity Press.

Senior, P. (1985) 'Groupwork with offenders' in H. Walker and B. Beaumont (eds) *Working with offenders*. Basingstoke: Macmillan.

Shaw, K. (1987) 'Skills, control and the mass professions', *The Sociological Review*, 35 (4): 775–93.

Sheath, M. (1990) 'Confrontative work with sex offenders: legitimized noncebashing?, *Probation Journal*, 37 (4): 159–62.

Shepherd, G. (1991) 'Management: short of ideals?', *Probation Journal*, 37 (4): 176–81.

Sim, J., Ruggiero, V. and Ryan, M. (1995) 'Punishment in Europe: perceptiom and commonalities', in V. Ruggiero, M. Ryan and J. Sim (eds) *Western European Penal Systems: a Critical Anatomy*. London: Sage.

Simmons, J. and Dodd, T. (eds) (2003) *Crime in England and Wales 2002/2003*. Home Office Statistical Bulletin. London: Home Office.

Simon, J. (1998) 'Managing the Monstrous: sex offenders and the new penology', *Psychology, Public Policy and the Law*, 4 (1/2): 452–67.

Smart, B. (1983) 'On discipline and social regulation: a review of Foucault's genealogical analysis', in D. Garland and P. Young (eds) *The Power to Punish*. London: Heinemann.

Smith, D. (1995) *Criminology for Social Work*. London: Macmillan.

Smith, A. (2001) *Specific Sentence Reports: A Survey of Probation Areas*. London: Association of Chief Officers of Probation.

Social Exclusion Unit (2002) *Reducing Re-offending by Ex-prisoners*. London: Office of the Deputy Prime Minister.

Souhami, A. (2003) *Transforming Youth Justice: A Local Study of Occupational Identity and Membership*. Unpublished PhD thesis. Keele: Keele University.

Spalek, B. (2003) 'Victim work in the Probation Service: perpetuating notions of an "ideal victim"', in W.H. Chui and M. Nellis (eds) *Moving Probation Forward: Evidence, Arguments and Practice*. Harlow: Addison Wesley Longman.

Sparks, R. (2003) 'States of insecurity: punishment, populism and contemporary political culture', in S. McConville (ed) *The Use of Punishment*. Cullompton: Willan.

Spencer, J. and Deakin, J. (2004) 'Community reintegration: for whom?', in G. Mair (ed) *What Matters in Probation*. Cullompton: Willan.

Stacey, T. (1989) 'Why tagging should be used to reduce incarceration', *Social Work Today*, 20 (32): 18–19.

Stenson, K. (2000) 'Someday our Prince Will Come: Zero Tolerance Policing and Liberal Government' in T. Hope and R. Sparks (eds) *Crime, Risk and Insecurity*. London: Routledge.

Stephen, J. (1993) *The Misrepresentation of Women Offenders*. Social Work Monograph 118. Norwich: University of East Anglia.

Taylor, I., Walton, P. and Young, J. (1972) *The New Criminology*. London: Routledge.

Thomas, T. (2000) *Sex Crime: Sex Offending and Society*. Cullompton: Willan.

Thomas, T. and Tuddenham, R. (2001) 'The supervision of sex offenders: policies influencing the probation role', *Probation Journal*, 49 (1): 10–18.

Thorpe, J. (1979) *Social Enquiry Reports: a Survey*. Home Office Research Study 48. London: HMSO.

Thurston, P. (2002) 'Just Practice in Probation Hostels' in D. Ward, J. Scott and M. Lacey (eds) *Probation: Working for Justice*. Oxford: Oxford University Press.

Tonry, M. and Hamilton, K. (eds) (1995) *Intermediate Sanctions in Overcrowded Time*. Boston: Northeastern University Press.

Travis, A. (2003) 'Correct Route', *The Guardian*, 7 May 2003.

Travis, A. (2004) 'Opinion', *Guardian*, 14 January 2004.

Trotter, C. (1999) *Working with Involuntary Clients*. London: Sage.

Tuddenham, R. (2000) 'Beyond defensible decision-making:towards reflexive assessment of risk', *Probation Journal*, 47 (3): 173–83.

Tutt, N. and Giller, H. (1984) *Social Inquiry Reports*. Lancaster: Social Information Systems (tape recording).

Tyler, T.R. (1990) *Why People Obey the Law*. New Haven: Yale University Press.

Underdown, A. (1998) *Strategies for Effective Offender Supervison – Report of the HMIP*. London: Home Office.

Unell, I. (2002) 'Controlling Drug Use: Where is the Justice?', in D. Ward, J. Scoot and M. Lacey (eds) *Probation Working for Justice*. Oxford: Oxford University Press.

van Swaaningen, R. and de Jonge, G. (1995) 'The Dutch prison system and penal policy in the 1990s: from humanitarian paternalism to penal business management', in V. Ruggiero, M. Ryan and J. Sim (eds) *Western European Penal Systems: a Critical Anatomy*. London: Sage.

Vass, A.A. (1990) *Alternatives to Prison*. London: Sage.

Vennard, J. and Hedderman, C. (1998) 'Effective intervention with offenders', in P. Goldblatt and C. Lewis (eds) Reducing offending: an assessment of research evidence on ways of dealing with offending behaviour. Home Office Research Study 187. London: Home Office.

von Hirsch, A. (1998) 'The Ethics of Community-Based Sanctions', in J. Petersilia (ed) *Community Corrections*. Oxford: Oxford University Press.

Waite, I. (1994) 'Too little, too bad', *Probation Journal*, 41 (2): 92–4.

Walker, N. (1991) *Why punish?* Oxford: Oxford University Press.

Walker, H. and Beaumont, B. (1981) *Probation Work: Critical Theory and Socialist Practice*. Oxford: Blackwell.

Walker, H. and Beaumont, B. (1985) *Working with Offenders*. London: Macmillan.

Walmsley, R., Howard, L. and White, S. (1992) *The National Prison Survey 1991*, Home Office Research Study 128. London: HMSO.

Ward, D. and Spencer, J. (1994) 'The future of probation qualifying training', *Probation Journal*, 41 (2): 95–8.

Webb, T. (1996) 'Reconviction prediction for probationers', *Probation Journal*, 43 (1): 8–12.

Welldon, E. (1988) *Mother, Madonna, Whore: the Idealisation and Denigration of Motherhood*. London: Free Association Books Ltd.

Welldon, E. (1996) 'Female sex offenders', *Prison Service Journal* 107: 39–47.

Weyell, E. (2003) *Legitimating community service: staff, procedures and perceptions of fairness*. Unpublished PhD thesis. Keele: Keele University.

White, L. (1984) 'Residential work: the Cinderella of the probation service?', *Probation Journal*, 31 (2): 59–60.

Whitehead, P. and Thompson, J. (2004) *Knowledge and the Probation Service*. Chichester: John Wiley and Sons Ltd.

Whitfield, D. (1993) 'Extending the boundaries', in D. Whitfield and D. Scott (eds) *Paying Back: Twenty Years of Community Service*. Winchester: Waterside Press.

Whitfield, D. (1995) 'Crime, surveillance and tagging: the thin end of the white elephant', *Criminal Justice Matters*, No. 20, Summer, 19.

Whitfield, D. and Scott, D. (eds) (1993) *Paying Back: Twenty Years of Community Service*. Winchester: Waterside Press.

Williams, B. (1994) 'Probation training in the UK: from charity organisation to jobs for the boys', *Social Work Education*, 13 (3): 99–108.

Williams, B. (ed) (1995) *Probation Values*. Birmingham: Venture Press.

Williams, B. (1996) *Counselling in Criminal Justice*. Buckingham: Open University Press.

Williams, B. (2002) 'Justice for Victims of Crime' in D. Ward, J. Scott and M. Lacey (eds) *Probation, Working for Justice*. Oxford: Oxford University Press.

Willmott, P. (1987) 'Introduction', in P. Willmott (ed) *Policing and the Community*. London: Policy Studies Institute.

Wincup, E. (1996) 'Mixed hostels: staff and resident perspectives', *Probation Journal*, 43 (3): 147–51.

Windlesham, Lord (1993) *Responses to Crime*. Vol. 2. Oxford: Oxford University Press.

Woolf, H. and Tumim, S. (1991) *Report into the Prison Disturbances* April 1990. Cmnd. 1456. London: HMSO.

Worrall, A. (1981) 'Out of place: female offenders in court', *Probation Journal*. 28 (3): 90–3.

Worrall, A. (1990) *Offending Women: Female Lawbreakers and the Criminal Justice System*. London: Routledge.

Worrall, A. (1998) 'Laws and orders: public protection and social exclusion in England and Wales', *Current Issues in Criminal Justice*, 10 (2): 183–96.

Worrall, A. (1999) 'Troubled or troublesome? Justice for girls and young women', in B. Goldson (ed) *Youth Justice: contemporary policy and practice*. Aldershot: Ashgate.

Worrall, A. (2000) 'Governing Bad Girls: changing constructions of adolescent female delinquency' in J. Bridgeman and D. Monk (eds) *Feminist Perspectives on Child Law*. London: Cavendish Publishing.

Worrall, A. (2002a) 'Rendering women punishable: the making of a penal crisis', in P. Carlen (ed) *Women and Punishment: The Struggle for Justice*. Cullompton: Willan Publishing.

Worrall, A. (2002b) 'Missed Opportunities? The Probation Service and Women Offenders', in D. Ward, J. Scott and M. Lacey (eds) *Probation, Working for Justice*. Oxford: Oxford University Press.

Worrall, A. (2004a) 'Twisted Sisters, Ladettes and the New Penology: the social construction of "violent girls"', in C. Alder and A. Worrall (eds) *Girls' Violence: Myths and Realities*. New York: SUNY Press.

Worrall, A. (2004b) 'What Works and the Globalisation of Punishment Talk', in G. Mair, *What Works in Probation*. Cullompton: Willan Publishing.

Worrall, A., Mawby, R., Heath, G. and Hope, T. (2003) *Intensive Supervision and Monitoring Projects*. Home Office Online Report 42/03. London: Home Office.

Worrall, A. and Mawby, R. (2004) 'Intensive projects for prolific/persistent offenders' in A. Bottoms, S. Rex and G. Robinson (eds) *Alternatives to Prison: Options for an insecure society*. Cullompton: Willan Publishing.

Young, P.(1989) 'Punishment, money and a sense of justice', in P. Carlen and D. Cook (eds) *Paying for Crime*. Milton Keynes: Open University Press.

Youth Justice Board (2003) *News*, Issue 19, September.

Youth Justice Board (2004a) *ISSP: The Initial Report*. London: Youth Justice Board.

Youth Justice Board (2004b) *News*, Issue 21, February.

www.audit-commission.gov.uk
www.dca.gov.uk/criminal/rccstat.htm
www.dspdprogramme.gov.uk
www.homeoffice.gov.uk
www.hmprisonservice.gov.uk
www.learndirect-advice.co.uk
www.legislation.hmso.gov.uk
www.moj.go.jp
www.nao.gov.uk
www.napo.org.uk
www.parliament.uk/post
www.probation.homeoffice.gov.uk
www.youth-justice-board.gov.uk

Index